MAIL &
FEMALE

Women and The Canadian Union
of Postal Workers

JULIE WHITE

Thompson Educational Publishing, Inc.
Toronto

Additional copies of this publication may be obtained from:
  Thompson Educational Publishing, Inc.
  11 Briarcroft Road, Toronto
  Ontario, Canada M6S 1H3
  Telephone (416)766-2763 Fax: (416) 766-0398
Please write for a full catalogue of publications.

Canadian Cataloguing in Publication Data

White, Julie
  Mail and female: women and the Canadian Union of Postal Workers

Includes bibliographical references.
ISBN 1-55077-008-X

1. Canadian Union of Postal Workers. 2. Women in trade-unions - Canada.
3. Sex discrimination against women - Canada. 4. Postal service - Canada -
Employees. I. Title.

HE6659.P4W45 1990   331.4'7811383'0971   C90-094380-7

Cover photograph by Paul Darrow, *Halifax Daily News.*
CUPW members on the picket line in Halifax face police brought in to protect
replacement workers, 1987 strike.

ISBN 1-55077-008-X Paper

Printed in Canada by John Deyell Company.
1 2 3 4 5   94 93 92 91 90

TABLE OF CONTENTS

LIST OF TABLES

ABBREVIATIONS

CLC	Canadian Labour Congress
CLRB	Canada Labour Relations Board
CNTU	Confederation of National Trade Unions
CPEA	Canadian Postal Employees Association, predecessor to the Canadian Union of Postal Workers
CPU	Council of Postal Unions, the joint negotiating body for the Canadian Union of Postal Workers and the Letter Carriers Union of Canada
CSAC	Civil Service Association of Canada, predecessor to the Public Service Alliance of Canada
CUPE	Canadian Union of Public Employees
CUPTE	Canadian Union of Professional and Technical Employees
CUPW	Canadian Union of Postal Workers
LCUC	Letter Carriers Union of Canada
PSAC	Public Service Alliance of Canada
PSSRA	Public Service Staff Relations Act, labour relations legislation covering federal government workers
PSSRB	Public Service Staff Relations Board, administrative body of the Public Service Staff Relations Act

ACKNOWLEDGEMENTS

The support and help of the members and officers of the Canadian Union of Postal Workers has been essential to this project. I would like to thank them for allowing me to draw upon their time and knowledge, for providing interviews that were frank and open, and for being prepared to debate controversial issues. I hope that the results will be of some use to them. I am also indebted to the Women and Work Strategic Grants Programme of the Social Sciences and Humanities Research Council of Canada for the financial support of this research. Geoff Bickerton, Deborah Bourke, Carl Cuneo, Allan Moscovitch, Janet Siltanen, and Don Wells took time from their busy schedules to read the manuscript and provide many detailed and useful comments.

Again I am grateful to Allan for withstanding the onslaught of another book-writing effort, and for doing so with love, insight and humour. Thanks are also due to Hannah and Noah who enabled me to maintain a proper perspective on the relative importance of research in the general scheme of life and who saved me, in the face of some pressure, from becoming a workaholic.

Despite these considerable contributions there may be errors of fact or judgment that remain my own.

This book is dedicated to my parents,
Molly and George White.

1

INTRODUCTION

In the late 1950s, when the Post Office first began to hire women full-time workers, the union of inside postal workers opposed their introduction with some vehemence.

> Postal work was men's work and we intended to keep it that way. Women, we argued, when they first began to appear in full-time positions, could not perform all the functions in a postal clerk's job description and therefore had no right to occupy such positions.[1]

When women were hired in increasing numbers as low-paid part-time workers, the union called for the abolition of part-time work from the Post Office and refused to allow part-time workers to join the union.

However, by the 1980s the Canadian Union of Postal Workers (CUPW) had negotiated a collective agreement generally regarded as one of the most progressive for women, including equality of pay and benefits for part-time workers. Moreover, in 1981 the union was on strike for six weeks with paid maternity leave as one of the central issues and the CUPW became the first national union to obtain fully-paid maternity leave.

The initial purpose of this research was to examine the reasons for this notable shift in union policy towards women workers. What had happened in the twenty years between the early 1960s and the 1980s to create such diametrically opposed positions within the same union? It seemed relevant to explore what had happened within the union of inside postal workers, not only to understand how such major changes could occur within one union but also to illuminate events within the union movement more generally.

Over the last twenty-five years the labour movement has experienced a radical change. The increasing participation of women in the labour force since the second World War has altered the composition of many unions. In 1962 a quarter of a million union women represented 16 percent of total trade union membership; by 1986 over one and a quarter million women unionists comprised 36 percent of all union members.[2] This large influx of women members has resulted in new concerns and directions. Women's committees, caucuses and conferences have been developed to meet the needs of an increasingly vocal sector of union

---

[1] Joe Davidson and John Deverell, *Joe Davidson*, James Lorimer, Toronto, 1978, p. 85.

[2] Statistics Canada, *Corporations and Labour Unions Returns Act*, Part—II, Labour Unions, Cat.71–202, Ottawa, 1962–1986.

TABLE 1: The CUPW Membership by Sex, 1962–1986				
Year	Total Members	Total Men	Total Women	Percentage of Women
1962	10537	10021	516	4.9
1964	10746	10166	580	5.4
1966	10748	10096	652	6.1
1968	14694	12877	1817	12.4
1970	17447	14050	3397	19.5
1972	19143	14570	4573	23.9
1974	21289	14591	6698	31.5
1976	24059	15770	8589	35.3
1978	24476	14785	9691	39.6
1980	24391	13763	10628	43.6
1982	23392	13702	9690	41.4
1984	23699	13377	10322	43.6
1986	24759	14834	9925	40.1

SOURCE: Statistics Canada, *Corporations and Labour Unions Returns Act*, Part II—Labour Unions, Cat. 71–202, 1962–1984; Unpublished data from Statistics Canada, Corporations and Labour Unions Returns Act Division, for 1986.

membership. Negotiations may now include sexual harassment, paid maternity leave and child care—issues unheard of in the union movement two decades previously. Internally the union movement has debated how to increase the participation of women in union structures, particularly at the higher levels.

While there is general agreement that important changes have occurred within the union movement in regard to women's concerns, little attention has been paid to the reasons for those changes. Where positive union action has been explored, explanations have focused almost entirely upon the activities of women themselves in forcing change within unions. Emphasis has been placed upon the growing proportion of women within unions,[3] the development of women's committees and caucuses,[4] and alliances with the women's movement.[5]

---

[3] M. Baker and M.A. Robeson, "Trade Union Reactions to Women Workers and Their Concerns," Katharine Lundy and Barbara Warme, *Work in the Canadian Context, Continuity Despite Change*, Butterworths, Toronto, 1981.

[4] Joy Langan, "Trade Union Women's Committees," *Canadian Labour*, Vol.21, No.3, September 1976; Francoise David, "Women's Committees: The Quebec Experience," and Debbie Field, "The Dilemma Facing Women's Committees," in Linda Briskin and Lynda Yanz, *Union Sisters, Women in the Labour Movement*, The Women's Press, Toronto, 1983.

[5] Carol Egan and Lynda Yanz, "Building Links: Labour and the Women's Movement," Linda Briskin and Lynda Yanz, *Union Sisters, Women in the Labour Movement*, Women's Press, Toronto, 1983.

The CUPW has experienced a rapid increase in women members over a relatively short period of time. Table 1 indicates just how radical this change in membership has been. In 1962, the earliest year for which information is available, women were less than 5 percent of the membership, but by 1980, just 18 years later, the union was almost 44 percent women.

Given this rapid increase in women members, it might be the case that this shift in membership explains the union's altered policies. And yet when the union decided to permit part-time workers to join the union in 1966, women comprised only 6 percent of the membership, hardly sufficient to force such a major change in policy. In 1981 when the union was on strike, in part for paid maternity leave, the union membership was 43 percent women, a significant minority, but still a minority.

While the actions of women in promoting their own interests are one important aspect of understanding change in unions, this argument alone is not sufficient explanation. It cannot explain why unions that have a predominantly female membership, such as nurses' unions, have not necessarily been in the forefront of obtaining improvements specific to women's concerns. Nor does it explain why some unions have made greater advances than others despite a similar proportion of women members.

A higher percentage of women in a union does not even guarantee the election of women to official union positions. The Women's Rights Committee of the British Columbia Federation of Labour conducted a survey of over 100 affiliated unions. The study found that where women formed between 50 and 66 per cent of the union's membership, the top leadership position was held by a man in 67 percent of cases. But, where the proportion of women was higher and comprised more than 66 percent of the membership, an even higher proportion (75 percent) of the top leaders were men. The study concluded: "The higher the percentage of women in the membership, the lower the percentage of women in leadership positions.[6]

The relationship between women, the employers that hire them and the unions that represent them is too complex to allow for any one factor explanation, including the suggestion that increased involvement by women is sufficient to create change. However, there has been relatively little interest in exploring more systematically why positive changes have occurred within the union movement. This study, then, began with the intention of discovering what factors had led to the CUPW's change in policies towards women. Examining one union in depth would make it possible to take into consideration the many factors involved in the interaction between women workers, the union and the employer.

But, inevitably, the question became more complex. Early on in the research my notion of the changes that had occurred within the CUPW received a sharp encounter with reality when two activists within the union commented drily that

---

[6] British Columbia Federation of Labour, "Union Activist's Summary. Women's Rights Committee Survey 1987," Vancouver, p. 1.

I might be right about my interpretation of the 1960s, but did I really believe that things had changed so much? It was brought to my attention that the CUPW had taken a decidedly cautious approach to women's issues inside the union, not actually opposing the development of women's committees and caucuses, for example, but also not encouraging them. Here indeed was a union with a very progressive contract for its women workers, that had never held a women's conference, had no national women's committee, no regular women's caucuses, and no educational programmes for women.

The research question took a new turn. It was necessary to ask not only why the CUPW had changed its perspective on women workers from one of antagonism to one of equality, but also why a union that had bargained a remarkably progressive contract for women would remain relatively backward on the organization of women within the union.

Further, it became clear that this was no simplistic issue of a union still predominantly male in which the men were able to outvote the women. Women members of the CUPW were themselves divided over many issues, so that some had, for example, opposed the development of women's committees. Meanwhile the support of men had been critical in the development of women's committees in certain union locals, while their opposition had just as certainly prevented or delayed their development elsewhere. As the research progressed even the initial research question altered somewhat. It no longer appeared that the union had moved directly from a position of opposition to women to one of support for women and their concerns. Rather the initial period of comparative hostility gave way to a situation in which gender was relatively unimportant. Women were treated as equals not because they were women, but because they were members of the union like any other members. When specifically women's issues emerged in the 1980s, such as maternity leave and women's committees, the union was supportive of some, but not all, of these concerns. The purpose of the research became to explain these rather more subtle shifts of union policy.

The reality of the position of women within the CUPW has proved far more complex than my original formulation of the issues allowed—and also very much more interesting.

This book is divided into three sections that deal, somewhat loosely, with the 1960s, the 1970s and then the 1980s. It does not deal generally with issues of concern to women inside postal workers over these three decades, but focuses upon specific themes that at the time were of particular importance. These themes have been selected not only because they were critical issues for the union of inside postal workers, but also because they reflect general problems that are regularly raised when the question of women and unions is discussed.

The first section on the 1960s considers specifically the exclusion of the predominantly female part-time workers from the union in the first half of the 1960s. At this time the question of part-time work, and also casual labour, was second in importance only to wage issues within the union. Moreover, from a more general point of view, there has been considerable debate in earlier research over the reasons why unions have adopted exclusionary policies towards women workers. In this case not only the reasons for the exclusionary policy are examined, but also the factors that caused the change in that policy in 1966.

The second section on the 1970s focuses upon the general theme of the union's negotiations with the employer. Within this framework three aspects of the CUPW's negotiations are examined. The first considers the union's response to the employer's introduction of a new classification of workers, called Postal Coders. These workers, the majority of them women, were to operate the new letter sorting machines, part of a massive shift to automated technology that began in 1972. The Coders were considered less skilled than the predominantly male manual sorters and received a lower rate of pay. Other research has suggested that unions have contributed to the ghettoization of women in the labour force by preserving higher paid jobs for men. Why did the CUPW undertake a major campaign over a period of two years to prevent the emergence of a predominantly female, lower-paid job category in the Post Office, and at a time when women comprised less than 30 percent of the union's membership?

The second negotiation issue examined returns to the situation of the part-time workers. Why did the union press determinedly to obtain equality for the part-time workers? This applied not only to pay and benefits in negotiations with the employer, but also encompassed changing the highly sensitive seniority arrangements to the disadvantage, and the dismay, of many full-time workers.

The third issue dealt with in the section on the 1970s considers the union's strenuous attempts to bargain restrictions upon the use of part-time work. Again, this has been a contentious issue, since it has been suggested that limitations upon part-time work have a negative impact for women who might prefer part-time to full-time employment. This chapter examines the reasons for the CUPW's position, the methods used to restrict part-time work, and the responses from part-time workers themselves.

The 1980s saw the emergence of specifically women's issues within the union, and this is the theme dealt with in the third section of the book. It would not be possible to write a book on women and the CUPW and not deal with the 1981 achievement of fully-paid maternity leave that followed a six-week strike. This chapter considers not only why the union took on the question, but also the controversy it aroused among the CUPW members and how that was handled inside the union.

The final chapter on the CUPW looks at the position of women inside the union structure and organization. It first examines the number of women in union leadership positions and then goes on to consider the development of policies on various women's issues that affect the internal functioning of the union, including women's committees, sexual harassment, child care for union meetings and education. The CUPW is a democratic union that encourages debate on controversial issues, and women's issues have proved to be very controversial. This chapter considers why the union has responded with caution to the emergence of women's issues inside the union and looks in some detail at how women members of the CUPW regard the situation.

Finding the answers to these questions has required an understanding of the context in which the union has functioned over the last thirty years; women's concerns have not been handled in isolation from other issues. Consequently, the general economic climate, government policy on the Post Office, labour relations legislation, management strategies and decisions, and technological change appear and re-appear as a backdrop against which to view and comprehend the development of the union and of its policies with regard to women. Two chapters, those that introduce the 1970s and the 1980s sections, examine these contextual questions in some detail.

Discussion of the relationship of this study of the CUPW to earlier research is reserved for the conclusion. Some readers may be interested in the history of the union without feeling an equal interest in the general state of research on women and unions. This final chapter examines the findings of this study in relation to other research on women and unions.

The primary research method for the study was the analysis of relevant documents, including materials on negotiations, documents pertaining to the internal functioning of the union, union publications and bulletins, and many government reports and studies of the Post Office. As well, interviews were conducted with a total of 63 CUPW members and officials, including 14 locals in nine provinces (excluding Prince Edward Island). Eight of those interviewed were national or regional union officers of whom three were women. Another woman was the full-time President of the Vancouver local. The remaining 54 people interviewed were working as inside postal workers in the Post Office, and of these three were men and 16 held some position on their local union executive. Five of the interviews were not taped because they were conducted by telephone or over lunch. All the remaining taped interviews have been placed with the National Archives in Ottawa (Moving Image and Sound Archives, Accession No: 1990–0102).

The interview material was most important in examining how women, and how part-time workers, regard the union's handling of their concerns. It also resulted in a general discussion of conditions of work on the shop floor of the Post Office that introduces the analysis of the union in the 1980s.

SECTION I

WOMEN JOIN THE UNION IN THE 1960s

"A Standing Ovation for the Ladies"

2

WOMEN'S WORK IN THE POST OFFICE AND THE UNION'S REACTION

Throughout the early 1960s the Post Office employed only a small minority of women workers. Out of a total staff that increased from 25,000 to over 29,000 between 1960 and 1965, the number of women workers grew from 3,000 to almost 4,000, always remaining at approximately 12 percent of the workforce.[1] But, the controversy that was engendered by the presence of these women within the union of inside postal workers was far greater than their proportion in the workforce would suggest.

In part the difficulties originated from the concentration of women into particular types of work. The inside postal workers who sorted the mail were represented at this time by the Canadian Postal Employees Association (CPEA), with a membership of 10,500. The Letter Carriers Union of Canada (LCUC) represented the workers who delivered the mail. Of the almost 4,000 women employed by the Post Office in 1965, the vast majority were employed as inside postal workers, constituting not 12 percent, but more than 30 percent of the total number of inside postal workers. It was these inside workers that concerned the CPEA, the predecessor of the Canadian Union of Postal Workers (CUPW). Of critical importance was the fact that only a small minority of the women workers were employed full-time, some were casual workers and the majority were employed part-time.

Women Full-Time Workers

After the second world war, the proportion of full-time women workers employed in the Civil Service had grown as the federal government expanded and more women entered the labour force to fill the increasing number of clerical positions. In 1953 the Civil Service dropped its prohibition on the employment of married women and from the early 1960s provided protection of employment during pregnancy. In 1965 women constituted almost 30 percent of the full-time workers employed by the federal government under the Civil Service Act. However, in the Post Office the number of women working full-time remained much

---

[1] Statistics Canada, *Federal Government Employment*, Cat.72–004, Ottawa, January 1960-December 1965.

lower, at less than 3 percent. A total of 619 full-time women employees compared to 23,025 men were working in the Post Office as full-time workers by 1965.[2] As one study noted: "In the Post Office Department men have traditionally held most of the clerical and carrier jobs.[3]

This tradition of male employment was due in part to the fact that the Post Office employed large numbers of war veterans, who were given preference in the hiring procedure. The War Service Preference resulted in greater employment of men in clerical jobs that would normally have been assigned to women.[4] Veterans were most likely to be hired into Departments with unskilled or semi-skilled jobs, such as the Post Office, where war service would be a deciding factor. Immediately after the war in 1946, more than 79 percent of the total appointments to the Post Office were those receiving War Service Preference. Even in 1960 the figure was still 16 percent, with only the Department of National Defense having a higher proportion.[5]

While the Post Office employed only a small number of full-time women workers, their introduction had not been accepted without complaint. There were almost no women working as letter carriers, so their presence primarily affected the union then representing the inside postal workers, the CPEA. Joe Davidson, who later became President of the union, described the position of the CPEA at that time:

> Postal work was men's work and we intended to keep it that way. Women, we argued, when they first began to appear in full-time positions, could not perform all the functions in a postal clerk's job description and therefore had no right to occupy such positions. This argument didn't cut much ice with management, since the only duty that gave women any problem at all was lifting mail bags and this was hardly the essence of the job. The full-time women stayed and we reconciled ourselves to their presence.[6]

However, management was not hiring women in large numbers and there are indications that the union's view was shared by postal officials. Women did apply for the full-time positions, perhaps attracted by the pay, which was equal to the men's pay for the same job, but this attraction created difficulties for the Post

---

[2] Pay Research Bureau, "Composition of the Public Service of Canada," Ottawa, 1965, Table 3(e).

[3] W. Donald Wood, "Analysis of Manpower Patterns and Trends in the Federal Public Service," prepared for the *Royal Commission on Government Organization*, Ottawa, 15 January 1962, p. 14.

[4] *Ibid.*, p. 87.

[5] *Ibid.*, p. 88.

[6] Joe Davidson and John Deverell, *Joe Davidson*, James Lorimer, Toronto, 1978, p. 85.

Office management. An interim report prepared in 1961 for the Glassco Commission on Government Organization states:

> Field post offices have noticed an increase in the number of female applicants for jobs in the entrance grades. Postal authorities (middle to lower level supervisors) aren't pleased because they have to find ways of rejecting female applicants for reasons other than their sex.[7]

According to this report the postal authorities, like the union, felt that "the physical tasks involved are too much for the women," and the report concluded "All indications are that postal authorities will continue to resist the employment of women in postal positions, except on a casual or part-time basis."[8] Denied access to the full-time and equally paid positions in the Post Office, it may not have been of much comfort to find the following comment in another report prepared for the Glassco Commission: " ... there is a valuable pool of skilled and experienced help available in the number of married women found in part-time and casual employment in the Public Service."[9]

The reconciliation of the full-time male workforce in the Post Office to the presence of women full-time workers was not complete by 1965. In that year the Ontario South West Regional Conference of the union sent to the National Convention the following resolution: "Be it resolved that this Convention urge the Civil Service Commission and the Post Office Department to discontinue the practice of employing full-time female Postal Employees (Mail Handling Class)."[10] Like many others, this was one of the resolutions that never reached the floor of the Convention for discussion. Later the same year the government established the Royal Commission of Inquiry into Working Conditions in the Post Office Department, commonly known as the Montpetit Commission. One local in New Brunswick stated in its brief to the Commission: "We are opposed to women P.Cs. (Postal Clerk, level 2) because they are too often given special treatment, they are always placed on jobs that require no physical effort ... We feel that if we are to apply the equal work for equal pay rule, they should be

---

[7] "Manpower in the Government Service, Project No. 2, Interim Report No. 11, Post Office Department," prepared for the *Royal Commission on Government Organization*, Ottawa, 2 June 1961, p. 4.

[8] *Ibid.*, p. 4.

[9] W. Donald Wood, "Analysis of Manpower Patterns and Trends in the Federal Public Service," prepared for the *Royal Commission on Government Organization*, Ottawa, 15 January 1962.

[10] Canadian Postal Employees Association, "Resolutions, Ninth Triennial National Convention," 22–24 September 1965, p. 123, No. 390.

THE CUPW NATIONAL CONVENTION 1968

The Convention floor with few women to be seen; at this time women were 12 percent of the union membership.

Elected officers, including the President, Willie Houle (centre, sitting) and the Vice-President, Joe Davidson (right of Houle). The first woman national officer was elected in 1983.

placed on any job that the male clerk is required to do."[11] There were sufficient complaints of this kind for the Commission to respond in its report:

> It was said that the Department has employed too many female employees. These employees constitute only about 2 percent of the full-time staff. The Department does not have full liberty of action in this matter. The Civil Service Act and Regulations give equal rights to men and women and the latter are not excluded from any competition provided they fulfil the conditions stipulated in the competition posters and that they possess the physical strength required.[12]

While some members and locals were still questioning the right of women to full-time employment, by the mid-1960s they were not a general concern within the union. Most union members were reconciled to the presence of the few full-time women workers: they were full members of the union, and concern for their welfare could be expressed on occasion. In a submission to the Montpetit Commission, the Saskatoon local expressed concern about working conditions, including the detail that there was no couch in the women's washroom.[13]

The number of women union members within the CPEA/CUPW increased marginally from 516 to 652 between 1962 and 1966—a shift from 5 to 6 percent of the membership.[14] While uncommon, a few locals elected women to the local executive, usually in the position of secretary. However, at the 1959 National Convention a woman was elected as the Regional Vice-President for Quebec North. The full-time women workers were few in number and thinly scattered at conventions, but they were not quite invisible. At the National Office of the union in Ottawa women workers were related to in another way, because the support staff employed by the union joined the Office and Professional Employees' International Union. These women negotiated their first contract with the CUPW in January 1967.[15]

However with so few women in the union, most of the ten thousand male members continued to send each other fraternal greetings, referred to the problems "the men" experienced at work, and belonged to the Postal Workers Brotherhood without much reason to consider the situation of women. Far more attention and concern was directed to the much larger number of women who

---

[11] Canadian Union of Postal Workers, Moncton Local, "Brief to the Royal Commission on Working Conditions," 22 November 1965, p. 2.

[12] Canada, *Report of the Royal Commission of Inquiry into Working Conditions in the Post Office Department*, Ottawa, October 1966, p. 62.

[13] Canadian Union of Postal Workers, Saskatoon Local, "Submission to the Royal Commission of Inquiry into Working Conditions in the Post Office Department," (no date), p. 14.

[14] Statistics Canada, *Corporations and Labour Unions Returns Act*, Part II—Labour Unions, Cat. 71–202, Ottawa, 1962–1966.

[15] Canadian Union Of Postal Workers, *The Postal Tribune*, Vol. XXXV, No. 1, January 1967, p. 1.

worked part-time in the Post Office. While the union had just 652 women full-time workers as members in 1966, in that year the Montpetit Commission reported 3,100 part-time workers in the Post Office, and almost all of them worked as inside postal workers.[16]

Women Part-Time Workers

The reluctant acceptance of female full-time workers was not repeated for part-time workers during the early 1960s. The opposition of the union to part-time work was absolute until 1966. Part-time workers could not be members of the union, a position that was reaffirmed at the 1965 Convention. In its publications, in its Convention resolutions and in its representations to the government, the union demanded the abolition of part-time work from the Post Office. In the union briefs to the Montpetit Commission and in its submissions before Judge Montpetit, the use of part-time workers within the Post Office was a primary grievance, expressed both by the National Executive and by locals across the country. There were three major reasons for union opposition to part-time work: the threat of cheap labour, the deskilling of the work that the unskilled part-timers represented, and the attitudes of the union members towards women.

Cheap Labour

The union perceived the introduction of part-time work as "cheap labour pure and simple,"[17] threatening the wages and the jobs of the full-time workers because the lower wages encouraged the employer to increase the number of part-time workers at the expense of the full-timers. Certainly there is no doubt that part-time workers were paid less than full-time workers. Initially in the 1950s part-time workers received a flat hourly rate of pay, lower than the hourly rate of any of the full-time workers. Then for a period they received the minimum rate for the job that they were hired to do, although they were not eligible for any pay increments nor for fringe benefits other than 4 percent addition to pay in lieu of vacation.

In 1963 the Post Office management created a new class of worker, the part-time Postal Helper. Before this change part-time workers were earning $1.55 an hour working as Postal Clerk 1 (PC1) or Mail Handlers, and $1.57 as Postal Clerk 2 (PC2). They also received the same 15 cents an hour for night work as the full-time workers. In 1963 the wages of these part-time workers

---

[16] Statistics Canada, *Corporations and Labour Unions Returns Act, Part II—Labour Unions*, Cat.71–202, Ottawa, 1966; Canada, *Report of the Royal Commission of Inquiry into Working Conditions in the Post Office Department*, Ottawa, October 1966, p. 9.

[17] Joe Davidson and John Deverell, *Joe Davidson*, James Lorimer, Toronto, 1978, p. 86.

were frozen, and any new part-time workers hired were classified as Postal Helpers and were paid just $1.43 an hour, with no additional 15 cents for night work. Thus, part-time workers hired before 1963 continued on their wages of $1.55 or $1.57 an hour while all new part-time workers earned only $1.43.[18]

In the years following 1963 the gap between the wages of part-time workers and full-time workers increased steadily. By 1966 the Postal Helper's hourly rate had been increased from $1.43 to $1.55. The wages of part-timers hired prior to 1963 had remained static at $1.55 or $1.57, with 15 cents extra for night work. Meanwhile, as of October 1966 the full-time workers had received increases so that their wages ranged from $2.07 for a Mail Handler to $2.25 for a Postal Clerk and $2.59 for a Dispatcher.[19] At this point, then, the part-time workers were earning 75 percent of the wages paid to the lowest paid full-time worker. The majority of part-time workers sorted the mail, and compared to the full-time Postal Clerks who also sorted the mail, they were earning only 69 percent of their pay rate. The Postal Helpers had received only a 12 cent increase in pay since 1963, while the part-timers hired before 1963 had received no pay increase for five years, since 1961.

Moreover, this does not take into account the increments received by the full-time workers for years of service, for which the part-time workers were not eligible. A full-time Postal Clerk at level 2 would start at $2.25 an hour, but with seven increments could reach the highest pay of $2.76 an hour. Regardless of the number of years that they worked in the Post Office the part-time workers received the same $1.55 an hour.

In 1969 a study by the Post Office estimated the cost of part-time staff compared to full-time staff in order to assess the impact of mechanization upon the cost of labour. The study said:

> At present, these part-time staff are paid at a much lower hourly rate than permanent staff, although in Montreal they sort approximately 60 percent of the City letter mail. Permanent staff in Montreal cost the Post Office twice as much on average (including fringe benefits and allowances for vacation and other absence) as part-time employees.[20]

By this point the part-time staff were receiving $1.75 an hour compared to $3 for full-time staff, and this study assessed that part-time workers received only 8 percent in benefits compared to 33 percent for the full-time workers. Consequently, the part-time staff cost just 47 percent of the cost of the full-time staff.

[18] Hearings of the Royal Commission of Inquiry into Working Conditions in the Post Office Department, "Part-time Help, Departmental Comments and Reply," File 50–1–30, 6 May 1966.

[19] Canadian Union of Postal Workers, *The Postal Tribune*, Vol. XXXIV, No. 12, December 1966, p. 45.

[20] Post Office Department, *A Canadian Public Address Postal Coding System*, prepared by Samson, Belair, Riddell, Stead Inc., November 1969, p. 66.

Unskilled Labour

Inside postal workers were employed in three basic categories, Postal Clerks, Mail Dispatchers and Mail Handlers. Postal Clerks, the large majority of inside postal workers, received, forwarded and sorted the mail and also acted as wicket clerks dealing with the public. Mail Dispatchers loaded and unloaded the mail bags; requiring a thorough knowledge of distribution, timetables and points of connection, they also supervised the Mail Handlers, and maintained records and reports. The Mail Handlers assisted the Dispatchers in their duties, especially in moving mail bags. It was the Postal Clerk position that was opened to significant numbers of part-time workers.

The skill involved in the Postal Clerk's job was the capacity to sort letters into pigeonhole cases, thus directing the mail to a specific area. A Postal Clerk had to memorize at least 2,000 destinations, and sorted letters into a pigeon hole case with up to one hundred separations. Cities were divided into sections, called postal zones and in Toronto, for example, sorting required a knowledge of the postal zones for 3,000 street names, including where the street crossed zone boundaries. The Post Office Department required every Postal Clerk to pass a sorting examination with a 90 percent accuracy rate, and to prepare for these exams the Postal Clerks practised in their spare time. Moreover these examinations were repeated every year for as long as the postal worker remained on the job, and penalties, including wage deductions, were applied for failure to meet the required standard. The nature of these examinations, their frequency and the penalties were a source of irritation to the postal workers, but the need for an initial testing period to ensure the necessary level of skill was never in question.

Deskilling the work involved the introduction of the ABC system in the city sortation. This meant that instead of sorting by postal zone the sorting was done on an entirely alphabetical basis by the first letter of the street name. Working on the ABC system required only a knowledge of the alphabet and could be done by untrained staff, who were not required to take any examinations.

The unskilled labour hired by the Post Office was part-time and predominantly female. Because there was a surge of mail arriving in the late afternoon or early evening from the street box collections and mail arriving from other post offices, part-time workers could be hired at this time for just three to five hours a day to handle the city sortation. Post Office management explained the creation of the lower-paid Postal Helper classification in 1963 by stating that the part-time workers were doing different, less skilled work than the full-time workers and that comparative studies with industry had suggested that they were paying their unskilled workforce more than the market rate.[21]

---

[21] Hearings of the Royal Commission of Inquiry into Working Conditions in the Post Office Department, "Part-time Help, Departmental Comments and Reply," File 50–1–30, 6 May 1966.

In their complaints to the Montpetit Commission, the union and its locals referred regularly to the low morale created among the full-time workers by the use of untrained part-timers.[22] Clearly the value of their knowledge was in question if the work could be done by untrained staff.

Female Labour

It is not clear exactly what proportion of the part-time workers in the Post Office were women during the 1960s, although it was certainly the large majority.[23] In 1966 the part-time workers employed in Montreal submitted a brief to the Montpetit Commission and it states that of the 940 part-time workers in that city 750 were women, that is 80 percent.[24] However, activists within the union at the time recall even higher proportions. Jean-Claude Parrot, who was a full-time official for the CUPW Montreal local in the 1960s, estimates that at least 95 percent of the part-time workers were women.[25] In some locals, such as Winnipeg, the part-time workers were entirely women.[26]

If women had not been warmly welcomed into the Post Office as full-time workers, their position as cheap, unskilled labour ensured the enmity of most union members. Many full-time male workers felt that women did not really need the income and were working only for extras, not out of necessity to support dependent families. The minority of male part-time workers were regarded as moonlighters, who had other jobs and were therefore also earning money for frills rather than food. At the 1965 National Convention a delegate stated: "Part-time workers are simply there to add a little income to their regular income and they are not interested in having the same working conditions as full-time workers."[27] To the Montpetit Commission the CUPW Field Officer for the Maritime Region commented about the situation at the Halifax post office:

---

[22] Canadian Union of Postal Workers, "National Brief of CUPW to the Royal Commission of Inquiry into Working Conditions in the Post Office Department," 12 April 1966, p. 2.

[23] The Post Office did not keep such records, and information from Statistics Canada by sex does not include a breakdown by full-time and part-time.

[24] Canadian Union of Public Employees, Local 976, Part-time Employees at the Montreal Post Office, "Submission to the Royal Commission of Inquiry into Working Conditions in the Post Office Department," 8 February 1966, p. 1.

[25] Interview with Jean-Claude Parrot, National President of the Canadian Union of Postal Workers, Ottawa, 14 July 1987.

[26] Interview with Pat Miller, CUPW National Director for the Western Region, Ottawa, 20 October 1988.

[27] Canadian Postal Employees Association, *Ninth Triennial National Convention Proceedings*, Toronto, 22–25 September 1965, p. 422.

In Halifax there is a staff of women, some of whom have worked at the Postmaster's discretion for the past ten years. These women are not career women. They do not want full employment and are only interested in earning pocket money.[28]

Most union members believed that the part-timers had only a part-time commitment to the job, and that they were not interested in improving their working conditions because they were not reliant upon the income. Consequently, they could not be relied upon to share the interests of the full-time workers and would not be prepared to press for improvements to the same extent. The part-time workers were perceived as a quite separate and different group of workers; one delegate at the 1965 Convention referred to full and part-time workers as "two opposite sections of workers.[29]

However, it seems that, given the choice, male part-time workers were preferable to female part-time workers. From the Maritime Regional Convention the following resolution was sent to the 1965 National Convention, and although it was not debated on the floor, it appeared as part of an approved list of Resolutions published by the National Executive: "Be it resolved that if it is necessary to employ part-time and casual help that these be hired from the unemployed group and that men be given preference over women."[30] In their brief to the Montpetit Commission later in 1965, the Halifax local reiterated this position and explained that hiring men would "train men who could later be hired on as regular men when the opening occurred." They described their problem further:

Most of these part-time and casual help are on duty from 5:00 p.m. to 9:00 p.m. These would total around 25 compared to about 11 men of the regular staff at the same time. Any stranger coming in off the street would think that we carried a staff of all women.[31]

The introduction of low-paid, untrained, predominantly women part-time workers presented a threat both to the status of the work and to the standard of living of the full-time inside postal workers. In this case the likelihood of negative effects was increased by three factors: the actions of the Post Office Department, the generally poor management-staff relations in the Post Office, and the relatively powerless position of the union to deal with any grievances, including this one.

---

[28] Canadian Union of Postal Workers, Field Officer for the Maritime Region, "Submission to the Royal Commission of Inquiry into Working Conditions in the Post Office Department," 23 November 1965, p. 3.

[29] Canadian Postal Employees Association, *Ninth Triennial National Convention Proceedings*, Toronto, 22–25 September 1965, p. 422.

[30] Canadian Union of Postal Workers, *The Postal Tribune*, Vol. XXXIV, No. 6, June 1966, p. 56, Resolution No. 51.

[31] Canadian Union of Postal Workers, Halifax Local, "Submission to the Royal Commission of Inquiry into Working Conditions in the Post Office Department," 15 November 1965, p. 14.

The Use of Part-Time Work in the Post Office

In response to complaints by the union, in July 1964 the Post Оᵢᵢ. ment issued a statement of policy on the use of part-time work. It clearly ᵢₙᵢ. cated that part-time workers were only to be used for peak period work and not to replace full-time workers. Part-time workers were not to be employed back-to-back to cover an eight hour period, nor were they to be used if there was eight hours of work to be done and eight hours available to meet the required service so that a full-time worker could be employed. The Post Office Circular did go on to mention that day-to-day situations might require such uses in practice, but stated that the policies were not to be ignored on a regular basis.[32]

However, in 1966 union locals across the country informed the Montpetit Commission that the use of part-time workers was excessive. For some locals it was their primary complaint and the National Office of the union listed the problem as second only to the question of inadequate pay rates. Union locals protested that contrary to departmental policy, part-time workers were employed on regular day shifts, preventing full-time workers from moving from night to day work. It was also claimed that work was created for part-time workers that could have been done by full-time staff.[33] In Montreal the Montpetit Report noted that mail was processed by part-time workers in the evening, but was not dispatched until the following morning. There was therefore no reason to employ part-time rather than full-time workers to sort the mail.[34]

Union complaints about part-time work had extended over many years, and it was during the 1950s that the number of part-time workers had been significantly expanded, as Table 2 indicates. Not only had the number of part-time workers been growing during the 1950s, but their proportion relative to the total number of workers had increased from 3 percent in 1950 to almost 10 percent by 1957. By the mid-1960s the percentage of part-time workers had risen to almost 11 percent.

Nonetheless, this proportion of part-time workers, while significant, does not appear to be excessively large, so that one might wonder why the union was so concerned over the issue. But, these figures relate part-time work to the total number of employees in the staff post offices, while the part-time workers were heavily concentrated within particular positions. In 1966 the non-supervisory

---

[32] Post Office Department, Director of Postal Service, "Part-time Employees," Circular Letter, Ottawa, 17 July 1964.

[33] Canadian Union of Postal Workers, "National Brief of CUPW to The Royal Commission of Inquiry into Working Conditions in the Post Office Department," 12 April 1966, p. 2. These issues are also raised in submissions from locals in Vancouver (20 October 1965), Regina (8 December 1965), Toronto (7 March 1966), Montreal (10 January 1966), Quebec (17 January 1966) and Halifax (15 November 1965).

[34] Canada, *Report of the Royal Commission of Inquiry into Working Conditions in the Post Office Department*, Ottawa, October 1966. p. 51.

TABLE 2: Part-Time Workers in the Post Office, 1950 to 1957 and 1967			
Year	Total Workers	Part-TIme Workers	Percentage Part-Time
1950	17,853	536	3.0
1951	17,953	634	3.5
1952	18,363	876	4.8
1953	18,644	1,053	5.6
1954	19,741	1,242	6.3
1955	21,176	1,522	7.2
1956	21,614	1,665	7.7
1957	22,619	2,142	9.5
1967	30,130	3,200	10.6

SOURCE: Canada Post Office, "Report of the Postmaster General," for the years ending 31 March 1950 to 1957, and 1967.

staff employed in post offices across the country comprised 12,200 inside postal workers, 10,400 letter carriers and 3,100 part-time workers.[35] Very few part-time workers were employed as letter carriers, so that of the inside postal workers 20 percent were employed part-time, a very substantial proportion.

Apart from concern about the large number of part-time workers employed as inside postal workers, accusations of nepotism and favouritism were made by the union against management. Part-time workers were not hired through the Civil Service Commission like full-time workers, but could be employed at the discretion of the local management in the post offices. Consequently, it was much faster and less complicated to hire and fire part-time than full-time workers. On this situation Montpetit noted: "It would be needless to conceal the fact that the hiring of casual employees and part-timers may give rise to favouritism or nepotism."[36] Joe Davidson put it more directly:

> There were few more galling experiences for anyone than to see some woman chatting with her male supervisor all through the shift without sorting much mail, check her tally to find that somehow it showed full production and then see her out with the same supervisor for a drink after work.[37]

While the union called for the abolition of part-time work, the Montpetit Report maintained that it was reasonable for management to hire these workers to deal with peak periods in the work load, but it was recommended that a

[35] Canada, *Report of the Royal Commission of Inquiry into Working Conditions in the Post Office Department*, Ottawa, October 1966, p. 9.

[36] *Ibid.*, p. 57.

[37] Joe Davidson and John Deverell, *Joe Davidson*, James Lorimer, Toronto, 1978, p. 88.

thorough check of the part-time situation be carried out to ensure that their numbers were kept to a minimum and that all part-time workers be hired through the National Employment Service to avoid nepotism.

Labour Relations in the Post Office

Whatever abuses of part-time work were taking place, certainly the poor state of management-union relations within the Post Office was conducive to dislike and suspicion of management motives and initiatives. Through the early 1960s the workers' patience was strained by delayed or cancelled wage increases, bad working conditions, and a disciplinarian management style. In this context it is not necessary to enter into great detail on all the grievances of the workers, but it is important to have some knowledge of the situation in order to better understand the union's response to part-time work.

It was "the almighty dollar, or rather the withholding of it"[38] that created the major tensions within the workforce during the 1960s. Before the introduction of negotiated collective agreements in 1967, the Civil Service Commission generally recommended pay increases for the entire public service, including the Post Office Department, to the Treasury Board. However, in 1958 and again in 1959 increases were cancelled and as the postal workers entered 1960 on their 1957 rates of pay, their demeanour was less than positive towards their employer. In July 1960 an increase of $450 was given, placing the top salary for inside postal workers at $4,320. But, again in 1961 and 1962 no pay raises were forthcoming, and the 1963 increase of $300 to $360 did not constitute a sufficient catch up for the static pay rates of previous years.

Yet again in 1964, the government was not ready to announce an increase and discussions with the union continued on into 1965. Between 1957 and 1965 CPEA members had received only two pay increases, instead of the annual increase that had previously been customary. They had seen their wages gradually fall behind those of other workers employed in public services, such as the police and firefighters. Consequently, for 1965 the CPEA was attempting to obtain an increase of $660 for all inside postal workers. When the government announced a raise of $300 to $360 the inside postal workers, led by the Montreal local, walked off the job. This 1965 strike was the first in the Post Office since 1924, and was illegal because in law federal civil servants did not have the right to strike.[39]

While pay was the major catalyst behind the dissatisfaction in the Post Office and the 1965 strike, many other grievances irritated the workforce on a daily basis. These grievances were aired through the Montpetit Commission, a Royal Commission to investigate conditions in the Post Office, established by the government in September 1965 as a result of the strike.

---

[38] *Ibid.*, p. 67.

[39] *Ibid.*, chapter 3.

The grievances covered every aspect of the work. There were complaints from many locals about poor physical working conditions creating a hazardous work environment, including inadequate lighting and heating, the absence of air conditioning, dusty and dirty workplaces, unhygienic washrooms and eating areas, and poorly maintained equipment. In 1964–65 there were 1,928 minor accidents in the Post Office and a further 1,983 causing different degrees and durations of disability.[40] Of all government departments, boards or agencies, only the Department of National Defense had a higher rate of work-related accidents. To compound this issue locals complained of the absence of adequate first aid facilities and medical care at the workplace. In its Report the Commission stated:

> We were not able to check everything but we have to admit that some post offices, postal stations or railway mail cars left rather distressing impressions. Whatever the reasons may be, the Department—and it must assume this responsibility with respect to its employees—was too often unconcerned if not negligent.[41]

Workers' dissatisfaction also stemmed from the hours of work, which involved shift, night and weekend work, timing of pay cheques and late payment of overtime, boot and clothing arrangements, vacations and other kinds of leave, the examinations and promotions, to name but a few.

The complaints were embittered by the perception of the workers that the Department management did not treat the complaints seriously and made little effort to deal reasonably with the problems raised. The atmosphere in the post offices was described as disciplinarian and intolerant. The Montpetit Report noted that "Except in one or two districts, the attitude of some supervisors and postmasters towards their employees leaves much to be desired" and that as a result some union representatives "are rebelling to the point that they are alarmingly unwilling to compromise."[42]

Post Office management established its expectations of its workforce through its Code of Discipline, an 18 page document that set the tone in its first sentence: "Discipline is essential to the maintenance of proper order, control, good behaviour and efficiency."[43] Apart from major misconduct, such as theft, other misconduct meant "an infraction of the rules of conduct made by the Department in respect to the behaviour of its employees" and included absenteeism, lateness,

---

[40] Canada, *Report of the Royal Commission of Inquiry into Working Conditions in the Post Office Department*, Ottawa, October 1966, p. 167.

[41] *Ibid.*, p. 170.

[42] *Ibid.*, p. 17.

[43] Post Office Department, Deputy Postmaster General, "Code of Discipline," Ottawa, 1 November 1966, p. 2.

inaccurate record entries, and the loss of keys. Quite complex arrangements were laid down for different levels of discipline for more than one infraction or for different breaches of discipline, entitled "cumulative irregularities."

For example, casual leave referred to sick leave for up to three days without a medical certificate, and the Code recommends that "if periods of short absences continue, enquiries should be made to ascertain the validity of the absences."[44] At the first perceived abuse of casual leave, counselling is recommended, including the suggestion that "management has a responsibility to impress employees with the important fact that abnormal absences *even if supported by a medical certificate* place in doubt the usefulness of the employee to the Department."[45] Casual leave could be withdrawn and restored by the supervisor, with no right of appeal by the worker. The union objected to the withdrawal of sick leave and complained that some managers snooped on their sick employees, paying home visits at odd hours of the day and night.[46]

For arriving late to work, the penalty was a reduction in salary and again these penalties were at the discretion of local management and could not be appealed by the worker involved. Another example is the loss of keys, which was considered a misconduct in the Code, even if due to carelessness. Three repetitions of this form of misconduct resulted in one to three days suspension from work without pay, and dismissal was recommended for a fourth "violation."

The Code contains a further list of miscellaneous acts of misconduct, covering 20 types of behaviour and including:

(a) Abuse of coffee and other breaks, washroom absences, smoking privileges, etc. ...
(d) Disorderly conduct; disturbing others (horseplay, wisecracking, talking) ...
(h) Lack of courtesy, discretion, neatness.

The union's description of managers' intolerant attitudes, high handed rules and petty obsession with regulations gain in credibility from a reading of the Department's Code of Discipline. Moreover, in the last six months of 1963 there were 1,235 salary reductions of $5-$10 for periods of from one to six months, and a further 408 such reductions in the first six months of 1964.[47]

The bad relations engendered by management's day-to-day attitudes and actions are reflected in the strength of the union's comments. The Quebec City local stated it generally in their brief:

---

[44] *Ibid.*, p. iii.

[45] *Ibid.*, p. iv.

[46] Canadian Union of Postal Workers, "National Brief of CUPW to the Royal Commission of Inquiry into Working Conditions in the Post Office Department," Ottawa, 12 April 1966, p. 3.

[47] *Hansard,* Ottawa, 17 February 1965, answers by Hon. Rene Tremblay, Postmaster General to questions by Mr. Orlikow, No. 2533, 1 December 1964.

The men can no longer accept being just numbers, can no longer accept being victims of a bureaucratic regime that measures everything in terms of the government before taking into consideration the human rights of the workers.[48]

It was under these general conditions of mistrust and suspicion that part-time workers were being introduced into the Post Office. However, the discontent and anger experienced by the postal workers was due not only to the actions of management but also to the incapacity of the union to rectify their grievances.

The Canadian Postal Employees Association

Until the enactment of the 1967 Public Service Staff Relations Act (PSSRA) the union of inside postal workers, along with all the other unions representing federal civil servants, did not have the right to bargain for a collective agreement with the employer. In fact, the public service "unions" prior to this time can only be very loosely referred to as such, given that they could do little more than make requests to the employer. The union itself described the situation with regard to management as "little more than the cap in hand relationship.[49] During the 1960s the union was unable to assert much influence with regard to salaries, even to obtain a salary increase, let alone the amount.

In 1961 the Civil Service Act was amended to provide for formal consultation with the staff organizations, but all final decisions remained with Treasury Board. The limitations of this concession included the fact that neither side in the consultations could divulge the salary increases that they suggested. As a result, the pages of the *Postal Tribune*, the union's national publication at the time, were devoid of any information on the proceedings, other than that meetings were taking place. The resulting secrecy surrounding the discussions did nothing to engender good feeling or trust among the union's members.

A discussion of the union of inside postal workers in the 1960s that did not mention the controversy over stools would be incomplete, and it serves here as an example of the lack of control exercised by the union, even over relatively insignificant issues. In the 1950s, sorting mail involved standing before the pigeonhole cases for 8 hours since stools were not provided for the workers. Joe Davidson described the situation in Toronto where the workers brought their own stools to work and then became involved in time-consuming efforts to protect them from other stool-hungry workers.[50] Years of requests and complaints by the union finally resulted in one stool being provided for every five workers, predictably resulting in a constant struggle among the workers to obtain one. In 1959

---

[48] Canadian Union of Postal Workers, Quebec Local, "Submission to the Royal Commission of Inquiry into Working Conditions in the Post Office Department," 15 January 1966, p. 1.

[49] Canadian Union of Postal Workers, "National Brief of CUPW to the Royal Commission of Inquiry into Working Conditions in the Post Office Department," 12 April 1966, p. 2.

[50] Joe Davidson and John Deverell, *Joe Davidson*, James Lorimer, Toronto, 1978, p. 52.

the Postmaster General promised to make stools available to every worker who needed one, but in 1965 the *Postal Tribune* was still lamenting the lack of them. The Post Office then limited their use to 75 percent of those who needed them, resulting in further union protests, consultations with headquarters and letters from the members. Finally, in February 1965, Post Office Circular No. 37 allowed stools for all workers sorting mail. The union was assured that they would be supplied "as soon as possible."[51]

Complaints and problems experienced by the workers, of which there were many, were not open to negotiation and the union obtained little success in its meetings with management. To the Montpetit Commission the union complained that grievances were often ignored, or were channelled up the bureaucracy to become subject to endless delays, and that too often management made decisions without reference to the union or its concerns. The union's solution to this situation was to propose the implementation of full collective bargaining within the Post Office. At the CPEA's 1950 National Convention the delegates adopted a policy of support for bringing federal government workers under the Industrial Disputes Investigations Act, the same legislation that regulated industrial relations for private industry and that provided for full collective bargaining and the right to strike. From that time forward the union continued in its lobbying to government to press for this resolution of labour relations within the Post Office, a goal that was not actually achieved until 1981.

Meanwhile the lack of influence wielded by the union in the 1950s and early 1960s only contributed to the fear engendered by the increased use of part-time work. Essentially the union could do nothing to deal with the situation, except meet with management to complain, with the same negative results as on most other issues. And yet here was a situation that was potentially more damaging to the full-time workforce and to the union than any other. Part-time work threatened not only the wages, but also the actual jobs of the regular workers, and given that part-time workers were excluded from the union, the continued growth of part-time work also threatened the organization itself.

Union Reaction to Part-Time Work

From regional conventions across the country, including Alberta, British Columbia, Ontario and the Maritimes, resolutions were sent to the 1965 National Convention of the CPEA to abolish part-time work in the Post Office.[52] Although this issue was not debated at the Convention it was referred with other issues to the National Executive to deal with, and was subsequently approved and listed as

---

[51] Canadian Union of Postal Workers, *The Postal Tribune*, Vol. XXXIII, No. 6, June 1965, p. 28.

[52] Canadian Postal Employees Association, "Resolutions. Ninth Triennial National Convention," Toronto, 22–24 September 1965, pp. 193–203.

Resolution No. 49: "Be it resolved that part-time work be abolished."[53] This then was the formal policy of the union.

Other adopted resolutions dealt with the mechanisms necessary to abolish part-time work. One resolution called for an increase in the number of full-time staff to adequately cover for workers on sick leave, so that part-timers need not be hired for this purpose. In a similar vein it was agreed that a formula should be established so that the hours covered by part-time and casual workers in a year should be the basis for increasing the full-time staff complement the following year.[54]

However, from Quebec came a different approach than just the desire to abolish part-time work, an approach that caused some heated debate at the 1965 Convention. The Quebec Provincial Convention sent a resolution that the Constitution should be amended to allow part-time workers to join the union.

The Constitution Committee recommended non-concurrence with the resolution, being entirely opposed to the expansion of membership to part-time workers.[55] The first delegate to speak on the resolution spoke for the majority when he said: "When did we start to take part-timers into our Association? I have been a member for 20 years and all I have heard during that time is don't take in any part-timers or casual help. I am against it."[56] Those who were in favour of the change argued that the part-time workforce was "here to stay," that there was nothing the union could do about their presence and that they had to be controlled by being within the union. Then at least the union could obtain equal pay for them, so that they could not be used as a source of cheap labour. It was argued that this in turn would reduce the use of part-time workers. One delegate explained:

> If we do not take them in with us it will hurt us because the Department will take advantage of this situation and pay them low wages, whereas if they come in with us we can try to get them better wages and better working conditions. In the long run the Department will realize that it is no cheaper to hire part-timers than it is to have full-time employees, and that will reduce the number.[57]

Some other delegates agreed: "I can tell you this much, the Post Office Department will not be so willing to get them in when it has to pay them the minimum wage (for the job)."[58]

---

[53] Canadian Union of Postal Workers, *The Postal Tribune*, Vol. XXXIV, No. 5, June 1966, p. 56, Resolution No. 49.

[54] *Ibid.*, Resolutions No. 52, 54.

[55] Canadian Postal Employees Association, *Ninth Triennial National Convention Proceedings*, Toronto, 22–25 September 1965, pp. 401, 413.

[56] *Ibid.*, p. 401.

[57] *Ibid.*, p. 419.

[58] *Ibid.*, p. 417.

Montreal delegates warned that if part-time workers were not accepted into the CUPW, other unions would organize them. This had already occurred in Montreal, where the Canadian Union of Public Employees had a local of part-time workers. Elsewhere the Civil Service Employees Association (later the Public Service Alliance of Canada) had organized a few locals of part-time postal workers. However, the main concern in Montreal was the Confederation of National Trade Unions (CNTU), which had been organizing workers in other unions and was perceived as a strong political organization. In the event it was not the CNTU that presented the gravest threat to the CUPW, but the Montreal delegates were correct in anticipating future difficulties around collective bargaining. In July 1965, just two months before the Convention, the Heeney Report had been submitted to the government recommending limited collective bargaining rights for federal government employees, and legislation was expected within a year. As a Montreal delegate observed with some foresight: "Whether we like it or not we must find a way to get the regular part-timer into our bargaining unit, otherwise we will run into trouble when we come to bargain collectively."[59]

This Convention was held in September 1965, just two months after the first strike by postal workers in 40 years, a strike that changed the participants and their union. It was at this Convention that the name of the union was changed to the Canadian Union of Postal Workers. Consequently, the role of the part-time workers in that strike was an important element in the discussion about their membership in the union. One delegate commented that the part-time workers had not known which way to turn during the strike, since management told them to work: "If we had them in our organization at least they will know that when we are out on strike they are out on strike and we will not have them crossing our picket lines."[60]

Montreal delegates pointed out that the part-time workers had supported them in the 1965 strike, although they were not members of the union and did not have to respect the picket lines. "We did not ask them, we had no control over them, but they decided to do that."[61] However, elsewhere the part-time workers had not struck with the other postal workers, and delegates had bitter words about their role. A Toronto delegate said: "I consider this group as a group which jeopardized my job in the Toronto Post Office during the last strike. They crossed the picket lines every day."[62]

In dealing with this resolution on admitting part-time workers, the Finance Committee to the Convention developed and recommended a formula for part-

[59] *Ibid.*, p. 414.

[60] *Ibid.*, pp. 417–418.

[61] *Ibid.*, p. 419.

[62] *Ibid.*, p. 421.

Women part-time workers on the picket line in Montreal during the 1965 strike.

time workers to pay half the dues of the full-time members, but they were to have only an associate membership without the right to vote. There were reservations about this proposal. As one delegate saw it: "Accept their money but do not give them a vote. Are we going to be hypocrites? That would simply be a case of taxation without representation."[63] But, to contemplate full membership for part-time workers was not within the scope of the discussion. At the final vote 68 of the delegates would have allowed part-time workers to join the union, but 101 voted against it, so the policy of excluding part-time workers was reaffirmed.

From the Part-Time Workers' Point of View

It is not really possible to know what most part-time workers felt about their situation within the Post Office during the early 1960s. However, that there was dissatisfaction in some areas is apparent, because it was expressed in submissions to the Montpetit Commission. Some groups of part-time workers had

---

[63] *Ibid.*, p. 422.

joined unions other than the CUPW and expressed their grievances to the Commission. The most revealing document is a brief presented by the part-time workers in the Montreal Post Office, who belonged to Local 976 of the Canadian Union of Public Employees (CUPE).

The submission states that at that time, in early 1966, there were 940 part-time workers employed in the Montreal Post Office and that 750 of them were women (80 percent). Contrary to the perceptions of the male full-time workers, the part-timers gave the following explanation for why they were working for pay:

> The women, who are the majority, have an average age of more than 40 years. Several of them are widows with dependent children and have only this income to live on. Others work to help a husband on a low wage and the extra they earn of an evening enables them to balance the budget.[64]

The brief goes on to say that the male part-time workers were also in the position of trying to earn enough to live on because their other income was insufficient, given the increased cost of living.

Many of their grievances reflected those of the full-time workers, including dirty workplaces, nowhere to eat, favouritism, intimidation, and the lack of adequate equipment. For example, the brief states: "Some employees, especially the women, have to work for hours standing up because there are not enough stools for all the staff."[65] Arriving in the middle or late afternoon, presumably the part-timers found that the limited number of stools were already taken.

Particular to part-time work, several problems are raised by the brief. The Montreal part-time workers complain of the unequal pay received by part-time workers. By this point Postal Helpers were receiving $1.55 an hour, but part-time workers hired before 1963 were earning up to $1.72 for doing the same work. However, this latter group had received no pay increase since 1961 and this was also cause for dissatisfaction. The brief refers to the lack of benefits for the part-time workforce, in particular the absence of sick pay. Under the Civil Service Act Regulations, Section 100, a part-timer was not entitled to any leave other than payment in lieu for vacation and statutory holidays. It is also noted in the brief that if a part-time worker was absent from work due to sickness for more than two months, they had to start again as a new employee. This meant a pay reduction to the level of Postal Helper. Also, since every new part-time worker had to be employed for 30 days before being eligible for the 4 percent vacation pay, it was required that this be repeated.

On the conditions of work, the part-timers complained that they often did not work the hours that they were hired to work, that their hours were irregular and often changed without prior warning. They also protested the use of the token

---

[64] Canadian Union of Public Employees, Local 976, Part-Time Employees at the Montreal Post Office, "Submission to the Royal Commission of Inquiry into Working Conditions in the Post Office Department," 8 February 1966, p. 2.

[65] *Ibid.*, p. 5.

system for their work, a system of individual work measurement. In 1963 the CPEA had managed to eliminate individual work measurement for the full-time workers, but it was maintained for the part-timers. Each time a tray of mail was sorted the worker placed a token in the tray and the supervisor could check the number of tokens for each part-time worker to ensure that production standards were maintained. However, the Montreal part-time workers strongly protested that the system led to favouritism by management. They complained that preferential treatment was also given to some part-time workers over hours of work and the number of reprimands.

Other than the CUPE local in Montreal, there were several locals of part-time workers across the country that belonged to the Civil Service Association of Canada (CSAC). The CSAC submitted a brief to the Montpetit Commission in which it complained of the treatment of part-time workers, in particular the "gross injustice" of the lower wages paid to part-timers. The brief stated: "The part-time employee provides a valuable and necessary service and because these employees are not full-time there should be no suggestion of cheap labour."[66]

While the Commission reviewed the complaints of the part-time workers, the Report recommended only that an allowance be made to the part-time workers in lieu of sick leave. Perhaps on this question of benefits, the Commissioner was influenced by the perspective of the Deputy Postmaster General. Questioned as to whether regular part-time workers should receive the same benefits as the full-time workers on a pro-rata basis, he responded:

> In most of the big offices where they are mostly married women I think it would drive us crazy, because there is quite a bit of absenteeism for one reason or another and while we do control it I think entitlement to leave for housewives and some of those other jobs (sic) they would take every bit of leave that they could get and would consider it as a right rather than a privilege.[67]

The Monpetit Report was not overly sympathetic towards the problems expressed by the part-time workers. Of the eleven recommendations that relate to part-time work, all but the one concerning the sick leave allowance pertain to the control and reduction of part-time employment. The Report makes no recommendation concerning the lower pay rates of the part-time workers, and states: "We do not wish to deprive part-time employees of an essential livelihood, but it is our responsibility to give our attention first of all to full-time employees."[68] This position is considered to be self-evident, so no further explanation is forthcoming, although one might question why the "essential livelihood" of the part-timer was less important than that of the full-time worker.

[66] Civil Service Association of Canada, "Submission to the Royal Commission of Inquiry into Working Conditions in the Post Office Department," 3 November 1965, p. 5.

[67] Hearings of the Royal Commission of Inquiry into Working Conditions in the Post Office Department, Ottawa, 9–10 May 1966, p. 12363.

[68] Canada, *Report of the Royal Commission of Inquiry into Working Conditions in the Post Office Department*, Ottawa, October 1966, p. 52.

	1960–1	1961–2	1962–3	1963–4	1964–5	% change
National	1702	2241	2717	3112	3357	97.3
Montreal	178	301	509	640	586	229.9
Toronto	230	239	229	252	282	22.7
Ottawa	24	65	89	84	106	334.8
Vancouver	39	23	65	33	54	37.5
Winnipeg	59	95	55	55	69	17.0

Table 3: Expenditures on Casual Workers, 1960 to 1965 ($000s)

SOURCE: Letter from Gaspé Taché, Assistant Director of Personnel, Post Office Department, to Mr. Faguy, Advisor to the Royal Commission of Inquiry into Working Conditions in the Post Office Department, 6 January 1966, p. 2.

Casual Women Workers

Apart from the few full-time women workers and the large number of part-time workers in the Post Office, women were also employed as casual workers.

The Post Office regulations laid down specific reasons for hiring casual workers. They were to be employed on a temporary basis for only two reasons: to replace the regular staff absent due to vacations, sick leave or other reasons, and to help reduce the amount of overtime by covering temporary surges in mail volume. Casuals were not to be employed for more than six months, but should this become necessary, requests for extensions had to be submitted to the District Director and forwarded to the Civil Service Commission in Ottawa for approval. Otherwise hiring casuals, as with the part-timers, was at the discretion of local management in the post offices.[69]

The union's complaints about casuals paralleled those about the part-time workforce: they were cheap unskilled labour, employed at lower rates of pay; their use was excessive and therefore they were replacing regular full-time workers; and because they were hired by the local management nepotism and favouritism were common.

All casuals were paid at the Postal Helper level: $1.43 in 1963 and $1.55 by 1965, considerably below the pay of the full-time workers. This lower pay rate was questioned by the Montpetit Commission, particularly since many casual workers were hired specifically to replace a full-time worker and therefore to do the same work. Casual workers were not eligible for any benefits, not even the statutory holidays that the part-time workers received. They were paid only for the number of hours worked and after five weeks of employment were eligible to receive 4 percent in lieu of vacation.

---

[69] Post Office Department, "Casual Employees," *Personnel Manual*, amended March 1965.

Between 1960 and 1965 the use of casuals in the Post Office doubled. In 1960 the number of casuals employed monthly varied from a low of 521 to 641 at the maximum. In 1965 the numbers had increased from 716 to a high of 1,340, with more than a thousand employed in most months.[70] It should be clarified that these figures do not include the Christmas help hired by the Post Office to deal with the surge in mail at that time of year, but the casual workforce employed every month of the year.

The increased use of casuals was not consistent across the country. Table 3 shows that expenditures on casual staff between 1960 and 1965 increased by 97 percent across the country, but varied among the five largest post offices from a 17 percent increase in Winnipeg to almost 335 percent in Ottawa.

By the mid 1960s it was in Montreal that the largest number of casuals were employed. The magnitude of the issue is better understood from the following details. As the table above shows, between 1960 and 1964 the expenditure on casuals in the Montreal Post Office more than tripled from $178,000 to $640,000, but then fell back the following year to $586,000. The reason that the expenditure on casuals dropped back in 1964–65 is that a large increase in the regular staff was made. A total of 236 full-time and 100 part-time staff were added to the regular staff of that Post Office "with a view to drastically reducing the casual help and over-time."[71]

This detailed information was obtained by the Montpetit Commission from their questions to the Post Office Department. It was also ascertained that in Quebec City 203 full-time postal clerks were employed, 56 part-time workers and the equivalent of 60 casual workers.[72] In other words more than one-third of the staff of that post office was part-time or casual. In a letter to the Commission the Post Office admitted that contrary to Post Office policy, 151 casuals had been employed continually for more than one year, including 32 in Quebec, 27 in London, 26 in Ottawa and 23 in Windsor.[73]

In discussing the issue of casual work with headquarters officials of the Post Office, Judge Montpetit warned them: "I must say to you that there are certain postmasters who have agreed before us that they do employ casuals on a regular

---

[70] Statistics Canada, *Federal Government Employment*, Cat.72–004, Ottawa, January 1960-December 1965.

[71] Letter from Gaspé Taché, Assistant Director of Personnel, Post Office Department, to Mr. Faguy, Advisor to the Royal Commission of Inquiry into Working Conditions in the Post Office Department, 6 January 1966, p. 2.

[72] *Ibid.*, 9 March 1966.

[73] *Ibid.*, 22 December 1965.

basis and who stay regularly there and have been there for quite a number of months, if not years."[74] The Deputy Postmaster General and the Director of Personnel were unable to explain the large number of casuals at some post offices, although they did agree that in Montreal there had been "excessive use of casuals" and that the situation in Quebec should be investigated.[75] Despite the recommendations of the Montpetit Report that the situation be closely checked and controlled, the use of casual workers continued to increase. While in 1965 1,000 casuals were employed on average each month in the Post Office, by 1968 the figure had doubled to 2,000 casual workers each month.[76]

It is interesting to find the Deputy Postmaster General reporting to the Montpetit Commission that the great majority of casual workers were women, because the data available suggest that this was not the case. According to Statistics Canada figures for 1962 to 1965, women were approximately half of the casual workforce, varying from 50 to 54 percent over those years.[77] Although the large majority of regular part-time workers were women, this was not the case with the casual workforce. It is likely that not only the Deputy Postmaster General was confused about just who was who in the Post Office. Union members would also have experienced considerable difficulty in identifying the different types of workers, especially in the larger post offices that employed hundreds of workers. The regular full-time workforce was almost exclusively male, so the women casual workers were more obvious, while the male casuals blended with the rest of the male workforce.

For the regular full-time workforce, watching the increasing number of part-time and casual workers arriving on their shifts, it must have been difficult to distinguish between the two. Indeed, some of the antagonism expressed by the union towards part-time workers was the result of perceiving the two kinds of work as the same. They were viewed by the union as presenting the same kinds of problems, since both were regarded as cheap, unskilled labour that threatened the full-time workforce, both were perceived as uncommitted to postal work, and both were in part female labour. The union protested the use of both types of work with one breath, insisting upon the abolition of casual and part-time work.

However, there were differences, in particular the fact that part-time workers were regularly employed by the Post Office and often remained in the job for many years. Although they had no regularity of hours and might be called in as needed, still part-time workers had more regularity of employment than the casual workers. The number of part-time workers did not fluctuate month to month and day to day like the casual workforce. Casuals usually worked full-

---

[74] Hearings of the Royal Commission of Inquiry into Working Conditions in the Post Office Department, Ottawa, 19–20 April 1966, p. 12091.

[75] *Ibid.*, p. 12114.

[76] Statistics Canada, *Federal Government Employment*, Cat.72–004, Ottawa, March 1968-December 1968.

[77] *Ibid.*, 1962–1965.

time, but would come and go, working in different positions as required. Their appearance was relatively unpredictable compared to the part-time workers. Although in practice the differences were sometimes hard to distinguish, casuals were temporary workers, and part-time workers were part of the regularly employed workforce.

Summary and Conclusions

By the end of the 1950s a few women began to appear as full-time mail sorters within the Post Office, despite the resistance of both management and the union. However, since they constituted only a very small part of the workforce and since they received the same wages and benefits as the men, they constituted no threat to the male workers and were gradually accepted, if largely ignored.

The introduction of women part-time workers into the Post Office in the 1950s was an entirely different and more controversial issue. The part-time workers were hired to work on a less skilled sortation method, were paid lower wages and received fewer benefits. Their hours varied according to management demands and they continued to be subject to individual work measurement after this was abolished for the full-time workers. By 1965 part-time workers constituted 20 percent of the total number of inside postal workers, representing a very real threat to the pay and conditions of the full-time workers.

At the same time the Post Office was increasing its use of casual workers, half of whom were women. They were hired on a temporary basis, paid at the same low rate as the part-time workers and they received even fewer benefits. By 1965 an average of 1,000 casuals were employed in the Post Office every month, while in some locations even Post Office officials were prepared to describe their use as excessive.

The threat to pay and conditions posed by the part-time and casual workers was exacerbated by a Post Office management that regularly ignored its own restrictive policies on the use of these workers, and by the lack of power of the CPEA/CUPW to rectify the situation, given that the union had no legal right to negotiate with the employer. As well, the predominantly male full-time workers believed that the women who worked part-time did not rely upon the income, were not committed to their jobs and therefore were not interested in improving their working conditions. In these circumstances the response of the union was to call for the abolition of part-time and casual work, and to refuse to permit these workers to join the union. The reaction of the union and its members to women working in the Post Office was the result of both their sex and their type of employment.

The fact that the Post Office was using the part-timers as a source of cheap labour provided no reasonable explanation for excluding them from the union, although this was the rationale used by the union at the time. The low pay and poor working conditions might have been cause for some concern for the part-time workers hired under these conditions, and could have supported an argument for involving them in the union so that they could better their situation.

However, concern for the material conditions of the part-time workers was almost never expressed by the union or its members.

Instead the union's position on part-time work contradicted other policies. In his Christmas message to postal workers in December 1965, the Executive Vice President of the union congratulated the members for having excluded part-time workers at the Convention earlier that year and stated that it could not be said "that the Union gives comfort to those who sell their labour too cheaply."[78] Such a position hardly concurred with the union's complaints that the full-time workers had been seriously underpaid, the main cause of the 1965 strike. Moreover, a primary rationale for any union is to improve the wages of its members, who otherwise might be forced to sell their labour too cheaply.

The members of the union were unable to extend their concern for their own material conditions to the situation of the part-time workers partly because these workers were women. It was assumed that as women employed part-time they were not reliant upon their incomes, but worked only for pocket money, and that therefore they were not interested in improving their conditions. The fact that some part-time workers had already joined other unions, and that indeed their readiness to do so was cause for concern within the CUPW, appeared not to influence the general consensus.

The extensive use of part-time workers did pose a real threat to the jobs of the full-time workers. However, the response of the union to press for the abolition of part-time work was not realistic as an approach to the problem, and actually restricted the capacity of the union to respond to the situation. It was not realistic because there was an element of postal work that could usefully be performed by part-time workers, namely the evening sortation when mail was heaviest. This reality was recognized by the Montreal local in their recommendation to the Montpetit Commission: "The hiring of part-timers should be held to the strict minimum and they should be used only in case of absolute necessity at peak hours."[79] However, this was contrary to the general position of the union that all part-time workers should be replaced with full-time staff.

By holding to a policy of eliminating part-time work the union restricted its capacity to deal with the problem. One delegate to the 1965 Convention expressed the difficulties clearly: "How can we possibly ask our National Officers to go to the Department and ask that they do away with part-time employees when at the same time we are accepting them as members and taking their money? Are we being a bunch of crooks?"[80] Since the union's goal was to entirely eradicate part-time employment from the Post Office, its position would

---

[78] Canadian Union of Postal Workers, *The Postal Tribune*, Vol. XXXIII, No. 12, December 1965, p. 5.

[79] Canadian Union of Postal Workers, Montreal Local, "Submission to the Royal Commission into Working Conditions in the Post Office Department," 10 January 1966, p. 9.

[80] Canadian Postal Employees Association, *Ninth Triennial National Convention Proceedings*, Toronto, 22–25 September 1965, p. 415.

certainly have been weakened by recognizing their presence through the offer of union membership. Likewise, it was not really possible for the union to argue for improved pay and conditions for part-time workers when they were not supposed to exist.

These difficulties were overcome quite suddenly in 1966, when the union reversed its policy and accepted part-time workers as members of the union.

3

UNION CHANGES AFTER 1965

In 1965 the CUPW reaffirmed its position that part-time work should be abolished and that these workers could not be admitted even as associate, non-voting members of the union. However, within two years part-time workers were accepted as full, voting members of the CUPW and the union was actively campaigning to organize these workers. What caused such a dramatic change? The CUPW did not change its policy on part-time work because it recognized the contradictions in its position, nor because it changed its perspective on women workers. Practical, rather than philosophical, matters prevailed.

Many of the practical problems had been raised at the 1965 National Convention by those delegates who had argued that part-time workers should be admitted to the union. Of the inside postal workers represented by the CUPW, the part-time work force was one-fifth of the total, a figure that threatened the capacity of the union to take effective action, as long as the part-time workers were not members of the union. This issue was accentuated during the 1965 strike, when some of the part-time workers continued to work, and was then clearly expressed by some of the 1965 Convention delegates: "We cannot be going around arguing and bickering with the part-timers and then expect them to cooperate with us."[1] The point was raised that the policy to abolish part-time work was unrealistic, that they were a permanent presence and had to be dealt with as such: "The part-time staff in the larger offices in Canada are there to stay and we have to concede this. There is nothing we can do about it."[2] By keeping them out the union had no control over them at all: "When we bring these part-timers into the CPEA we will be able to control the part-timers and be working with them. We would also control how many come into the post office."[3] However, in any event not even these substantial problems caused the alteration of union policy.

The crucial factors came from outside the CUPW: the changing legal situation and the resulting rivalry for members with other unions.

[1] Canadian Postal Employees Association, *Ninth Triennial National Convention Proceedings*, Toronto, 22–25 September 1965, p. 416.

[2] *Ibid.*, p. 416.

[3] *Ibid.*, p. 416.

Changing Union Policy

In response to the illegality of collective bargaining and strikes within the federal civil service, in 1950 the Canadian Postal Employees Association (CPEA) National Convention endorsed a policy that federal public servants should be governed by the Industrial Relations Disputes Investigations Act. This legislation covered employees in the private sector who came under federal jurisdiction, and provided the right to form associations, negotiate and strike, with third party arbitration as a non-binding method to facilitate disputes. The CPEA strongly expressed its opinion that the many problems experienced by its members would best be resolved via the process of free collective bargaining.

This was not the perspective of other organizations representing federal civil servants. The Civil Service Association of Canada and the Civil Service Federation of Canada both comprised large numbers of civil servants, the latter being a loose federation of various organizations representing federal workers. In 1966 these associations merged to form the Public Service Alliance of Canada (PSAC). It was not until 1953 that the Civil Service Federation passed a resolution calling for collective bargaining, but with binding arbitration. This meant that the workers would not have the right to strike, but would submit any issues unresolved during collective bargaining to an arbitration board and its decision would be binding. The CPEA argued that binding arbitration did not constitute real collective bargaining, because workers deprived of their right to strike were also deprived of their leverage in the bargaining process. In 1962 the CPEA formally withdrew from the Civil Service Federation because of this controversy.

Pressed by the various organizations for some resolution of the issue, in 1963 the government appointed Arnold Heeney to study the question of collective bargaining in the federal civil service. Despite constant lobbying by the CPEA, Heeney's Preparatory Committee on Collective Bargaining followed the wishes of the majority of civil service associations and recommended collective bargaining with binding arbitration and without the right to strike.[4] The report was released in July 1965. Just weeks later the inside postal workers were on strike, illegalities notwithstanding, and consequently the legislation that was drawn up in the following months was a compromise. When Bill C–170 was presented for its first reading in the House of Commons in April 1966 it contained two routes for collective bargaining. The union could choose, before negotiations commenced, to opt for binding arbitration, or it could select a process that included the right to strike.

The legal compromise did nothing to reduce the antagonism between the CPEA/CUPW and the other civil service associations. Fundamental questions remained concerning the certification of unions under the new legislation. It was not clear just how the new legislation would function, in particular which unions would be certified to represent which workers. Although the wording of the

[4] Canada, *Report of the Preparatory Committee on Collective Bargaining in the Public Service*, Ottawa, 1965.

legislation seemed to allow for the postal workers to certify as a separate bargaining unit, there were real fears that they might be absorbed by the more conservative civil service associations.

Early in 1966 the Civil Service Federation publicly proposed that all civil service workers, including postal workers, be represented by the Federation in "one big bargaining unit," or alternatively that occupational categories be established as separate bargaining units.[5] Since both of these proposals threatened the existence of the CUPW, sharp retorts about "such nonsense" appeared in the press.[6] Eventually the internal structure of the PSAC did cut across workplaces and departments by combining workers according to their occupational group for purposes of bargaining. Thus, for example, all the clerical workers were incorporated into one bargaining unit, regardless of where they worked. This was entirely opposed by the CPEA/CUPW, that wanted all the workers within the Post Office Department in one union.

In the midst of the legislative changes the CUPW was threatened by the civil service associations because of their size and the approval that they were receiving from the government as responsible organizations. At this time, the CUPW represented 10,500 workers, while the two civil service associations had over 100,000 members. The associations had not supported the CUPW during the 1965 strike although their members had benefitted from the wage increases that followed. Their position in opposition to strikes in the federal civil service had won the government's recognition that they were reasonable and rational organizations. By mid-1966 the CUPW was publicly attacking the civil service associations as management-orientated, company unions.[7]

The real danger from the civil service associations came not only from their proposals to the government, but from their actual organizing within the Post Office. During 1965 and 1966 the Civil Service Association of Canada and then its successor, the PSAC, organized several locals of clerical workers and part-time workers in the Post Office. The PSAC also moved to organize the railway mail clerks, a dwindling number of 350 Post Office employees who worked on the trains, who did join the PSAC in 1968. With such a foothold of members in the Post Office, and given the uncertainty around the certification process, it seemed that the PSAC might be able to fulfil its goal to represent postal workers as well as other civil servants.

This fear was enhanced by the establishment of the Bureau of Classification Revision which, in the midst of these other changes, was re-organizing the occupational categories within the federal government. The CUPW informed the Bureau that it would not accept any reclassification that would prevent the union

---

[5] Canadian Union of Postal Workers, *The Postal Tribune*, Vol. XXXIV, No. 2, February 1966, p. 19.

[6] *Ibid.*, Vol. XXXIV, No. 3, February 1966, pp. 5, 15.

[7] *Ibid.*, Vol. XXXIV, No. 6, June 1966, pp. 27–28.

from representing all inside workers employed by the Post Office. The Bureau responded that administrative and clerical workers would not be included with the inside postal workers in the new category called Postal Operations.[8] and indeed it was the PSAC that was certified to represent the clerical workers in the Post Office, along with the clerical workers in all other government departments.

In this context the issue of the part-time work force posed a central dilemma for the CUPW. The 1965 National Convention had recently reaffirmed the union's policy of excluding part-time workers from the union, but if the PSAC organized them it seemed likely that the CUPW would be denied certification as the bargaining agent for the inside postal workers. The CUPW would then cease to exist. The resulting strategy was Project A.

In November 1966 the CUPW National Executive announced that its locals could start signing up part-time workers, though under particular conditions. Project A was introduced as a study in the feasibility of associate membership for part-time workers. Part-time workers were to pay half the dues of the full-time members in return for an associate membership which did not give them the right to vote on any union or contract issues. The union offered to fight for the same basic hourly rate of pay as the full-timers, pro-rata fringe benefits and protection from arbitrary action by the employer. The dues from the part-time workers were to be maintained in a separate fund for Project A and no money from the general CUPW treasury was to be used to organize part-time workers. It was planned that there would be a full discussion of Project A on the first day of the next National Convention in 1968.[9]

The PSAC complained to the Canadian Labour Congress (CLC) that the CUPW was encroaching upon its jurisdiction. Since the PSAC had first begun organizing the part-time workers in the Post Office, the CLC applied sanctions to the CUPW on a charge of raiding. This was duly ignored by the CUPW and its locals proceeded to sign up the part-time workers.

The Public Service Staff Relations Act (PSSRA) finally became law in March 1967. In the same month the CUPW joined with the Letter Carriers Union of Canada (LCUC) to form the Council of Postal Unions. This was not a merger of the two unions, but a joint council established for the purposes of certification and negotiation. Both the letter carriers and the inside postal workers were part of the same occupational category within the federal government, called Postal Operations. The legislation seemed to require that in order to be certified a union must represent the majority (50 percent plus one) of an occupational category. Neither the LCUC not the CUPW could do this alone, so the Council of Postal Unions (CPU) was formed in response to perceived legislative requirements. The close relationship between the unions was not new because they had worked together in the Postal Workers Brotherhood for common goals since the 1940s,

---

[8] *Ibid.*, Vol. XXXIV, No. 9, pp. 27–31.

[9] *Ibid.*, Vol. XXXIV, No. 11, November 1966, p. 45.

and there had been much fruitless discussion of a complete merger of the two unions.

Hence, as a result of the new legislation it was the Council of Postal Unions (CPU) that applied to the Public Service Staff Relations Board (PSSRB) for certification for postal workers in April 1967. The PSSRB was the body established to administer the new legislation. Both the Treasury Board and the PSAC intervened to attempt to prevent the certification. The Treasury Board claimed that the CPU was not properly constituted, while the PSAC was itself seeking certification for the part-time postal workers. After four months the PSSRB turned down the CPU's application and this decision had an immediate impact upon the status of part-time workers in relation to the CUPW.

The certification was formally refused on technical grounds; the CUPW was told that it did not have sufficient mandate from its members to have formed the CPU for purposes of negotiation of a collective agreement. This was dealt with by a referendum of the membership of the CUPW to obtain the required direct consent. However, in its decision the PSSRB gave warning to the CUPW concerning the position of part-time workers within the union. In his report the chair of the PSSRB, Jacob Finkelman, noted the "restrictive membership" of the CUPW with regard to the part-time workers. He observed that Project A did not allow these union members any voice or vote at local meetings and questioned how the union planned to represent them under such circumstances. The lawyer for the CPU appearing before the PSSRB could only suggest that the views of the part-timers would be taken into account by the full-time workers when they voted. Finkelman concluded, and quite accurately: "In short, the Postal Workers were prepared to go no further at the present time than to extend to part-time employees a sort of second class membership." While remarking that the PSSRB was not called upon to decide whether this situation would necessarily disentitle the CPU to be certified as a bargaining agent for these workers, the report expressed its concern so that the unions "may be able to fully consider their position."[10] Despite the restrained tone, the position was clear. The PSSRB made this decision on August 18th 1967 and later that same month the CUPW organized a referendum of its members on the following question:

> Are you in favour of amending Article I, section 5 of the Constitution of the Canadian Union of Postal Workers so that it will read as follows: "to unite fraternally all employees in the Post Office Department excepting Postal Officers and those employed as letter carriers," thereby enabling part-time employees ... to hold full membership in the CUPW and amending all other provisions of the Constitution relating to part-time employees ... to conform with this amendment.[11]

---

[10] Public Service Staff Relations Board, *Decisions*, File No. 146–2–13, 18 August 1967, p. 15.

[11] *Ibid.*, File No. 146–2–83, 4 January 1968, p. 12.

On the ballot 8,226 union members voted in favour of the amendment, while 705 voted against it.[12] From that time Project A was abandoned and part-time workers were signed up as full members of the CUPW.

Thus, the pressure exerted by the new labour relations legislation and the PSSRB was the immediate reason for the inclusion of the part-time workers as full members of the union. Joe Davidson put it quite bluntly: "We had to reconsider our attitudes toward the women or go the way of the dodo, so reconsideration won out."[13] However, while the union had reconsidered in order to survive, what did this mean for the process of organizing the part-time workers, and for the place of part-time workers within the union? The antagonism had been long and hostile and it might be expected that the path to full involvement would be less than smooth. Some difficulties there were, but the large majority of part-time workers did join the CUPW and they were met with a decidedly warm reception. The following sections explore the new relationship and the reasons for the apparent ease of transition.

Organizing the Part-Time Workers

The initial attempt to organize part-time workers under Project A was not an outstanding success. Between the fall of 1966, when the project was initiated, and September the following year, the CUPW had signed up only 334 part-time workers out of a total of 2,621 employed by the Post Office.[14] The failure to sign up a large number of part-time workers caused delays in the certification of the CPU to represent the part-time workers, and there were several hearings before the PSSRB.

Whether the part-time workers rejected the secondary status offered by Project A or whether the fault lay with inadequate organization is not clear. Certainly there were serious complaints from the full-time union members that the drive to sign up the part-time workers had been poorly organized. In fact the Director of Organization was brought to task at the 1968 National Convention over this issue. It was claimed that the system of field officers was not working well, so that little assistance was forthcoming to organize the part-time workers and consequently few gains were made for a year after Project A was launched.[15]

However, in the months following the union's decision to give part-time workers full and equal membership, the CUPW was successful in signing up the majority of part-time workers. The PSSRB's warning had not only prompted the CUPW to treat its part-time workers equally, but forced the realization that

[12] *Ibid.*, p. 12.

[13] Joe Davidson and John Deverell, *Joe Davidson*, James Lorimer, Toronto, 1978, p. 86.

[14] Public Service Staff Relations Board, *Decisions*, File: 146–2–83, 21 May 1968, p. 1.

[15] Canadian Union of Postal Workers, *Tenth Triennial Convention Proceedings*, Montreal, 27–29 May 1968, pp. 36–45.

certification for the part-time workers would not be automatic; the union would have to make a serious effort to organize them. Moreover, in January 1968, the PSSRB determined that the part-time work force should constitute a separate bargaining unit because of the long background of animosity between the full and part-time workers.[16] This meant that in order to be certified to represent the part-time bargaining unit the union had to show a majority of members among those workers. The *Postal Tribune* printed a Bulletin with the following call to action:

> The decision of the Public Service Staff Relations Board that part-time postal workers are an appropriate bargaining unit under Section 32 of the Act makes it urgently necessary that every member of the union participate in a crash recruitment campaign designed to sign up the required 50% plus one immediately.[17]

National and local executives were urged to participate in the campaign, with the National Office bearing any expenses incurred. The Bulletin goes on to say: "Full-time and part-time employees must accept the fact that they are employed in a mutual environment requiring mutual respect between the two groups."[18] By March 1968 the union reported 1,553 part-time members.[19]

The CPU was certified to represent the full-time workers in January 1968, but because of the PSSRB decision to certify the part-time workers separately and as a result of delays by the PSSRB, the final decision on certification for the part-time workers was not made until 18 months later. In February 1969 the PSSRB insisted upon a representation vote, although it was clear by this point that the majority of part-time workers had joined the CUPW. In June 1969 the employer listed 2,557 part-time employees, of whom 2,218 voted. In favour of being represented by the CPU were 1,990, while only 185 were opposed.[20] Finally the CPU was certified to represent the part-time workers in the Post Office.

The part-time workers joined the CUPW because, despite the animosity, it was the obvious choice, given that all the full-time workers were in that union. Moreover, the CUPW had a considerable advantage over the PSAC in that its representatives were in every post office across the country, in contact with the part-time workers every day and able to sign them up. Despite the false notion of

---

[16] Public Service Staff Relations Board, *Decisions*, File No: 146–2–83, 4 January 1968, p. 13.

[17] Canadian Union of Postal Workers, *The Postal Tribune*, Vol. XXXVI, No. 1, January 1968, p. 13.

[18] *Ibid.*, p. 13.

[19] Canadian Union of Postal Workers, *Tenth Triennial National Convention Proceedings*, Montreal, 27–29 May 1968, p. 50.

[20] Public Service Staff Relations Board, *Decisions*, File No: 146–2–106, 25 June 1969, p. 1.

many full-time workers that the part-timers were not interested in improving their conditions this proved not to be the case. At the 1968 Convention a delegate from Montreal said "We went after the part-timers but we found we did not have to go after them, they were really coming to us."[21]

The campaign to unionize was a success despite a harsh approach, at least in some areas. In Toronto Joe Davidson was then the local President and described his tactics as follows:

> "We don't want part-time workers," I told groups of them on numerous occasions. "The CUPW policy is for full-time jobs. If there are lay-offs, it's the part-timers who should be laid off first. Where part-time jobs can be combined into full-time, that's what we're fighting for. But, as long as you're here, you should be getting the same wages and benefits as the full-time, and we'll fight for that too."[22]

It has been suggested that the part-time workers may have appreciated this approach as an honest one, knowing quite well the policies of the CUPW toward part-timers in the past. Perhaps they were convinced that while the CUPW favoured full-time work it would also really struggle for equal pay and conditions for part-time workers.[23]

In many respects the situation of the part-time workers was worse than that of the full-timers. Their pay was lower, their benefits were almost non-existent, their hours of work varied unpredictably and they were still subject to individual work measurement and the favouritism that resulted from it. Setting aside the notion that they worked just for pin money, and accepting that they needed the income just like the full-time workers, it seems probable that they would be eager to improve their conditions through unionization.

Initial Negotiations

Once the CUPW accepted part-time workers as members under Project A in November 1966, the union initiated discussions on pay increases for them, holding meetings with Treasury Board and Post Office officials in January 1967. At this time the part-time workers were still earning $1.55 per hour, just 75 percent of the pay rate for the lowest paid full-time worker, and only 69 percent of the pay of the Postal Clerks who, like themselves, sorted the mail. The union's position was that part-time workers should be paid the minimum full-time rate for the job. Instead of there being one lower rate of pay for all part-time workers,

---

[21] Canadian Union of Postal Workers, *Tenth Triennial National Convention Proceedings*, Montreal, 27–29 May 1968, p. 353.

[22] Joe Davidson and John Deverell, *Joe Davidson*, James Lorimer, Toronto, 1978, p. 87.

[23] Interview with Jean-Claude Parrot, National President of the Canadian Union of Postal Workers, Ottawa, 14 July 1987.

each part-time worker should receive the same rate as the full-time workers doing the same work.

Under some pressure following the 1965 strike and the outcry over part-time work expressed to the Montpetit Commission, the Post Office Department agreed to reclassify a large proportion of part-time workers to the equivalent levels as the full-time workers, and with the concomitant increase in pay. The union received assurances that at least 1,600 of the existing part-time staff would be reclassified as Postal Clerk 2, over 60 percent of the part-time work force.[24] The pay rate for these part-time workers increased from $1.55 to $2.25 an hour as a result of this agreement. There were also a small number of part-time workers reclassified to other full-time classifications.

However, the Post Office retained, or re-introduced, the classification of Postal Helper, with a separate job description and insisted upon a lower pay rate for this group. These part-time workers were largely those who worked in the City section on the unskilled ABC system, whereas the part-timers who worked in other areas that required the same knowledge and skills as the full-time workers were reclassified. "The CUPW took strong exception to the introduction of this classification at a lower rate of pay," and anticipated problems of abuse with "local management hiring part-time workers as Postal Helpers rather than Postal Clerks." The Postal Tribune urged "It is essential that all Locals police the Department's part-time employment policies in the next few months."[25] The union had wanted to ensure all its members of at least the 25 cent per hour rise obtained for the full-time postal workers, but the Postal Helper wage rate was set at $1.75 an hour, a 20 cent increase. However, even this raise in pay was far greater than any other received by the part-time workers in the previous five years.

Following these discussions with the CUPW, more than sixty percent of the part-time workers were to be reclassified at the minimum rate for the full-time workers and received very substantial pay increases. Other part-time workers, still called Postal Helpers, remained in a separate classification and received a lower wage, but they also obtained a significant increase in pay.

Part-Time Workers in the Union

By the CUPW National Convention in May 1968, the majority of the part-time workers belonged to the union although they were still not formally certified, and there had been a virtual transformation in the attitudes expressed toward the part-timers, in comparison to those of the 1965 Convention. This change was reflected in many of the discussions at the Convention. First, there were the complaints, referred to above, that the part-time workers had not been organized fast enough and that insufficient resources and organization had been

---

[24] Canadian Union of Postal Workers, *The Postal Tribune*, Vol. XXXV, No. 2, February 1967, p. 5.

[25] *Ibid.*, p. 5.

expended under Project A. There was some discussion around dues for part-time members and it was agreed that they should pay half the full-time fee. Most delegates agreed that it was only fair that those earning a part-time wage should only pay partial dues, but it was clearly stated that nonetheless: "They should not be part-time members, they should be full members of the CUPW."[26]

At the time of the Convention the union had initiated negotiations of its first collective agreement for the full-time workers. But, the bargaining was at a standstill and a strike was anticipated, and indeed occurred within two months. An emergency resolution from the floor proposed that if a contract had not been signed by June that the union should strike and not return to work "without first having received substantial pay increases for the part-timers."[27] This resolution was not passed because the delegates were convinced to wait until the union was in a legal position to strike under the PSSRA before taking such action. However, the following resolution was passed with the support of the Resolutions Committee and without need for any debate:

> Whereas our members who are employed as part-time Postal Workers are entitled to full membership rights; it is resolved that our Union negotiate a collective agreement, on behalf of part-time Postal Workers, and that all the terms and conditions be the same, on the basis of parity, as the collective agreement applying to full-time Postal Workers.[28]

The CUPW was not yet certified to represent the part-time workers and there were no part-timers as delegates to the Convention. However, a Vancouver delegate introduced Miss Jones, a part-time worker who wished to say a few words to the Convention. She said:

> This is a great moment for me to be able to speak on behalf of the part-timers from Victoria to Newfoundland ... we now have a great union with over two thousand members. We all know that this great Convention is behind us and you must know that we are behind you in any strike that comes.[29]

Following this a woman from Montreal, identified as a "lady delegate" was encouraged to speak: "I am glad to have heard this lady say what she has just said. We also will support you in case a strike comes."[30] These were the only women to speak at the Convention; none had spoken in 1965.

---

[26] Canadian Union of Postal Workers, *Tenth Triennial National Convention Proceedings*, Montreal, 27–29 May 1968, p. 169.

[27] *Ibid.*, p. 53.

[28] *Ibid.*, p. 348.

[29] *Ibid.*, p. 352.

[30] *Ibid.*, p. 352.

Words of goodwill and mutual support flowed. "If the part-timers go out on strike we will never cross their picket lines," "the part-time workers have supported us in the past and it is now up to us to support them," "there is no question as to the loyalty of the part-time Postal Workers and the full-time Postal Workers."[31] At the opening of the following day's session a delegate rose before an enthusiastic audience to suggest: "I should like to ask the delegates to this Convention to give a standing ovation to the ladies."[32]

Understanding the Change in Attitude

The immediate reason for the CUPW to organize part-time workers was the fear that the union might be denied certification for the inside postal workers under the new legislation if the part-timers were not full participants in the union. However, once the members had ratified the necessary changes to the constitution and once it had become clear that the CUPW would be successful in signing up the majority of part-time workers this fear was removed. It was not necessary for the union to welcome the part-timers as warmly as they did, express such support and solidarity, nor proceed to bargain such favourable pay increases. None of this related to the original reason for accepting the part-timers, that is the problem of certification, since that reason was no longer operative as soon as the part-time workers joined the union as full members. How can the changed attitudes of the CUPW be explained?

Certainly at the 1968 Convention, the full-time members were relieved that the part-time workers had joined the CUPW, thereby eradicating the fears with regard to the PSAC and certification problems. They were also pleased that their campaign had been such a success, despite the organizing attempt of the PSAC. As one delegate phrased it: "The Alliance was right there in Montreal, the Alliance was right there trying to get them in their ranks, but the majority of the part-timers chose the CUPW as their representative."[33]

The part-time workers were in the union, but none of the serious difficulties envisioned earlier had come to pass. In fact it was quickly apparent that the aspirations of the part-time workers with regard to pay and working conditions were not dissimilar to those of the full-time workers, and that they too were prepared to take action to obtain these goals. Despite former misgivings it was now recognized that the part-time workers would not weaken the union by their lack of interest or militancy. The part-time workers had even more reason to be dissatisfied with their working conditions than did the full-time workers, and this

[31] *Ibid.*, pp. 357, 358.

[32] *Ibid.*, p. 500.

[33] *Ibid.*, p. 353.

was quickly established in their support for the strikes that followed in 1968, 1970 and later. Since the part-time workers were in a separate bargaining unit their strike vote was counted separately and in some instances their vote in favour of strike action was even stronger than that of the full-time workers.[34] Joe Davidson later wrote:

> Whether our earlier fears that women would weaken the union were realistic is open to debate, but in 1975 they were a source of strength and their voting patterns on strike decisions were, if anything, more militant than those of the full-time staff. Most of them were at work because, just like the men, they needed to be, and it showed.[35]

The fears of a different group of workers had evaporated and the status of the union was assured. Thus, the delegates to the 1968 Convention had every reason to be satisfied with the situation.

The attitudes of the union and its members to the newly joined part-time workers were also influenced by the general politics of the union and its situation in regard to the employer. The inside postal workers had become increasingly discontented during the 1960s. Some of the reasons for the dissatisfaction have already been outlined, the poor working conditions, the infrequent wage increases, and the management style in the Post Office. Contrary to the union's expectations the introduction of collective bargaining and the right to strike did not reduce the tensions. The PSSRA placed considerable restrictions upon what could be negotiated, and upon the process of negotiation. The resulting limitations and delays will be examined in more detail in the following chapter, but they resulted in frustration for the union members and made a strike more, rather than less, likely. For example, in the first round of negotiations under the PSSRA, which resulted in the 1968 strike, the first three months of negotiation produced no agreement whatsoever. The union's negotiator, Romeo Mathieu, reported to the 1968 National Convention: "I have spent all my life in the labour movement and I can assure you, and please believe me, they are the most complex, the most difficult negotiations I have ever had anything to do with."[36]

The difficulties experienced by the Post Office workers in the 1960s led directly to an increasingly militant union. As late as 1965, the Postmaster of the Toronto Post Office was invited to open the 1965 National Convention of the

---

[34] Interview with Jean-Claude Parrot, National President of the Canadian Union of Postal Workers, Ottawa, 14 July 1987. Parrot recalls this being the situation in the Montreal local on more than one occasion.

[35] Joe Davidson and John Deverell, *Joe Davidson*, James Lorimer, Toronto, 1978, p. 87.

[36] Canadian Union of Postal Workers, *Tenth Triennial National Convention Proceedings*, Montreal, 27–29 May 1968, p. 119.

Union, welcoming the delegates to Toronto and hoping that management and unions would be able to operate "with a firm feeling of understanding and trust."[37] But, in 1968 the CUPW President launched proceedings with the following words: "If we have to force society to give us justice, then it is up to us workers to fight for it. We are part of the working force in Canada and we must fight for our rights."[38] The change in the membership was reflected in changes in the national and local executives, as the representatives found to be not militant enough for the members were voted out of office. The CUPW's publication, the *Postal Tribune*, shifted away from its "ladies and gentlemen" tone, replete with social notices of baseball games and dinner dances, to a publication that concerned itself with pay and working conditions and the struggles of the union. Thus, during the 1960s the employer faced a work force that was growing more militant, represented by an increasingly assertive and determined union.

A new era of labour relations was not the only problem facing the management of the Post Office. In its 1966–67 Annual Report the Post Office for the first time was forced to focus upon the increasing deficit of the Department. In the ten years from 1957 to 1966 the average yearly deficit was $20.6 million, but in 1966–67 the deficit reached almost $47 million, a 55 percent increase over the previous year and a 107 percent increase over the average of the previous decade. The rising deficit and the strikes in 1965 and 1968 led the government to undertake a series of studies on the Post Office, resulting in a report entitled *Blueprint for Change*.

The report identified the lack of autonomy within the Post Office as a major problem. The Post Office Department had to refer for decisions to Treasury Board, the Civil Service Commission, the Public Works Department and Parliament itself, leaving the Post Office with insufficient control over the running of the Department, resulting in inefficiency. Meanwhile, the volume of mail handled by the Post Office had been rising rapidly, producing an increase in staff and therefore increased labour costs, but no attention had been given to obsolete equipment and buildings. And there had been no increase in mail rates to balance the increased cost of operations. The primary recommendation was that the Post Office should become a Crown Corporation, operating with independence from the government in its management decisions, and free to bargain with its unions without reference to the government. It also concluded that modernization and automation were necessary to move the mail more efficiently.

The Post Office management was beleaguered with negative government reports, and under pressure to reduce the deficit and in particular to control labour costs. Post Office workers were discontented with their pay and working conditions, insistent upon improvements, and they had elected successively more mili-

---

[37] Canadian Union of Postal Workers, *Ninth Triennial National Convention Proceedings*, Toronto, 22–25 September 1965, p. 7.

[38] Canadian Union of Postal Workers, *Tenth Triennial National Convention Proceedings*, Montreal, 27–29 May 1968, p. 4.

tant leaders in order to obtain their goals. Conflict was inevitable and the sense of struggle on the part of the union was strong. In this situation of bitter antagonism, part-time workers outside of the union were regarded with suspicion and antipathy. However, once inside the union, the part-time workers became a part of the workers' struggle, joined on the right side of the lines of battle. Part-time workers were accepted into the union so enthusiastically partly because of the embattled nature of the situation. The standing ovation to "the ladies" given at the 1968 National Convention occurred just two months before the union went out on strike.

The union's decision to admit part-time workers had an immediate and dramatic impact upon the composition of the membership. In 1966 there were just 652 women in the CUPW, 6 percent of the total membership. These women were the few full-time women workers that belonged to the union. But, between 1966 and 1967 the number of women members jumped from 652 to 1,189 and from 6 to 10 percent. By 1970 the number of women in the union had increased remarkably to 3,397, so that almost 20 percent of the membership were women, the majority of them part-time workers.[39] How did the union respond to its new constituency? Did the expressions of support for part-time workers translate into policies and action? These question will be explored in the following section on the 1970s.

---

[39] Statistics Canada, *Corporations and Labour Unions Returns Act*, Part II—Labour Unions, Cat.71–202, Ottawa, 1966–1970.

SECTION II

BARGAINING FOR EQUALITY
IN THE 1970s

"To the Advantage of Both"

4

THE 1970s CONTEXT

During the 1970s women continued to enter the Post Office and join the CUPW in large numbers. In 1970 women comprised close to 20 percent of the union's membership; by 1975 this proportion had increased to 29 percent and by the end of the decade in 1980, almost 44 percent of the CUPW's membership were women. Over this ten year period the number of women members in the union leapt from 3,397 to 10,623.[1] The rapid increase of women working in the Post Office in this decade constituted a second wave of hiring women workers. In the 1950s and 1960s the women had been hired primarily as part-time workers. In the 1970s not only part-time, but also full-time women workers were hired, many of them to operate the new machinery that was introduced as a result of technological change.

During the 1970s the CUPW's bargaining policies and strategies had a dramatic impact upon the status of women postal workers. Since it is not feasible to consider in depth the many problems that were subject to negotiation over these years, three issues of particular concern to women have been selected: the Coder dispute of 1972 to 1974, bargaining equality for part-time workers, and negotiating restrictions upon the use of part-time work.

Women were entering the Post Office and joining the CUPW during a period of massive automation that began in 1972 and continued throughout the 1970s. It has been argued that conditions of technological change and the resulting insecurity are the most likely to lead to antagonism between men and women within a union, given that women are often used as a source of cheap labour.[2] In the very first stage of automation a dispute arose between the Post Office and the CUPW over the introduction of a new low-paid classification of worker to operate the new machines; the majority of these Postal Coders were women. It is important to examine how the union responded to this second challenge of cheap female labour; this time from full-time women workers and in the context of extensive automation.

The use of part-time work and casuals continued to be contentious issues for the CUPW throughout the 1970s. The union had promised to bargain equal pay and conditions for the part-timers, while maintaining that full-time work was its

---

[1] Statistics Canada, *Corporations and Labour Unions Returns Act*, Part II—Labour Unions, Cat.71–202, Ottawa, 1970–1980.

[2] Cynthia Cockburn, *Brothers: Male Dominance and Technological Change*, Pluto Press, London, 1983.

first priority. How did the union actually handle the part-time work question, having brought this predominantly female work force into the union? The union's approach to negotiating pay and conditions for the part-time workers will be considered, as well as the CUPW's other major policy on part-time work, that is the determination to restrict the number and use of part-time workers.

Before turning to an examination of these issues, it is necessary first to consider the context in which these concerns were located, because the framework within which the CUPW operated had a profound impact upon how the union perceived and dealt with these problems. It is necessary to understand the impact of technological change, the role of the Public Service Staff Relations Act (PSSRA), and the influence of the economic situation, both generally and within the Post Office.

Automation

In 1966 the Montpetit Report noted with surprise that "little mention was made of mechanization and automation by the postal clerks who will evidently be the first ones affected."[3] The report went on to advise everyone concerned to investigate the situation immediately because of the profound impact that would result from technological change.

It was perhaps not so surprising that the CUPW had not yet considered the question of automation. Even by 1969, the only letter sorting machine operating in Canadian Post Offices was the Burroughs machine that had been introduced into the Winnipeg Post Office. It was a "primitive, noisy brute which required constant adjustments and seemed to tear more mail than it sorted."[4] It also did not replace the sorting knowledge since it only paced the speed at which letters were presented and it was never introduced into other Post Offices. Other than this unsuccessful experiment, in the late 1960s mail was sorted by hand into pigeon hole cases, looking not much different than it had in the 1950s. A government report commented: "Mail processing in the Canada Post Office is essentially a manual operation" and referred to "the failure of the Canada Post Office, in comparison to major post offices elsewhere, to introduce mechanical sortation processes."[5]

However, in 1969 the CUPW did send study groups to see the mechanised postal stations in the United States, although the impact of the coming changes was not yet acknowledged. It was also in 1969 that a major government report,

[3] Canada, *Report of the Royal Commission of Inquiry into Working Conditions in the Post Office Department*, Ottawa, October 1966, p. 25.

[4] Joe Davidson and John Deverell, *Joe Davidson*, James Lorimer, Toronto, 1978, p. 123.

[5] Canada Post Office, *Blueprint for Change*, Ottawa, November 1969, p. 23.

Blueprint for Change, recommended fundamental changes in the structure and operation of Canada Post, including complete mechanization of the letter sorting process.[6] By the 1971 CUPW National Convention, delegates from the far-sighted Montreal local were castigating the national officers for having ignored the issue,[7] and at that Convention a report on automation was passed as the policy of the union.

A critical aspect of the automation of the Post Office was the speed with which it was accomplished. The first computerized machinery was introduced in Ottawa in 1972 and over the following 10 years a billion dollars was spent to transform sorting the mail from a basically manual process into a highly mechanized operation. The results were dramatic for a considerable proportion of the workforce, particularly in the 29 centres where new machinery was installed. The bulk of the work changed to maintaining, operating and working with and on the machines. Retraining was necessary and changes were made in shifts and schedules. The location of the work changed as new buildings were erected in some cities to house the machinery, sometimes at considerable distance from the previous work place. Many issues had to be dealt with, including who would work in the new positions on the new machines, how and where retraining would be provided, and on what basis workers would apply for or be moved to the new jobs. Health and safety questions arose concerning both working directly on the machines and the noise they emitted. These issues arose at different locations across the country, with varying local conditions and concerns.

In 1969 the government's study, *A Blueprint for Change*, was critical in the decision to proceed with technological change in the Post Office. The report's recommendations stressed the importance of cooperation from the workers in the process of technological change and indicated that postal workers should benefit from automation. It said:

> The introduction of automated facilities presents a major managerial challenge, particularly in terms of relations with employees whose understanding and support of the broad goals and advantages of automation in terms of employment opportunities are vital.

and:

> The change to automation should be undertaken with the objective in mind of equipping the Canada Post Office to fulfil its responsibilities to the country while at the same time upgrading the work content, morale and job satisfaction of postal employees.[8]

Throughout the 1970s automation and its effects were the major concern of the CUPW. The policy of the union was clear and unchanging: workers should

---

[6] *Ibid.*

[7] Canadian Union of Postal Workers, *National Convention 1971, Proceedings*, Calgary, 3–5 June 1971, pp. 14–24.

[8] Canada Post Office, *A Blueprint for Change*, Ottawa, November 1969, pp. 24, 133.

AN AUTOMATED MAIL SORTING PLANT, GATEWAY IN TORONTO

Looking down on the plant; a person can be seen walking on the pathway at the left.

A view from the ground of a letter chute and the Optical Character Reading machine (OCR). Workers are visible on the left and one in the centre.

not only be protected from the negative effects of technological change, but they should benefit from the progress of automation. The union reiterated this position many times, for example in 1973:

> The Canadian Union of Postal Workers does not oppose policies to increase the efficiency of the postal service. They do oppose, however, and will endeavour to stop, any policy that will mean a lowering of wages or a worsening of working conditions for postal workers.[9]

And again in 1975:

> To the members of this Board, the union reiterates unequivocally its belief that, in principle, the advent of new technology in the Post Office is not only necessary but desirable. This is because technology has the potential to improve the Postal Service, and also to bring benefits to the workers.[10]

The union argued that if automation increased productivity then postal workers should benefit with reduced hours of work and earlier retirement, as well as higher classification and improved pay rates. However, CUPW found itself remarkably restricted in its attempts to protect and improve the pay and conditions of its members, restricted by the Public Service Staff Relations Act (PSSRA). It is not possible to understand the CUPW's actions in relation to technological change in general or the Coder dispute in particular, without first understanding the far-reaching impact of this legislation.

The Public Service Staff Relations Act

The most critical limitations imposed by the PSSRA were the restrictions placed upon what could be negotiated. Section 86(3) of the PSSRA indicates that the following areas are not subject to negotiation: "the standards, procedures or processes governing the appointment, appraisal, promotion, demotion, transfer, lay-off or release of employees." In a period of technological change these limitations were severe, because it was precisely in these areas that change was taking place and that the workers required some protection. It meant, for example, that training was not negotiable; but training was a crucial area because new machinery was introduced for which retraining was necessary. Perhaps most important, the prohibition on negotiating lay-offs meant that the union was legally prevented from bargaining job security for its members. This problem with job security was expressed by the 1972 Conciliation Board headed by Owen Shime:

> The introduction of technological change requires that there be a full range of discussion in all matters affecting both the operations of the Post Office and its

---

[9] Canadian Union of Postal Workers, *CUPW*, Vol. 2, No. 7, July 1973, p. 2.

[10] Canadian Union of Postal Workers, "CUPW Brief to the Conciliation Board," 18 August 1975, p. 5.

employees. For example, section 86(3) prohibits the board of conciliation from making recommendations concerning lay-off, but the issue of lay-off is an important matter for the employees who are threatened by the impact of technological change. An employee, and quite properly so, wants to know if a new machine will render him surplus and thereby cause him to lose his job.[11]

Another part of the PSSRA places yet further limitations upon what can be negotiated. Section 7 states: "Nothing in this Act shall be construed to affect the right or authority of the employer to determine the organization of the Public Service and to assign duties and classify positions therein." This question of classification is fundamental because when new jobs are created in periods of technological change, questions arise as to how they will be classified within the system, which in turn decides the level of pay. The 1972 Conciliation Board report maintained that employees should be able to discuss the impact of new job descriptions and classifications and called Section 7 "an additional limitation which prevents a realistic approach to advancing technology."[12] This legal restriction upon the negotiation of classifications was of central importance in the Coder dispute.

A further legal problem posed by the PSSRA for the union was that those items that could not be negotiated under the legislation also could not be grieved through the usual grievance procedure, which included, at the fourth level, an independent adjudication. So, for example, if a union member felt that a job had been classified wrongly or had a complaint about a promotion, that grievance could only be handled within the Post Office Department, with no independent means of appeal. Thus, grievances against the employer that fell under the restrictions of the PSSRA could only be taken to the employer for a decision.

It was a constant complaint of the CUPW that instant, rubber-stamp denials at the first three levels were commonplace, and that a remarkable number of grievances had to be taken to the fourth level, costing the union time, energy and money. In a dispute between a worker and the employer, leaving the decision with the employer was a process hardly likely to inspire confidence, or a sense of justice.

However, the grievance procedure of any union is important not only because of the individual justice that it allows the union members to seek, but also because it is the major method by which the union ensures that the employer adheres to the collective agreement. It is commonplace for unions to note that a collective agreement is only as good as the capacity to enforce it, and the primary mechanism for that enforcement is the grievance procedure. The CUPW was limited on several critical issues in what it could negotiate in the collective agreement, and where the union might obtain arrangements through discussions

---

[11] "Report of the Conciliation Board to the Chairman of the PSSRB," Chaired by Owen B. Shime, Ottawa, 14 December 1972, pp. 12–13.

[12] *Ibid.*, p. 14.

outside of the collective agreement such provisions could not be enforced through the grievance procedure.

Under the PSSRA the union did not have the right to strike upon the expiry of the collective agreement. The parties were required to attempt to bargain in good faith to reach a new agreement. Should this process fail, either side could make a request to the Public Service Staff Relations Board (PSSRB) for the establishment of a Conciliation Board. This Board comprised a union nominee, a management nominee and a mutually agreed-upon chairperson, and its terms of reference were established by the PSSRB. Evidence to support their differing positions could be presented by both the union and the employer, and the Conciliation Board would produce a report with non-binding recommendations on items still in dispute. Not until seven days after the presentation of the report was the union in a legal position to strike.

Far from acting as a cooling-out process, or facilitating successful negotiations, the union maintained that the resulting delays led to an absence of good faith bargaining on the part of the employer and increased frustration among their members. After the PSSRA was enacted, the first agreement took six months to negotiate. The next three agreements each took more than one year to obtain. Then the agreement that expired in June 1977 took almost two years to replace. At the 1974 National Convention a resolution was presented to limit the length of negotiations before a strike. Although it was not passed there was some sympathy for the delegate who said: "The members are getting sick and tired of waiting 10, 12 months and then being told that they have got to go out on strike."[13] In other words, what was the purpose of lengthy negotiations that did not result in an agreement, while the members waited under their old contract?

Throughout the 1970s the PSSRA was a source of constant friction between the CUPW on one side and the Post Office and Treasury Board on the other; the most serious conflict occurring over the restrictions upon what could be negotiated. The union did not accept that it could not bargain for its members the issues that were of most concern, not if it was to maintain any semblance of representing its members' interests, of being a union in fact. Consequently, the union proceeded by ignoring the restrictions of the PSSRA in its demands and its negotiations, insisting for example upon negotiating job security, staffing and classifications. The union maintained that, according to their legal counsel, nothing in the legislation prevented the Post Office and Treasury Board from voluntarily agreeing to bargain these issues.[14] However, the employer worked within the PSSRA, refusing to negotiate many aspects of the technological changes that were taking place. The legislation contributed to the unceasing conflict and remarkably poor labour relations within the Post Office throughout the 1970s.

---

[13] Canadian Union of Postal Workers, *National Convention 1974, Proceedings*, Quebec, 3–8 June 1974, p. 379.

[14] Canadian Union of Postal Workers, "CUPW Brief to the Conciliation Board," 18 August 1975, Article 8.

The Economic Climate

The economic recession that affected Canada from the mid–1970s until into the 1980s resulted in inflation and rising rates of unemployment. In this situation unions were under pressure to bargain improved wage increases to cover the rising prices and maintain standards of living, while at the same time reduced in strength because of the insecurity created by high levels of unemployment. Unions were further weakened by the government's policy of general wage controls, introduced in October 1975, which effectively reduced negotiated wage increases, but failed to control rising prices. The government's other policy response was to cut back on spending, both within the government at the federal level and in general through reductions in expenditures on services such as education, health care and unemployment insurance.

The CUPW members were affected by the general economic climate, particularly since they were at this very time undergoing a massive restructuring of their work through automation. The high rates of unemployment accentuated fears of what would happen if jobs were lost through technological change. In 1977 the union asserted "The present unemployment situation is clearly intolerable and the spectre of being unemployed certainly haunts all workers, be they in the private or public sector."[15] The union's struggle to obtain protection from technological change for its members was accentuated by the general economic recession and its effects.

Within the federal government, the Post Office was seriously affected by the new pressure to control spending and cut costs that was part of the government's response to inflation. The previous chapter referred to the rising deficits in the Post Office deficits during the late 1960s and even at that time pressure was building to attain an efficient, that is self-sufficient, operation. But the deficit increases of the 1960s were trivial compared to the early 1970s. The 1970 deficit was almost $53 million, but by 1973–74 it had reached $177 million, and at its height in 1976–77 it was $578 million.[16] The Post Office came under increasing pressure to reduce the deficit, and given that 70 percent of the expenditures were labour costs, that meant holding the line on wages and reducing staff where possible. This situation helps to explain some of the actions by Post Office management to be discussed in the following sections, particularly in regard to the use of cheap labour. However, of importance to this study is that the economic context of the 1970s contributed to a contentious relationship between a union determined to protect its members' jobs and improve pay and conditions and a management under economic pressure to cut costs.

This then was the context in which increasing numbers of women were employed by the Post Office and joined the CUPW. It was against this background of technological change, legislative restrictions and economic recession that pay

---

[15] Canadian Union of Postal Workers, "Negotiations 77," Submission by the CUPW to the Conciliation Board, 10 April 1978, p. 131.

[16] Canada Post Office, *Annual Report*, Ottawa, 1970, 1973–1974, 1976–1977.

and conditions for part-time workers were negotiated, and that the union developed its policy of controls upon the use of part-time work; it was in these circumstances that a major dispute arose between the CUPW and the employer over the introduction of a new job classification.

THE CODER DISPUTE 1972–1974

Coders and Women

In the very first stage of automation in the Post Office a major confrontation developed between the employer and the union—a confrontation that involved the use of women in the work force. The first computerized letter sorting machines were introduced into the Alta Vista Post Office in Ottawa in 1972 and the Post Office established a new classification of postal worker, with a new job description, to operate the machines. When the first Postal Coders were hired in Ottawa in August of that year over 60 percent were women. While the Post Office did not intend to hire women in particular, for two reasons the job was likely to be filled primarily by women: the type of work and the pay.

A Coder sits with eleven other Coders at a Coding Desk Suite, which is a part of the computerized Letter Sorting Machine. Letters are presented at a window in front of the Coder, who reads the postal code and keys it onto a keyboard, similar to that of a typewriter except that it is smaller and used with only one hand. The machine then marks the letter with a phosphorescent bar code, which is read by the machine as it is sorted to its appropriate destination. If the postal code is missing or cannot be read, the Coder presses a reject button and the letter is sent to a location from which it will be sorted manually. The Coder is expected to maintain an average speed of 1,800 letters an hour, and applicants for the position have to pass a dexterity test. Indeed, the Coder job is similar to that stronghold of women's employment, typing, although considerably more tedious and repetitive. The 1972 job description candidly pointed out: "there is limited scope for independent action."[1]

The Coder job was a full-time position and was classified by the Post Office as level PO 1, to be paid an hourly rate of $2.94. At this time, under the collective agreement for the full-time workers there was no level PO 1 position, although under the agreement for the part-time workers, Postal Helpers were classified at level PO 1. The lowest classification for any full-time postal worker was a level PO 2 for the position of Mail Handler, with a pay rate of $3.12 an hour. However, the Postal Clerks who sorted the mail manually were classified as level PO 4, and paid $3.44 an hour. Thus, the Postal Coder was classified at

---

[1] Canada Post Office, Position Analysis Schedule, Descriptive Title: Postal Coder, Ottawa, 1972.

TABLE 4: Number of Full-Time Workers in the Postal Operations Category (non-supervisory), by Sex, Classification and Pay Rate, 1972

Level	Job Title	Rate ($)	Number of Men	Number of Women	% Women
(PO 1)	(Postal Coder)	(2.94)	(12)	(19)	(61.3)
PO 2	Mail Handler	3.12	2,140	8	0.4
PO 3	Letter Carrier, Mail Services Courier, Supervisory Mail Handler	3.31	11,871	99	0.8
PO 4	Postal Clerk	3.44	10,684	1,888	17.7
PO 5	Mail Dispatcher, supervisory (Relief) Letter Carrier	3.52	2,302	6	0.3

SOURCE: Agreement between The Treasury Board and The Council of Postal Unions, Postal Operations Group (non-supervisory), Code: 608/10/70, Expires March 26, 1972; Pay Research Bureau, Public Service Staff Relations Board, "The Composition of the Public Service of Canada, September 1972," Ottawa, September 1973, p. 17.

the bottom of the heap and paid 50 cents an hour less than the workers who sorted the mail manually.

Table 4 shows the classifications and pay rates for full-time postal workers, with the number of men and women workers in each classification. These figures include both the inside postal workers represented by the CUPW and the letter carriers who belonged to the Letter Carriers Union of Canada (LCUC). Because the two unions bargained together at this time as the Council of Postal Unions, they were covered by the same collective agreement and the available data combines the two groups. However, the memberships of the two unions can be distinguished without much overlap. The vast majority of the membership of the LCUC are found at the PO 3 level: the letter carriers, although they also represented some mail service couriers, also at level 3, and a few supervisory letter carriers working just on a relief basis at level 5. The CUPW's membership is concentrated at the PO 4 level, the Postal Clerks who sorted the mail. The CUPW also represented some Mail Service Couriers (sharing this group with the LCUC), the Mail Handlers at level PO 2 and the highest paid Mail Dispatchers at the PO 5 level.

Although it did not appear in the collective agreement, for comparative purposes I have included the Coder position as it was classified by management at level PO 1, and I have inserted the number of men and women workers initially hired in Ottawa in August 1972.[2] It is clear from the table above that the only full-time position into which women had entered in any significant number was the Postal Clerk at level PO 4, and even here women represented just under 18 percent of the workers. Consequently, it is remarkable to note that in the new full-time Coder classification women comprise more than 60 percent of the workers hired.

In summary, the outcome of the new classification was to create a predominantly female full-time occupational category, with a lower classification and lower rate of pay than the full-time occupational categories dominated by men.

The Dispute

The Beginning of the Dispute

Management introduced the new Coder classification suddenly and with almost no prior warning. Union representatives had attended meetings on technological change with the employer in 1971, but the possibility of new classifications had been raised only as a potential development far into the future. In fact the union had received some reassurance that the new work that would be done on the machines would be made available to their members. At a meeting in January 1971, Mr. Jerry Fultz, Director of Coding and Mechanization for the Post Office, responded to the concerns of the union for the future job security of its members, by saying:

> I can tell you this; we have no intention of following the system that was used in one country where no postal clerks worked on the coding desks. We plan to use our present staff on the machines when they go in and we'll worry about what happens to the residue after our present staff have been looked after.[3]

And in December 1971 during a discussion of training, the Post Office Department's minutes record: "Mr. Fultz went into an explanation of the operation of the training machines ... It would take approximately 60 to 80 hours to train a Postal Clerk to work on the machines and they would be replaced at their normal workplace on the same basis as at present."[4]

Despite these reassurances, at a union-management meeting on 20th June 1972 the union was informed that workers on the machines would be called Coders, had been classified at the PO 1 level and would be paid $2.94 an hour.

---

[2] Public Service Commission, Eligible List No: 72-PO-CC-OTT–68, Postal Coders, Postal Operations Level 1, 8 August 1972.

[3] Canada Post Office, "Briefing on Coding and Mechanization," Verbatim report of a meeting between representatives of the Post Office and the Council of Postal Unions, Ottawa, 7 January 1971, p. 12.

[4] Canada Post Office, "Minutes of a Union/Management Consultation Meeting," Ottawa, 13 December 1971, p. 2.

Management intended that the Coders should work exclusively on the machines for eight hours per day, and planned the creation of "a separate division with its own seniority list, called tentatively the Machine Mail Processing Division."[5] The Post Office management had not only prepared the posters advertising this new position, but intended to post them immediately and planned to hold meetings with the Ottawa staff in the following week to explain the program and encourage their support. It was already arranged that, should there be insufficient internal applicants, management would hold an external competition to hire from outside the Post Office. If Postal Clerks applied for the positions, they would be paid $2.94 an hour, thereby accepting a 15 percent cut in pay. They would also lose all their seniority.

The union representatives at the meeting were appalled and vigorously protested the new classification. They called the pay rate "disgusting," said it was tantamount to legalizing casuals and that it represented a downgrading of jobs from PO 4 to PO 1. They objected that the union had not been consulted, but management replied "on the question of classification it was not necessary to consult," referring to the restrictions of the Public Service Staff Relations Act (PSSRA). At the insistence of the union representatives, a further meeting was arranged and management agreed to delay posting the competitions and meeting with the Ottawa workers for a week, pending further discussions.[6] The union immediately perceived the importance of the issue and moved to deal with it in three different ways: through further meetings and discussions with management, by informing and mobilizing the union membership, and through the legal mechanism of placing a complaint before the Public Service Staff Relations Board (PSSRB). These three strategies are threads running throughout the response of the union to the Coder issue, and indeed have been important in many other concerns dealt with by the CUPW. Their relative success in terms of the Coder dispute will be assessed later in this chapter.

Meetings with Management

At further meetings on 23rd and 26th June, the national officers of the union pressed for the issue to be negotiated. The collective agreement had expired in March 1972 and negotiations were in process at this time. Management refused to refer the Coder issue to the negotiating table on the basis that under the PSSRA, classification was not subject to negotiation. The union proposed that a joint management-union application be made to the PSSRB to determine whether classification was negotiable under the law. Management refused, indi-

---

[5] Canada Post Office, "Minutes of a Meeting Held Between the Post Office Department and the Council of Postal Unions," Ottawa, 20 June 1972, p. 4.

[6] *Ibid.*

cating that the union was free to apply itself if it wished. The union recommended that the use of the machines and the hiring of Coders be delayed until an agreement could be reached. Management refused. The union proposed that the Coders be classified temporarily at the PO 4 level and with the PO 4 pay rate, pending further discussions and agreement. Again, management refused. The meetings ended with no resolution of the union's concerns and management stating that it meant to proceed with hiring for the new Coder jobs.[7]

The closed competition for the Postal Coder position was posted in the Ottawa Post Office on 5th July. No-one applied. Consequently, an open competition was held and by 7th August the Public Service Commission had established a list of eligible workers from outside the Post Office. By 21st August the first Coders had been hired at the Alta Vista Post Office in Ottawa.

The Legal Route

On 18th July the union formally complained that the employer had violated Section 51 of the PSSRA. This section is meant to protect workers between the expiry of one collective agreement and the signing of another, by prohibiting the employer from making any changes in pay or working conditions during that period. The expired collective agreement continues in effect until the new agreement is signed. The agreement that expired in March 1972 guaranteed that if new classifications were created, their rates of pay would be fixed by "mutual agreement" between the union and management.[8] The union claimed that the employer had violated this provision by failing to consult over the introduction of the new classification, and sought an order requiring the Post Office to refrain from proceeding with the new classification.

The hearings were not held until September (after Postal Coders were already employed in the Ottawa Post Office) and the PSSRB decision was not announced until 18th October. The Board decided that the Post Office was within its rights to classify the Postal Coders at PO 1 and to set an interim rate for the job. However, the Post Office "did not carry out its obligation to confer with the Applicant in appropriate fashion in an endeavour to establish an agreed rate for that classification."[9] The Post Office was ordered to meet with the union in order to reach an agreement on the pay rate for the Postal Coders. While the union had thus demonstrated the lack of consultation over the issue, the right of management to create new classifications without reference to the union was upheld.

[7] Canada Post Office, "Minutes of a Meeting Held Between the Post Office Department and the Council of Postal Unions," Ottawa, 23 June 1972; Canadian Union of Postal Workers, "Special Meeting," Ottawa, 23 June 1972 and 26 June 1972.

[8] Agreement between The Treasury Board and the Council of Postal Unions, Postal Operations Group (non-supervisory), Code: 608/10/70, Expires: 26 March 1972, p. 65, Article 32.

[9] Public Service Staff Relations Board, *Decisions*, File No: 148–2–7, Ottawa, 18 October 1972, p. 5.

Mobilizing the Membership

Immediately following the first meeting with management on the Coder issue on 20th June, the CUPW national officers took steps to inform and mobilize their members. On 22nd June a telex was sent to the fifteen locals then expected to be converted to mechanized Letter Sorting Machines, recommending that they meet that day or the next with local management to ask a long list of questions about mechanization. The telex said: "For our meeting tomorrow at headquarters John Mackay must know that our 15 locals are aware of his double-cross and that the CUPW is prepared to mobilize."[10] At this time John Mackay was the Deputy Minister to the Postmaster General. On 23rd June, the morning of the second meeting with management, the workers in Ottawa walked off the job for the morning in protest over the new classification.

Over the following weeks, the union issued information bulletins, front page articles appeared in the CUPW newspaper, and the issue received considerable coverage by the national press. The Postal Coder issue became a central concern for the union's members. In August demonstrations were held by postal workers across the country demanding that Postal Coders be reclassified to the PO 4 level. The union declared: "At this point we, the Postal Workers, have every reason to believe that we have been betrayed by our employer."[11]

In the Ottawa local the newly hired Coders were signed up as members of the CUPW and on 14th October a meeting was held for them to discuss the situation. The CUPW National President at the time, Jim McCall, attended the meeting and reported on it the next day in a letter to the Ontario National Director. All 31 Coders attended the meeting and had many complaints about changing shift schedules, working most Sundays, erratic pay checks, and safety problems. Shop stewards were elected from among the Coders to start dealing with some of these problems at the local level. The President noted: "the boss has angered them by his treatment. Consequently, we now have a new group of solid militant members."[12]

In September 1972 the union initiated a campaign, Boycott the Postal Code. The CUPW national officers contacted the Canadian Labour Congress and the provincial federations of labour requesting that they and their affiliates and union members not use the postal code on their mail. The purpose of this campaign was to bring some pressure to bear on the Post Office management by reducing the

---

[10] Canadian Union of Postal Workers, Telex from CUPW National Office in Ottawa to all National Directors and Winnipeg, 22 June 1972.

[11] Canadian Union of Postal Workers, *CUPW*, Vol. 2, No. 8, August 1972, p. 1.

[12] Letter from J.B. McCall, National President of the Canadian Union of Postal Workers, to Arnold Gould, National Director, Ontario Region of the Canadian Union of Postal Workers, 5 October 1972, p. 1.

use of the postal code and thereby obstructing the effectiveness of the mechanization programme. It also served as a means to increase public awareness about the problems in the Post Office, and at the same time gave locals and members a campaign to organize around. It took some time to get off the ground, becoming a more important element of the union's strategy in 1973, and it was maintained until 1975. The union claimed that the Post Office was affected by the boycott. In 1975 the Post Office did introduce additional fees for bulk customers not using the postal code on their mail, although it had previously claimed that use of the postal code would be voluntary. The CUPW suggested that the Post Office had taken this step because of the effectiveness of the boycott campaign.[13]

The Struggle Continues

Meanwhile negotiations for a new collective agreement were continuing. No agreement having been reached, a Conciliation Board was established, chaired by Owen Shime, that reported in December 1972. The report proposed the establishment of a Manpower Committee, a joint union-management committee with an external advisor to discuss all issues of concern around automation, including the Postal Coder.[14] The union nominee to the Board agreed with this proposal, while the management nominee dissented, stating with some foresight: "I do not understand how consultation can achieve what negotiation has so far failed to achieve."[15]

Following the Shime report there was some tension and conflict within the CUPW. A referendum of the membership was held on whether or not to accept the report as a basis for settlement, but the wording of the referendum appeared to create some confusion. It was accepted against the recommendation of the negotiating team and consequently the Manpower Committee became enshrined in the full-time and part-time collective agreements that were signed in February 1973. The position of Coder, being unresolved, appears in the full-time workers' collective agreement as a separate title, unrelated to the other classifications, and not as PO 1.

In February 1973 the CUPW national officers met with the Coders in the Ottawa local and explained that their situation was still to be resolved in the Manpower Committee. The union expressed a cautious approach to the value of the Committee. A front page article in the union's newspaper pointed out that in the Manpower Committee for the first time the union would have the right to

[13] Letter from W.B. Kidd, National Director of Education and Organization, Canadian Union of Postal Workers, to Donald MacDonald, President of the Canadian Labour Congress, 18 October 1972; Canadian Union of Postal Workers, *CUPW*, Vol. 2, No. 5–6, May-June 1973, p. 1, and Vol. 5, No. 3, September 1975, p. 3.

[14] "Report of the Conciliation Board to the Chairman of the PSSRB," Chaired by Owen B. Shime, December 1972.

[15] B.H. Stewart, "Dissenting Report to Recommendations of the Conciliation Board by the Employer Nominee," Toronto, 14 October 1972.

discuss classification and job evaluation with management. However, it was understood that the outcome of those discussions would depend upon the goodwill of both sides in reaching agreement, and that the Manpower Committee could not prevent the employer from continuing its own program of mechanization.[16] In fact, the Manpower Committee never functioned to discuss or resolve anything. It took months to organize meetings and discuss terms of reference, which were not agreed upon until January 1974, 10 months after the contract had been signed.

Meanwhile the union was experiencing other difficulties. In August 1973 detailed information was requested from the Post Office on the mechanization program and its impact upon postal workers. No information was provided by management until January 1974 and then it was only partial and incomplete. Meanwhile tension was mounting as more plants were mechanized in the west and plans proceeded with little union input. Frustration among the members was growing because of the failure of the Manpower Committee to produce results and criticism was developing of the CUPW national office and the President in particular for the handling of this, and other issues concerning technological change.

These tensions finally erupted in April 1974, when 300 workers in Montreal were suspended for wearing T-shirts to work printed with the slogan "Boycott the Postal Code." The Montreal local refused to have the CUPW President, Jim McCall, negotiate on its behalf, and consequently he resigned and was replaced by the Vice President, Joe Davidson. Davidson immediately called a national strike, the main issue being the Coder position. The strike lasted from 19th to 26th April, and was technically illegal because a collective agreement was in force. The workers returned to work on the basis of an agreement mediated by Eric Taylor. The terms were that a Special Settlement Committee to be chaired by Taylor would decide the Coder issue, thereby removing the issue from the exclusive jurisdiction of the employer; that Taylor would also hear other areas of dispute; that all suspensions and disciplinary measures that had caused the dispute would be lifted; and that there would be no reprisals for the strike action.[17] When the members returned to work, it was clear that some resolution of the Coder question was to be forthcoming.

The Solution

Eric Taylor chaired the Special Settlement Committee with the union nominee, Mr. Tirrell and the management nominee, Mr. Savoie. Both parties presented quantities of material to substantiate their positions and appeared before the Committee to make presentations and answer questions. It is useful to look at

---

[16] Canadian Union of Postal Workers, *CUPW*, Vol. 2, No. 3, March 1971, p. 1.

[17] "Recommendations of Eric G. Taylor appointed under the Public Service Staff Relations Act in Respect of a Dispute Between the Council of Postal Unions and the Treasury Board," Ottawa, 24 April 1974.

CODERS AT WORK

Letters drop down into a screen, the Coder reads the postal code and inputs it using a keyboard, 1,800 times an hour. *(Photograph by Louise de Geosbois.)*

Each Coder Desk Suite has places for twelve Coders. *(Photograph by Louise de Geosbois.)*

these presentations in some detail because each side mustered their most complete and fully argued case.

The union began by arguing that technological change should benefit workers and provide improved opportunities, an opinion widely held but also expressed in particular by their own employer. In 1970 in the House of Commons, Eric Kierans, then Postmaster General, had stated that "the national code will entail an upgrading of job skills in the Post Office."[18] In agreement, on this occasion, with the Postmaster General, the CUPW's position was that the skills of the manual sorter and the mechanical sorter should be combined, and all should be classified at the PO 4 level. The union argued that this would allow for job rotation between workers, reducing the routine and repetitive tasks that lead to tension, health problems and low morale. At the same time it would provide management with a more flexible work force, able to perform a variety of tasks as the need arose, and not confined to sitting at the coding desk as the Coders were presently. The union maintained that the job was sorting mail, and whether it was done manually or mechanically, it was the same function and should be paid at the same rate. Evidence was presented to show that in England, Japan and Belgium no distinction was made between workers sorting on or off a machine.

The union held that the current system effectively denied the existing manual sorters the opportunity to take the jobs on the machines because they had to accept a substantial cut in pay to do so. Moreover, the lower paid Coder position would have the effect of downgrading pay levels for all postal workers. In fact, by the time of the Special Settlement Committee, Coders were employed not only in Ottawa, but also in Winnipeg, Regina, Saskatoon and Edmonton, although there were still only 95 in total. However, based upon information supplied by the Post Office for 14 of the Post Offices to be automated, the number of Coders was to increase to 1,065 by 1977 (and these figures exclude the large Montreal Post Office). Over the same period there was to be a loss of 2,647 positions at the PO 4 level.[19] This meant that there would be more low-paying jobs and fewer higher paid jobs as automation progressed.

On the other side, the employer argued that coding work was a distinct and separate function, requiring unskilled workers and little training. Evidence was submitted on the classification process and how it was decided that a Coder was PO 1 on the basis of job evaluation and a points system. Since the work was unskilled it was argued that the PO 1 classification was appropriate.

The other aspect of the employer's presentation was a legal one. First, management was concerned that the Special Settlement Committee should operate within the same legal framework as a Conciliation Board, constrained by the requirements of the PSSRA. Therefore, the Post Office representatives provided

[18] Letter from Eric Kierans, Postmaster General, to Willie Houle, National President of the Canadian Union of Postal Workers, quoting his comments to the House of Commons, 17 February 1970, p. 3.

[19] Canadian Union Of Postal Workers, "Submission to the Special Settlement Committee," Exhibit C 22, 6 May 1974.

the Committee with the terms of reference of the Shime Conciliation Board, which indicated that the Board was constrained by Section 7 of the PSSRA, namely that classification was a management prerogative. This engendered the following debate at the Committee hearings between Eric Taylor and Mr. E.W. Greenslade, Director of Staff Relations at the Post Office:

Mr. Greenslade—You will find that the Committee has to keep within Section 7 of the Act, Section 56.2 and Section 83.3.

Mr. Taylor—That's the report of the Conciliation Board. We are empowered, by agreement between the parties, to hear and decide on this matter.

Mr. Greenslade—It was not my intention to enter into any kind of a legal debate. Whatever your findings are, you will have to take cognizance of the legislation.

Mr. Taylor—You are asking us to be aware of these provisions and to take cognizance of the Acts and the provisions.

Mr. Greenslade—And any restraints that may fall therefrom on such a committee as this.

Mr. Taylor—We are not a statutory board of any kind. We are a special committee to decide.[20]

The employer also stressed the legalities of the situation in the development of the Coder dispute. In his presentation to the Committee, Mr. Greenslade stated management's position succinctly: "The Post Office Department was not required by law to negotiate the classification and unilaterally introduced the Coder classification."[21] Mr. Fultz concluded "We did everything in strictest accordance with the law of the country and it is on this basis that our case must be judged."[22] This last statement might be questioned since the PSSRB had found that the Post Office had violated the law by failing to confer with the union upon a rate of pay for the new job. However, what is important here is that management's primary concern was adherence to the legislation. At the end of management's presentation, Mr. Taylor concluded: "I listened this morning to a statement where a great deal of emphasis was placed on legal rights, legal processes and I recollect that the discharge of these has produced the problem that we are confronted with ... There is a human relations problem here that has to be responded to."[23]

Adherence to Section 7 of the PSSRA raised an important contradiction which was dealt with directly by the Committee. The collective agreement in force in 1972 required that the rate of pay for any new classification be mutually agreed

[20] Special Settlement Committee Hearings, Ottawa, 7 May 1974, pp. 2–3.

[21] Canada Post Office, "Post Office Exhibit Re PO 1-PO 4 Issue," prepared by E.W. Greenslade, Assistant Director, Staff Relations Branch, 3 May 1974, p. 4.

[22] Canada Post Office, "Presentation to the Special Committee," prepared and presented by J.G. Fultz, Director of Coding and Mechanization, 7 May 1974, p. 19.

[23] Special Settlement Committee Hearings, Ottawa, 7 May 1974, p. 29.

upon by the union and the employer. But, how could the union participate in setting the rate for the job, if the employer unilaterally decided the classification, because the classification imposed limitations upon what the pay rate could be? The classification set the level for the job (in the case of the Coder, level 1), and the union could only negotiate rates of pay for the different levels, but not a rate for the job. This created some confusion for the Committee members and resulted in the following debate:

> Mr. Tirrell—If the Coder is in level 1, how can you negotiate? I am talking about negotiating for a rate for a job and not a level. I am not prepared to sit here and face a ridiculous situation. Other people can negotiate a rate without anything stopping them.

> Mr. Greenslade—This is the system within which we are operating.

> Mr. Tirrell—I think it behooves the official side to take a very close look at that problem.

> Mr. Greenslade—You can negotiate a set of rates for levels.

> Mr. Tirrell—The employer, by the Act, theoretically and ultimately places all of these jobs into a level 1. What kind of bargaining is this for rates? This is not realistic. The only person who has any say where these jobs fall is the employer. It is all one-sided.[24]

Finally the Special Settlement Committee neatly side-stepped the legal problem by establishing a higher rate of pay for the Coder position without any determination of the classification issue. The minimum rate of pay for Coders was set at $3.88, a rate that was between the PO 2 and PO 3 levels but fitted into neither. The union called it the PO 2 3/8 level. The Committee's report indicated that the union and management would still have to decide what to do with the Coder position in terms of classification, possibly creating a separate category for Coders.[25] The new pay rate for the Coder undermined the employer's classification system and did in effect end the employer's right to unilateral classification, because the Committee had set a pay rate that could not be accommodated within the PO 1 level. This led in turn to the final resolution of the Coder issue.

Part of the agreement that ended the April strike was that Eric Taylor would hear any other matters arising out of the dispute and consequently a series of meetings were held between May and December 1974. In these union-management meetings Taylor was appointed by the PSSRB and acted as chair and advisor. The meetings focused on the automation of the Post Office in Toronto, on the understanding that agreements reached would apply across the country. In December 1974 Taylor reported that agreement had been reached on questions of classification, including the Coder dispute.[26]

---

[24] *Ibid.*, p. 6.

[25] "Decision of A Special Settlement Committee," Ottawa, 7 June 1974.

[26] "Report by Eric Taylor," Ottawa, 31 December 1974.

The agreement brought about important changes in the classification system for the inside postal workers. In future contracts there were only three classification levels, the Mail Handlers at PO 3 (upgraded from PO 2), the Postal Clerks and the Supervisory Mail Handlers at the PO 4 level, and the Mail Dispatchers at PO 5. Under this new system the Postal Coders were reclassified to level PO 4 and the duties of the Postal Clerk and the Coder combined, the position advocated by the CUPW for two and a half years.

The Union's Motivation in the Coder Dispute

Clearly the CUPW fought long and hard to prevent the formation of a separate, lower paid classification that would have been predominantly occupied by women. Before looking at why the union acted as it did, it is interesting to consider the fact that the possibility of protecting only their existing members and permitting the creation of a lower paid category of work was posed to the union as a realistic alternative.

When the union applied to the PSSRB in July 1972, their application contained the following comment:

> In a further statement by the employer, it has been said that if the bargaining agent does not wish its members to perform the above-mentioned functions (i.e. Coder), then they should not be concerned because the employer was prepared to hire new employees for the above functions and that the bargaining agents' prerogative, in his opinion, is only to represent existing employees and classifications.[27]

Clearly the union was aware of this possible perspective on the issue. The employer denied having made such statements and it may indeed be the case that they were not made as directly as the union's assertion here implies. However, Post Office management did make comments that were open to this interpretation.

In its attempts to allay the union's fears, management gave reassurances that the existing work force would not be directly affected. At the meeting on 20th June 1972, at which the union was first informed of the new Coder position, "Management confirmed that the start up in operating would not have any adverse effect on the job security of existing part-time or full-time employees in the Post Office."[28] Following the morning walkout of workers in the Ottawa Post Office on 23rd June, the Regional General Manager for Ontario wrote to explain the situation to all Ontario supervisors. Having expressed his regret at the mail disruption he noted the facts of the case, including:

---

[27] Council of Postal Unions, "Application to the Public Service Staff Relations Board," 18 July 1972, pp. 2–3.

[28] Canada Post Office, "Minutes of a Meeting Held Between the Post Office Department and the Council of Postal Unions," Ottawa, 20 June 1972, p. 2.

Meetings have taken place between Management and the staff of the Ottawa Post Office at which time it was stated that no full-time or part-time regular employees will lose their jobs because of the LSM's. Nor will the classifications of any of these employees be affected by the LSM's.[29]

However, the idea that if present employees were protected, then the union had little to concern itself with, was expressed more directly by the Conciliation Board under Owen Shime, than by the employer. The Shime report of December 1972 suggested that the union had "over-reacted" on the Coder issue, commenting that it was not an attempt "to displace the *existing* work force and to force a lower rate on the employees."[30] During the Conciliation Board meetings the employer had agreed to renew the letter of understanding guaranteeing job security to all present full-time employees. This letter, signed by the Postmaster General, had been obtained by the CUPW after rotating strikes in 1970 and stated:

The planned modernization program will not result in lay-offs of present full-time employees during the life of the present agreement provided employees will accept relocation, reassignment and retraining.[31]

The format of a letter attached to the agreement was used because, under the PSSRA, the union could not negotiate lay-offs and therefore nothing could appear in the collective agreement on the issue. In 1972 the employer agreed to add a second letter assuring that none of the existing full-time workers would experience any change in pay rate for the duration of the collective agreement.[32] The Shime report states that, given these guarantees, the Coder issue need no longer be a concern for the union. In other words, if the union's present members are fully protected, there is no reason for concern for new workers in a new classification.

The employer's nominee to the Conciliation Board, Mr. B.H. Stewart, wrote a dissenting report in which this view is more determinedly expressed. Stewart regarded the employer's offer as providing unprecedented wage and job security

---

[29] Letter from J.C. Corkery, Regional General Manager, Ontario Postal Region, to all Supervisors, Ontario Postal Region, Toronto, 29 June 1972.

[30] "Report of the Conciliation Board to the Chairman of the PSSRB," Chaired by Owen B. Shime, 14 December 1972, p. 36.

[31] Agreement between the Treasury Board and the Council of Postal Unions, Postal Operations Group (non-supervisory), Code: 608/3/73, Expires: 31 December 1974, C, Letter of Understanding.

[32] *Ibid.*, D–1 and D–2, Letter of Understanding.

to postal workers and objected to the Manpower Committee as unnecessary capitulation to the union's demand for participation in the creation of new jobs. He wrote that the union had pressed for the "elaborate machinery" of the Manpower Committee, despite the fact that no present employee would suffer financially now or during the term of the agreement.[33]

The CUPW completely rejected this perspective on the Coder issue. Why? First, it is important to point out that there is no evidence that the union was responding to pressure from its women members. In 1972 women comprised almost 24 percent of the union's membership.[34] There were no women on the National Executive, nor any women in paid union positions within the union structure. There is no way of knowing how many women went as delegates to the National Conventions, but at the 1968 Convention that lasted for five days, two women spoke. At the 1971 Convention that lasted six days, women spoke on just six occasions.[35] It is clear that women did not have a strong voice within the union at this time. Women's committees and caucuses had not been developed even locally at this point and were not discussed at a National Convention until 1977. It was not because of pressure from women within the CUPW that the union turned the Coder issue into a dispute.

Moreover, the Coder dispute was not regarded by the union or its members, male or female, as an issue of particular concern to women. In all the documentation, I found only one comment that related to gender. When the 15 locals were asked to meet with their local managements to question them about mechanization, copies of the minutes of those meetings were forwarded to head office. The Quebec City local asked an additional question: "If women would be favoured because of the kind of work involved?" The answer was the same as to most of the other questions: "I don't know."[36] Apart from this sole exception, in union bulletins, articles, debates, submissions and briefs there is never any reference to the possible impact of the Coder classification for women. There are no references to the fact that the Coders might be, or were, predominantly women, nor any suggestion that the separate lower paid classification might be particularly unfair to women workers or might create a ghetto of female employment.

---

[33] B.H. Stewart, "Dissenting Report to Recommendations of the Conciliation Board by the Employer Nominee," Toronto, 14 December 1972, pp. 42–43.

[34] Statistics Canada, *Corporations and Labour Unions Returns Act*, Part II—Labour Unions, Cat.71–202, Ottawa, 1972.

[35] Canadian Union of Postal Workers, *Tenth Triennial National Convention Proceedings*, Montreal, 27–29 May 1968, and *National Convention 1971 Proceedings*, Calgary, 31 May–5 June 1971.

[36] Letter from André Marceau, Staff Representative, Canadian Union of Postal Workers, Quebec City, to W.B. Kidd, Director of Organization, Canadian Union of Postal Workers, 28 June 1972.

On 20th June 1972, when the CUPW national officers first heard of the new classification, their response was immediate. Before any Coders were actually hired and therefore before the union could know that the Coders would be predominantly women, locals were informed and mobilized against the new classification and it was condemned in union bulletins and in the national paper. Moreover, once the Coders were hired in August 1972 their sex made no impact upon how the issue was argued, or the union's policy or actions. Although the Coders posed some threat to the pay rates of the other CUPW members, there was no hostility expressed towards them at any time.

The CUPW Ottawa local immediately signed up the Coders as members and organized a meeting at which the Coders appointed their own shop stewards.[37] By 29th August the union stated in a summary of the events to that point: "Our dispute in this matter is entirely with the employer. We have no dispute with the Coders, in fact, they are already members of our union."[38] After a meeting with the Coders in October 1972 the National President reported: "I have met and come to admire some very fine people. They do not deserve to be treated in such a way or paid such a rate of pay." He went on to say that the union was now representing the "individual worker on this job" as well as the national issue with all its legalities and negotiations.[39]

Thus, the fact that the Coder dispute had particular implications for women was not recognized by the union, in either a negative or positive way. On the one hand the union did not draw strength from arguments concerning women's equality, nor from any particular expression of concern by its women members about the Coder issue, but neither was there any hostility expressed towards the women Coders, nor any sexism in the union's approach. The union did not deal with the issue differently because a high proportion of women were involved, nor did it influence the union participation of the Coders or the degree of protection provided to them as union members.

If neither pressure from women, nor consciousness of women's issues played a role in the union's response, what were the reasons?

First of all the union realized that despite management's reassurances, the existing workers would be negatively affected by a lower paid job classification in both the short and longer term. Immediately, lower paid workers might act as a downward drag on wages in general and depress the increases negotiated for all the classifications. The union representatives were also shrewd enough to recognize that even if there were no immediate lay-offs or pay reductions for

[37] Letter from J.B. McCall, National President of the Canadian Union of Postal Workers, to A.R. Gould, National Director, Ontario Region of the Canadian Union of Postal Workers, 5 October 1972.

[38] Canadian Union of Postal Workers, "CUPW Statement on Coder Dispute," 29 August 1972, p. 8.

[39] Letter from J.B. McCall, National President of the Canadian Union of Postal Workers, to A.R. Gould, National Director, Ontario Region of the Canadian Union of Postal Workers, 5 October 1972.

existing workers, hiring patterns would change so that there would be fewer higher paid workers and more lower paid positions. This would have a broad impact upon the level of wages for work in the Post Office and could adversely affect the ability of the union to bargain higher pay rates in the longer term.

The union campaigned against the Postal Coder classification on the basis that it was likely to have an impact upon the whole work force, not just the few Postal Coders then employed, nor even just the CUPW members in the 15 locals immediately affected. From the union's perspective, the letters of understanding guaranteeing no lay-offs or wage reductions meant nothing if classifications, and thereby wages, could be manipulated. A Bulletin to all union members stated:

> It would be fatal for postal workers to believe that declassification would only take place with Postal Clerks in the fifteen major centres. To accept management's position that they have the absolute right to classify would mean that any time within the life of a collective agreement they introduced a mechanical aspect to any job, then that worker could be downgraded ... There is not one postal worker in any office in Canada that could not be adversely affected by this concept.[40]

The union was proved correct in at least some of its fears. It emerged that the Post Office had plans for other new classifications as well as the Coders. Stewart's dissenting report for the Conciliation Board in 1972 mentioned that the Post Office had a "pay for skills" program and planned several new job functions, of which the Coder was just the first.[41] Before the April 1974 strike the CUPW was aware that another new position, called a Keyer-Facer, was to be introduced that was intended to replace the highest paid position in the bargaining unit, the Mail Dispatcher at level PO 5. It was not until January 1974 that the Post Office released its staffing projections for the 15 locals to be automated, but it was then clear that the number of workers at the PO 1 level was to expand, while the higher paid PO 4 level positions were to be decreased.

Also of primary importance in the CUPW's struggle around the Coder dispute was the union's philosophy of equality for its members—a philosophy that was translated into policies and action. This had nothing to do with equality for women particularly, but related to notions of what was generally fair and just. As a consequence, the union had maintained for years that pay discrepancies within the bargaining unit should be decreased, partly by across the board increases and also by a goal to finally negotiate everyone in the bargaining unit into the same, single classification. These policies, and the action taken on them, will be examined in detail in the following section on part-time work, but they were a strong influence within the union and affected the response to the Coder issue.

---

[40] The Council of Postal Unions, Negotiating Committee, "Bulletin No. 7, To All Members," 28 June 1972.

[41] B.H. Stewart, "Dissenting Report to Recommendations of the Conciliation Board by the Employer Nominee," Toronto, 14 December 1972, p. 42.

The introduction of another classification at a lower pay rate ran in direct contradiction to the union's policies of decreasing the pay gap between the lowest and highest paid workers. It was felt to be blatantly and obviously unfair that a separate group of workers should be hired to sort the mail at a much lower rate of pay. In a summary of the state of the Coder dispute prepared in August 1972, the union stated: "We do not want them (Coders) to lose the jobs for which they have been hired, but we want them to be reclassified to their rightful position of a P.O. Level 4 (Postal Clerk)."[42] From this point of view the technicalities of the level of skill involved were irrelevant; a rate had been established for sorting mail and it was not acceptable to downgrade the pay.

Another reason why the CUPW did not accept the employer's creation of a new classification is that the union and its members did not trust much that the employer initiated. The bad labour relations atmosphere of the 1960s had not been improved by the advent of collective bargaining and strikes had resulted in 1968 and 1970. The negotiations in 1972 were not going well when the Coder classification was introduced. Management was proposing numerous rollbacks, including reduced job security and pay rates that would vary across geographical regions. The Shime report commented upon the difficulty of introducing any change in an atmosphere where anything done by management raised suspicion and distrust. The level of hostility was expressed by one delegate to the 1974 National Convention: "We are in a stage of all-out war. I am dealing, day in and day out, with the most immoral, crooked, lying, two-faced management you ever saw in your life."[43] Under these circumstances it was not likely that the union would quietly accept the introduction of a lower job classification.

The CUPW was anxious to protect its members, aroused by the inequality of pay for the Coders, and suspicious of employer initiatives, but it also had the ability to undertake the struggle around the Coder classification and then carry it to a successful conclusion. The union's capacity to do so depended upon the solidarity and militancy of the membership. For two and a half years the union refused to accept legislated restrictions upon its right to negotiate classifications, maintaining throughout that its members should have the same right to free collective bargaining as workers in private industry. It is notable that in its early discussions with management, in contract negotiations, in the Conciliation Board process, and in the Manpower Committee established under the collective agreement, the union made no progress. The turning point was the April 1974 strike, initiated by the union's most militant local, and then carried to a national strike by the whole union. The fact that the union's members were prepared to strike without legal sanction in 1974 obtained for them the settlement of the Coder dispute.

---

[42] Canadian Union of Postal Workers, "CUPW Statement on Coder Dispute," 29 August 1972, p. 8.

[43] Canadian Union of Postal Workers, *National Convention 1974 Proceedings*, Quebec, 3–8 June 1974, p. 540.

While a committed and motivated membership is often the critical element in any employer-union dispute, the union's structure and leadership are also important. The union's internal organization must allow for the expression of the members' discontent, and the union leadership must be able to give overall direction and develop strategy to mobilize the members. The CUPW was developing on both these points. The 1965 strike had been opposed by the union's national leadership and consequently they were promptly ousted at that year's National Convention. Again in 1968 and 1971 leadership changes reflected the increased militancy of the members and their dissatisfaction with leaders who lagged behind. In the midst of the Coder dispute this issue became critical when the Montreal local forced the resignation of President Jim McCall. Joe Davidson stepped in and called the national strike that led to the resolution of the problem.

Concern about the inadequate structure of the union in the late 1960s led to the adoption of a new constitution at the 1971 National Convention, a constitution that established highly democratic processes within the union and assured the expression of membership concerns. Other changes included regular and required communications of events from head office to the locals, the development of shop stewards to deal with issues in the workplace, and a system of education for union members. These developments in turn produced a more informed and unified membership.

While the public was becoming exasperated by the series of postal strikes, the workers were drawing their own conclusions:

> Unions that are polite, restrained and non-aggressive invariably end up with the worst agreements. They may enjoy a good public image, but their members pay for it in paltry pay cheques and poor working conditions. The postal unions had a good public image until they began to resort to the strike weapon six years ago. Since then their image has gone down about as fast as their wages have gone up.[44]

The growing reputation of the CUPW for militancy was not just a reputation, but the foundation upon which the union relied when consultation, discussion, mediation, conciliation and negotiation failed.

---

[44] Canadian Union of Postal Workers, *CUPW*, Vol. 2, No. 10, October 1972, p. 1.

6

BARGAINING EQUALITY FOR PART-TIME WORKERS

A t the National Convention in 1968 part-time workers were welcomed warmly into the CUPW by the full-time workers with a standing ovation. Part-time workers were now members of the union, but they were still a source of cheap labour for the employer. Despite the improvements obtained by the union even prior to 1968, a substantial minority of part-timers were still classified as Postal Helpers and paid less than the full-timers, no part-time workers were eligible for pay increments, and the only benefits they received were pay in lieu for annual vacations and statutory holidays. In considering what action was taken to improve conditions for "the ladies," the following discussion examines pay and classification, then benefits and working conditions, and finally seniority. Was the new-found goodwill toward the part-time workers maintained and was it translated into action?

Pay and Classification

The First Collective Agreement

The union signed its first agreement for the full-time workers in August 1968, and a second in September 1970. Because of the delays in certification for the part-time workers, the first collective agreement for part-time workers was not signed until November 1970. Since the Public Service Staff Relations Board (PSSRB) had certified full and part-time workers into separate bargaining units, they had separate contracts that were ratified by a separate vote. However, they always expired on the same date, so that the contracts and negotiations for both groups ran simultaneously.

In the full-time contract for 1970 the level PO 1 had been dropped and the positions classified upwards, so that there were now four levels from PO 2 to PO 5. The PO 2 was a Mail Handler, PO 3 was a Mail Service Courier or supervisory Mail Handler, PO 4 was a Postal Clerk and PO 5 was a Mail Dispatcher. In the part-time contract there was no level PO 5, but the part-time PO 2, PO 3 and PO 4 positions were paid the same rate for the job as the full-time workers ($3.01, $3.20, and $3.33 respectively). However, in the part-time contract the level PO 1 was retained, this being the part-time Postal Helper position, and these part-timers received an hourly rate of $2.83 under this first agreement. Although still lagging behind the pay rates of other part-time workers and the minimum full-time rates, under this first contract the Postal Helpers received a substantial 62 percent pay raise, from $1.75 to $2.83. However, none of the part-time workers were eligible for pay increments for length of service.

In 1966, before unionization, part-time workers had been earning 75 percent of the lowest full-time rate. By 1970 the majority of part-time workers were earning the same minimum rates as the full-time workers, while even the Postal Helpers were earning 94 percent of the lowest full-time rate. It is hardly surprising that the part-time workers ratified their first collective agreement by "an overwhelming majority."[1]

Breakthrough in 1974

By 1974, work in the Post Office was divided into the classifications and pay rates shown in Table 5. While more than half of the part-time workers (57 percent) were classified in the same way as the full-time workers and received the same minimum rate of pay, 43 percent remained postal helpers at a lower rate of pay. At this point the Postal Helpers were earning 95 percent of the Mail Handlers pay, although only 88 percent of the Postal Clerk's pay rate, the rate received by the majority of full-time workers.

For 1974 there is no information on the number of men and women in these positions. The only data available is from the Pay Research Bureau for 1972 and is of questionable reliability, particularly with regard to the part-time workforce. However, since it is the only material broken down by sex, I provide it here, with the reservation that the number of part-time workers is underestimated, and that this inaccuracy may affect the proportion of men and women shown by the figures. According to this data the part-time workers in the CUPW bargaining unit were almost 65 percent women, while the full-time workers were just 11 percent women.[2] Numerically, there were slightly more women working as part-time than full-time inside postal workers, 2,053 compared to 2,001, although it is most likely that the number of women part-time workers is here underestimated.

As described in the section on the Coder dispute, following the strike in April 1974 and the interventions of Eric Taylor, changes in the classification system were agreed upon by the end of 1974. These changes were of benefit not only to the Coders, but also to the part-time work force and therefore to a large number of women employed as part-time workers. The level PO 1 was eliminated, not only for the full-time Coders, but also for the part-time Postal Helpers. As a result more than 40 percent of the part-time workers in the Post Office were reclassified, mostly to the PO 4 level as Postal Clerks, a change which entailed a

---

[1] Canadian Union of Postal Workers, *National Convention 1971, Proceedings*, Calgary, 31 May–5 June 1971, p. 26.

[2] Pay Research Bureau, Public Service Staff Relations Board, "The Composition of the Public Service of Canada, September 1972," Ottawa, September 1973, p. 17, table 2. To arrive at a figure for the CUPW bargaining unit, workers at level 3 are excluded, these being the Letter Carriers and Mail Services Couriers, who belonged primarily to the LCUC.

TABLE 5: Classification and Pay in the CUPW Bargaining Unit, Full-Time and Part-Time Workers, May 1974				

Level	*Job Title*	*No. Workers*		*Pay Rate*
		Full-Time	*Part-Time*	
PO1	Postal Helper	-	1571	3.59
PO 2	Mail Handler	2473	502	3.77 3.98 (max)
PO 3	Mail Services Courier*	1926	75	3.96 4.19 (max)
PO 4	Postal Clerk	14161	1544	4.09 4.34 (max)
PO 5	Mail Dispatcher	2462	-	4.17 4.43 (max)

Note: The maximum pay rates applied only to the full-time workers.
* Mail Services Couriers were divided between the CUPW and the LCUC.
SOURCE: Canada Post Office, "Submission to the Special Settlement Committee," chaired by Eric Taylor, 1974, Exhibit E2.

very substantial increase in pay. The last contract to contain a lower pay rate for part-timers at the PO 1 level expired in December 1974.

Equality, 1975

The CUPW meant 1975 to be a big year for its members. The union's newspaper announced "This Is The Year," the slogan for that round of negotiations.[3] There were several reasons why the union's members felt that major gains were in order. The Manpower Committee established in the previous collective agreement had produced nothing for the union. While the meetings with Eric Taylor had resolved the Coder dispute, the union regarded this as little more than retaining the status quo. It meant that Postal Clerks at level PO 4 would continue to sort the mail, but did not represent any advance in obtaining benefits from the automation program. Meanwhile mechanization was proceeding apace and it was felt that perhaps this would be the last opportunity to really influence the situation before it would be virtually a fait accompli. Moreover, the union had only discovered in July 1974, during the meetings with Eric Taylor, that the automation program was far more extensive than had been indicated in their

---

[3] Canadian Union of Postal Workers, *CUPW*, Vol. 5, No. 1, January-February 1975, p. 1.

earlier meetings with management. Instead of a $96 million program involving 15 cities, the union now had information indicating that 36 automated facilities were to be established in 26 cities at a cost of $847 million.[4]

Another major factor was that 1975 was the first year that the CUPW was negotiating for its members alone, having broken away from the Council of Postal Unions. The debate over this move had taken place over the years since 1971, when the Montreal local first proposed a separation from the Letter Carriers Union of Canada (LCUC). The dissimilarity between the working conditions for the two groups of workers led to differing interests at the bargaining table. The letter carriers worked with little supervision, on a shorter work day, with minimal impact from automation, and part-time work was virtually non-existent. Consequently, the struggles and concerns of the inside postal workers were not shared within the Council of Postal Unions. As one Conciliation Board report pointed out, as much negotiation took place between the two unions within the Council as between the unions and the employer.[5] Following a membership referendum, CUPW resigned from the Council of Postal Unions and applied to the PSSRB for independent certification. This obtained, the CUPW was in the position of being free to place its demands on the negotiating table, without first having to obtain consensus within the Council of Postal Unions.

The separate certification for CUPW under the PSSRA had other consequences. One was that the union lost its membership among the Mail Services Couriers, previously divided between the two unions, who voted to be represented by the LCUC. The second result was that the part-time workers were no longer certified in a separate bargaining unit. The union applied to represent the full and part-time workers in a single bargaining unit and this was accomplished. This major step forward for the part-time workers meant that they would be covered by the same collective agreement as the full-time workers. Negotiating equal conditions and benefits was easier with the same agreement covering both groups of workers.

The 1975 negotiations resulted in a bitter 42 day strike from 21st October to 2nd December. Since the union did not gain in wages from this strike, finally accepting the Post Office's pre-strike wage offer, the press suggested that the strike had been unnecessary. But the CUPW had made other gains over those 42 days, including an article on technological change and increased control over the use of casual workers. For part-time workers the strike had obtained eligibility for the same shift premiums as the full-time workers and pay increments for length of service. The arrangement was that while the full-time workers increased their pay rates in three stages over three years, the part-time workers received their pay increments every two years, taking six years to reach the

[4] Canadian Union of Postal Workers, "Negotiations 77," Submission to the Conciliation Board, 10 April 1978, p. 22.

[5] "Report of the Conciliation Board to the Chairman of the PSSRB," Chaired by Owen B. Shime, Ottawa, 14 December 1972, p. 15.

maximum pay rate. From the point of view of the pay packets of the part-time workers the strike was certainly not a wasted effort. In the 1979 collective agreement the CUPW negotiated that the part-timers would receive their increments at the same time as the full-time workers, after each year for three years, thus finalizing the push to equal pay.

Benefits and Conditions of Work

As indicated in the previous chapter, prior to unionization in 1966, part-time workers were eligible only for a 4 percent addition to pay in lieu of wages. This vacation pay was lower than the vacation benefits received by the full-time workers and they were ineligible for sick leave, special leave and pensions. If they were absent from work for more than two months for any reason the job was lost and they had to reapply as a new employee. Part-time workers also complained that their hours of work were erratic and subject to change without notice, and that the individual work measurement to which they were still subject was stressful and led to favouritism.

The first contract obtained by the CUPW in 1970 addressed some of these concerns. For the first time part-time workers could accumulate sick leave, at a rate of 5 hours of paid leave per month, although they could only take the paid sick leave after five days of unpaid leave. Part-time workers continued to receive 4 percent payment in lieu of vacation (the equivalent of two weeks vacation), but this was now increased to 6 percent after 8 years of employment and they had the right to take 2 or 3 weeks of unpaid leave for their vacation. Part-time workers were no longer subject to losing their jobs if they took a leave of more than two months. For the first time part-time workers were protected by seniority, which applied to shifts, vacations and certain assignments. The hours of work were not to exceed 30 per week and had to be scheduled and posted a week in advance, while clearly defined rest periods and lunch times were provided. The part-time collective agreement, like that for the full-time workers, contained the union security clause of the Rand formula and the same grievance procedure for complaints against the employer.[6]

The full-time workers still had superior benefits. For example, full-time workers had 3 weeks vacation increasing to four weeks after 18 years of service; paid sick leave started on the first day of illness; and they could accumulate special leave for marriage, bereavement, the birth of a child and other reasons. Full-time workers were also provided with severance pay and some job security in the form of reassignment to other positions and other post offices. However, the first agreement for the part-time workers was still a significant step forward, dealing with several of the part-time workers' major complaints.

When the union negotiated letters of understanding in 1970 and 1972, first covering job security and then guaranteeing no reduction in wages, these letters

---

[6] Agreement Between the Treasury Board and the Council of Postal Unions, Postal Operations Group (Part-Time Employees), Code: 678/11/70, Expires: 26 March 1972.

were attached only to the full-time collective agreement and therefore did not protect the part-time workers. It was after the strike in 1974, and included as a part of the return-to-work package, that the part-time workers were also given this security. In 1975 these protections were included in the single collective agreement that covered both full and part-time workers from that time on.

As well as the pay increments that were obtained in 1975, the other major breakthrough was the abolition of individual work measurement for part-time workers. In 1963 the union had obtained the elimination of individual work measurement for the full-time workers but part-time workers had continued to mark their trays of sorted mail, a constant source of complaint and irritation. The CUPW had always opposed individual work measurement but it was not until 1975 that part-time workers were released from its constraints.

Following the signing of the 1975 collective agreement, the National Vice-President and chief negotiator, Jean-Claude Parrot, stressed that the negotiating committee had tried to obtain gains for groups of workers who had been previously neglected, including the Mail Handlers and the part-time workers. He said: "The part-timers are full and equal members of the Union and the improvements in their wages and benefits are a very positive development."[7] However, despite the gains in pay increments and the abolition of individual work measurement, two years later the 1977 National Convention heard complaints about the inequality of benefits for part-time workers. Delegates to the Convention who were part-time workers pressed the union to obtain pro-rated benefits to equalize the position of the full and part-time workers and thereby prevent the employer from using one group against the other.[8] In fact, while the other gains were a major step forward, the 1975 agreement made barely any changes in the benefits of the part-time workers from the previous agreement.

Full-time workers were eligible for 3 weeks of vacation, while part-time workers had to wait until after 4 years of service to get the equivalent (6 percent) in lieu of wages. Part-timers accumulated paid sick leave, but could not receive it until after three days without pay, and they had to produce a medical certificate. Full-time workers received paid sick leave from their first day of illness and for the first three days were not required to produce a medical certificate (up to a maximum of seven such casual sick days per year). Both full and part-time workers were eligible for special leave with pay for bereavement and for the birth or adoption of a child (one day), although the part-time workers had to wait until they had been employed for 6 months. However, only full-time workers could take 5 days of paid leave when they married. The contract provided both full and part-timers with 11 days of paid holidays, but in order to be eligible the part-time workers had to have been employed for 30 days and to have received

[7] Canadian Union of Postal Workers, *CUPW*, Vol. 6, No. 1, p. 1.

[8] Canadian Union of Postal Workers, *Thirteenth Triennial Convention Proceedings*, Halifax, 25–29 July 1977, pp. 1009–1012.

pay for 15 days in the previous thirty. Part-time workers were still not eligible for severance pay.

Although not equal, these benefits for part-time workers were a definite advance over those outlined above for the first part-time contract, and over the years, contract by contract, the improvements continued. In 1979 part-time workers obtained marriage leave and severance pay. In the same contract sick leave arrangements were equalized, with part-time workers receiving sick pay from the first day of illness, and also eligible for the same 7 days of casual sick leave per year as the full-time workers before having to produce a medical certificate. In 1979 part-time workers obtained paid rest periods, and in 1981 meal periods were pro-rated to 15 minutes after 5 hours of work. Vacations for part-time workers were gradually upgraded until in 1981 a fully equalized arrangement was negotiated. Full-time workers received 3 weeks, rising to 4 weeks after 10 years, 5 weeks after 20 years, 6 weeks after 30 years and 7 weeks after 35 years. The part-time workers' pay in lieu rose from 6 percent to 14 percent in the same stages and they had the right to the equivalent number of weeks of unpaid vacation leave. Also in the 1981 contract, part-time workers became eligible for statutory holidays automatically like the full-time workers, without any requirement for 30 days of employment or 15 days of paid work.

Other details were also equalized and by 1981 it is difficult, reading the collective agreement, to find much evidence of inequality between the full and part-time workers. Only one major issue remained; part-time workers were unable to participate in the pension plan. Under the PSSRA pensions were one of the non-negotiable items and part-time workers were specifically excluded from coverage under the Public Employees Superannuation Act that provided for the full-time workers.

Seniority

Seniority has always been and remains a critical issue for the inside postal workers. This is because it regulates several vital aspects of working life. Shifts are determined by seniority, which takes on real meaning when it is understood that CUPW members may work on the night shift for 10 years or longer before obtaining sufficient seniority to move onto days. Seniority is also the decisive factor in obtaining preferred assignments, which refers predominantly to the wicket jobs, that is serving customers in postal stations. Again, this is of crucial significance because compared to sorting and moving mail for 8 hours a day in large, automated plants, these jobs are relatively clean, relaxed and interesting, so every inside postal worker wants to be a wicket clerk.

The third important aspect of working life influenced by seniority within the CUPW is the choice of vacation time. Only a certain number of workers can be on vacation at any one time, if the mail is to continue to move. The highly-desirable summer months are divided into blocks and the workers choose their time period according to seniority. Again, it may take many years before an inside postal worker gets a vacation during the children's school holidays. Consequently, seniority is described as "sacred" to postal workers, and for very good reason. As one CUPW officer explained, "In a small office if someone is one spot ahead of you on the seniority list it means an extra five or six years on midnight shift, or it means another few years with no summer holidays."[9]

From the 1960s and throughout the 1970s the full and part-time workers had separate seniority lists that operated rather differently. Full-time workers collected seniority from their date of employment, but only within their own classification (or class, as it is referred to in the contract language). Postal Clerks collected seniority as Postal Clerks with a separate list for that group, while the Mail Handlers had their own seniority list and so on. If a full-time inside postal worker moved from one classification to another, the seniority accumulated up until that point was lost, and the worker began afresh to accumulate years of service in the new position.

Seniority for the part-time workers was arranged differently, because they accumulated seniority as part-time workers, regardless of whether they were Postal Helpers, Mail Handlers or Postal Clerks. So they retained their seniority if they moved from one part-time position to another. However, if a part-time worker moved to any full-time position, all accumulated seniority was lost.

The resulting loss of seniority was a source of aggravation because part-time workers who moved into full-time jobs or full-time workers who changed classification moved to the bottom of the heap in choice of shift, vacation period and the chance at a preferred assignment. Consequently, there was considerable dissatisfaction with the seniority-by-class arrangements. The solution to the problem was to change to a universal system, by which every worker would retain seniority regardless of any changes in class or moves between full and part-time work. However, making such a change was no easy matter. Any shift in the method of accumulating seniority would benefit some, but disadvantage others. Those who had shifted from one class to another, or between full and part-time work, would benefit because all their years of work as inside postal workers would then be counted in their seniority and they would move up the list. But, this necessarily meant that anyone else who had not moved would find themselves lower on the list. Consequently, while seniority was a constant theme throughout the 1970s, and resolutions on universal seniority were presented at every National Convention from 1971 onwards, it was not until 1985 that the seniority system was changed.

The part-time work issue was central in the debates on seniority and in the hesitation over action. While some full-time workers moved from one class to another, the majority remained as Postal Clerks and consequently were not affected by the loss of seniority. It was the part-time work force that most commonly shifted—into full-time positions—and thereby suffered most from the loss of seniority. Adopting universal seniority meant that those who had always been

---

[9] Interview with Deborah Bourke, First National Union Representative, Canadian Union of Postal Workers, Ottawa, 12 October 1988.

full-time workers had the most to lose, while those who had shifted from part-time to full-time, or would do so in the future, had the most to gain. When part-time years could be counted for seniority the shuffling in seniority lists would be disadvantageous to those who had always worked full-time. Moreover, the impact would be felt almost immediately because bidding by seniority for vacations occurred every year and bidding for different positions and shifts often happened more frequently.

Fears about the results of universal seniority with regard to full and part-time workers, were heightened because of the automation of the Post Office. One delegate to National Convention asked: "If I have 14 years service and a part-time would have 15 years service and automation moves in, would he be able to take over my job?"[10] However, in 1971 after much discussion the delegates did pass a resolution that a referendum of the membership should be held on the issue.

By the 1974 Convention the referendum had not been held and again there was a lengthy discussion on what should be done. As one delegate argued:

> For many years our Union has discriminated against all members, full-time and part-time whenever they wanted to move from one class to another, to better their position financially or socially. They have lost their seniority and had to start from the bottom.[11]

Despite general agreement with this position, by 1974 there were other concerns. The CUPW was in the process of disaffiliating from the Council of Postal Unions and at this point it was unclear what the results would be and who would actually be in the union after the PSSRB decision. If seniority were made universal under these circumstances, the impact for members of the CUPW was unclear. On this occasion, the resolution was tabled and never returned to the floor.

By the 1977 Convention it was clear that the delegates were in favour of changing the method of calculating seniority, but two further problems emerged. The first was just what universal seniority would mean. The delegates were presented with three options, one of which was to change the seniority only for the full-time workers, so that they would be able to move from one class to another and retain their seniority, while part-timers moving to full-time positions would continue to lose their seniority. Delegates protested strongly that this was simply not an option in a union that claimed to treat its full and part-time members equally; the only possible choice was universal seniority for all members, full and part-time, from the first day of employment.[12]

---

[10] Canadian Union of Postal Workers, *National Convention 1974, Proceedings*, Quebec, 3–8 June 1974, p. 346.

[11] *Ibid.*, p. 233.

[12] Canadian Union of Postal Workers, *Thirteenth Triennial Convention Proceedings*, Halifax, 25–29 July 1977, pp. 1038–1042.

However, action was again delayed because of fears that any attempt to change seniority would create divisions within the union, and the CUPW was then in the midst of negotiations. One delegate said: "If we send out a referendum now while negotiations are going on, with the type of division that would cause—and I know because it's always been a contentious issue...all hell is going to break loose."[13] In a union beset by massive automation, lengthy negotiations and repeated strikes, raising a potentially divisive issue like universal seniority was no easy task. In all these debates the question was referred to as "touchy" and "contentious," an issue likely to stir up internal dissension.

A referendum on seniority was held in 1979, with three options presented. Only a small number of members voted and the result was to retain the status quo. Nonetheless, at the 1981 Convention seniority was again a source of concern because in 1980 the union had negotiated the peak period for part-time workers. The peak period will be discussed in more detail in the following chapter, but it meant that most part-time workers were confined to working the evening shift and therefore could not use their seniority to transfer to day shifts. If they transferred to full-time work they would lose their seniority as before and therefore still find themselves working undesirable shifts. One delegate to the 1980 Convention stated that under these circumstances seniority was "a sham" for the part-time workers, applying in reality only to the choice of vacation.[14]

A resolution before the 1980 Convention called for a new referendum, this time to include an option for pro rata seniority, an option perhaps less threatening to the full-time workers and more likely to obtain a majority vote. Such a system would allow part-time workers to accumulate seniority according to the hours that they worked and not from their date of employment regardless of the hours worked. Apart from the question of what constituted equality, the problem with this option was that part-time workers' hours varied so much that it would have been an impossible task to calculate seniority individually. The committee that advised rejection of the resolution pointed out that there had already been a referendum and that it had excited so little interest that, outside of Quebec, less than 10 percent of the members had bothered to vote. Delegates countered that the situation had changed because of the peak period arrangement and argued that the part-time workers must be offered some possibility to obtain day time work.[15]

The resolution calling for a referendum with a pro-rata option was lost, but the message was clear that the situation for at least some part-time workers was untenable and creating considerable dissatisfaction. In October 1982 a new referendum was held. It provided a clear option of yes or no to universal, not pro-rata,

---

[13] *Ibid.*, p. 1046.

[14] Canadian Union of Postal Workers, *National Convention 1980, Proceedings*, Ottawa, 28 July–1 August 1980, p. 397.

[15] *Ibid.*, pp. 381–382.

seniority. This time the CUPW members agreed to the change to universal seniority, although by the slimmest margin of just 51 percent.

Given the slim majority the National Executive Board decided not to apply the results immediately and waited until 1984 to negotiate the change with the employer. It was done prior to the main contract negotiations to avoid it becoming an issue for debate and division during the bargaining process. Even so it was suggested that the dissatisfaction caused by changing the seniority would "enormously affect the militancy of our members" who might not be prepared to support the national officials in negotiations.[16]

It is clear from the interviews conducted for this study in locals across the country that implementing universal seniority was "a hot issue." In the St John local a part-time worker with long seniority immediately moved to a full-time position, knowing he had enough seniority to start work on days, and the feeling was strong that people in this position had not "done their time" on the midnight shift. In Vancouver many full-time workers saw their chance at a day position move 4 to 5 years away as workers who had previously been part-time increased their seniority and moved up the list. It was such a difficult issue in Edmonton that the local held a vote on whether to have the usual annual shift bid that year or delay it to allow tempers to cool. In Winnipeg some workers were bumped off their day shift and had to move back to evening or nights. In Toronto the National President, Jean-Claude Parrot, faced a hostile meeting of full-time workers to attempt to explain the justice of the issue.[17]

However, although a good number of those interviewed still felt that a pro-rata system would have been more just, there was general agreement that most of the anger faded away after several months and that universal seniority was now accepted without serious opposition. The issue did not affect the members' support of the negotiating committee; universal seniority was implemented in January 1985 and a new contract was signed in April. In 1986 the President of CUPW was able to report:

> We must not hide the fact that the referendum on universal seniority was a divisive issue among our members. The result of the referendum proves it. It was by a very small majority that the members decided in favour of the universal seniority ... Today, even though differences may still exist, I think that, generally speaking, our members across the country realize that universal seniority is not necessarily the calamity they thought.[18]

---

[16] Canadian Union of Postal Workers, "Report of the National President to the 1986 National Convention," Ottawa, 1986, p. 8.

[17] Information from the following interviews: St John, 12 January 1989; Vancouver, 31 October 1988; Winnipeg, 4 November 1988; Jean-Claude Parrot, National President of the Canadian Union of Postal Workers, Ottawa, 14 July 1987.

[18] Canadian Union of Postal Workers, *National Convention 1986, Proceedings*, Ottawa, 7–11 April 1986, p. 30.

Pre-culling: an initial sort when the mail is first emptied out of bags and falls down chutes onto a conveyor belt.

After machine sortation, containers of flats (large size letters) are stacked ready to be moved to dispatch. *(Photograph by Louise de Geosbois.)*

Why the Union Bargained for Equality

The CUPW not only held to a policy of equality for part-time workers, but was remarkably successful in implementing that policy. Moreover this commitment went beyond the task of bargaining equal pay and benefits. Even internally, the CUPW proved itself capable of making changes, tackling the sensitive area of seniority. Why did the CUPW make such strenuous efforts on behalf of the part-time workers? There are four reasons to be considered: the protection of full-time jobs, the union's philosophy of equality, maintaining solidarity among the members, and the role played by the part-time workers themselves.

Protecting Full-Time Work

Part-time workers were a source of cheap labour as long as their wages were lower, and the union had reason to fear that the employer would increasingly replace full-time with part-time workers. Union delegates to the 1965 National Convention suggested that part-time workers should be organized and their wages improved so that the Post Office would have no reason to hire them in preference to full-time workers. However, the gradual equalization of pay and benefits did not reduce the employer's use of part-time work, the percentage of part-time workers remaining stable during the 1970s. The union was concerned to limit the use of part-time workers, but it attempted to do so using the far more direct method of negotiating restrictions, which will be examined in the following chapter.

The CUPW was also concerned that the presence of a substantial group of lower-paid workers would act as a drag on the union's ability to bargain effectively for its members. Likewise a lower level of classification for the part-timers could have a negative impact upon the full-time classifications. Such fears were actually realized during the Coder dispute. When the union argued that Coders should not be classified at level PO 1 because there was no PO 1 classification in the full-time contract, the employer responded that there was a precedent for a PO 1 level, namely the Postal Helpers in the part-time contract, and the $2.94 rate of pay that management established for the full-time Coders was the same as the rate for the part-time Postal Helpers.

While protecting the security and standards of full-time jobs was considered essential by the union, it was not the sole reason for the push to obtain equality for the part-timers. The union itself expressed a dual motivation:

> Both the simple principles of justice and the necessity to protect the security of the regular full-time employment available leads to the conclusion that part-time workers must be entitled to the same wages and benefits enjoyed by full-time workers in accordance with their proportionate working hours.[19]

---

[19] Canadian Union of Postal Workers, "Negotiations 77," Submission to the Conciliation Board, 10 April 1978, p. 73.

Justice and Equality

From 1966 onwards, the union accepted that part-time workers were a permanent section of the Post Office staff. Consequently, it was clearly understood as an issue of justice that they should receive equal pay, benefits and conditions of work. Within the CUPW there was a general conviction of what was fair and acceptable, an understanding that was applied to part-time workers as well as other groups of workers. It is within this context that the union's action on seniority can be explained and it is important to explore this issue in some detail.

In the 1960s, without any direct expression of policy, the CUPW had taken action to reduce pay differentials between workers in the Post Office. For example, the wages of Mail Handlers, a predominantly male group, had fallen behind and it was a constant demand of the union that the Mail Handlers' pay should be substantially increased to reduce the pay differential that had developed. This continued to be an issue during the 1970s and the union obtained a catch-up increase for Mail Handlers during the 1975 strike. Similarly, in the late 1960s the union argued that the Postal Clerk 1 position should be upgraded to the Postal Clerk 2 position, with the consequent increase in salary, because there was no substantial difference in the work performed. In its first negotiated collective agreements the CUPW not only narrowed the gap in wages and benefits for the part-time workers, but also increased the pay of the Mail Handlers relative to other inside postal workers, and upgraded Postal Clerks from level 1 to level 2. Part-time workers were not the only group of lower-paid workers for whom the union negotiated improvements relative to other workers.

The union also supported across the board wage increases in preference to percentage increases from an early date. While percentage wage increases widen the gap in pay between the highest and lowest paid, the same dollar raise for all workers continues to maintain the same dollar wage gap. At the 1965 National Convention a resolution was adopted to abolish percentage increases in favour of across the board pay raises in order not to discriminate against lower paid workers.[20]

Following this policy, in 1965 the union sought an across the board increase of $660 for all its members, and protested the two level pay raises that were finally imposed. In 1966 the CUPW wanted an increase of $1 per hour across the board, and actually obtained 25 cents for most of its members. The fact that not all the workers obtained the same increase was perceived as a failure by the union and the Postal Tribune reported:

> At one stage in the game we thought we had convinced the Postmaster General that for this round of negotiations the settlement must be on the basis of a uniform formula. It became evident, however, that the P.M.G.'s chief advisors

---

[20] Canadian Union of Postal Workers, *The Postal Tribune*, Vol. XXXIV, No. 6, June 1966, p. 57, Resolution 71.

TABLE 6: The Wage Gap Between the Lowest and Highest Paid Workers (Minimum Rates) in the CUPW Bargaining Unit, 1965 to 1985

	1965 Aug. 1	1970 Sept. 28	1975 Dec. 1	1980 Jan. 1	1985 Oct. 1
Lowest Pay Rate ($)	1.55	2.83	5.02	8.66	13.12
Highest Pay Rate ($)	2.38	3.41	5.42	8.96	13.44
Wage Gap (%)	34.9	17.1	7.4	3.3	2.4

SOURCE: Canadian Postal Employees Association, *The Postal Tribune*, Vol. XXXIII, No. 8, August 1965, pp. 14, 63; Collective Agreements between the CUPW and the Treasury Board and the Canada Post Corporation, 1970 to 1985.

were convinced that the 25 cent per hour formula, across the board, was too much.[21]

During the 1970s the CUPW became more confirmed in its push to equalize the situation of its members, and its stance was expressed in its bargaining demands and policy statements. In the 1975 round of negotiations the CUPW was proposing: "There shall be only one classification for postal workers in the bargaining unit, that of a PO 5 or its equivalent."[22] The union's position on wage increases was clearly stated:

> The CUPW strongly prefers across-the-board increases stated in money terms rather than percentages. It is imperative that the gaps between lower and higher income Canadians be narrowed, an objective incompatible with the common practice of percentage wage and salary increases. We support the concept of narrowing the income differentials between occupational groups both within our own Union and in society at large.[23]

The CUPW did not merely express this opinion; it was decidedly successful in putting this philosophy into practice. This is clear in Table 6 which shows that between 1965 and 1985 the pay gap between the lowest and highest paid workers in the bargaining unit narrowed from 35 percent to 2 percent.

In 1966, before the union had organized part-time workers, the lowest paid part-timer was earning $1.55, while the highest paid full-timer was earning $2.38 an hour, a wage gap of almost 35 percent. By the end of September 1970 the

---

[21] *Ibid.*, Vol. XXXV, No. 2, February 1967, p. 5.

[22] Canadian Union of Postal Workers, *CUPW*, Vol. 5, No. 1, p. 2.

[23] Canadian Union of Postal Workers, "CUPW Brief to the Conciliation Board," 18 August 1975, Wage Proposal section.

wage gap between the lowest paid part-timer and the highest paid full-time worker had been narrowed to 17 percent. For the first time in the 1975 contract there was no longer a lower classification of Postal Helper for the part-time workers, so the lowest hourly rate is no longer just for part-time workers, but also for full-timers. At this point, in December 1975, the wage gap between the lowest and highest paid workers in the CUPW bargaining unit was reduced to 7 percent. However, it is clear from the table that the push to narrow the wage gap was not limited to upgrading the part-time workers, because even though full and part-time workers had equal minimum rates by this point, the narrowing of the gap continued. By 1980 the wage gap had been reduced to 3 percent, and it dropped again to 2 percent by 1985.

The CUPW pressed for the upgrading of lower paid workers, negotiated across-the-board wage increases, and narrowed the gap between the highest and lowest paid workers because of an approach that stressed equality between workers. The improvements obtained for the part-time workers were a part of this more general process. It was not an approach that was intended to benefit women specifically, any more than any other section of the workforce. It was a perspective that benefitted any low paid group of inside postal workers, and as such was effective in obtaining equal pay for women, both as part-time workers and as Coders.

Equality and Solidarity

The CUPW perceived an important link between equality and solidarity. From the union's perspective it was necessary to maintain solidarity among the members in order to deal with the employer and splits within the union would detract energy from the union's main goal of obtaining improved conditions. As Joe Davidson expressed it: "One of the reasons trade unionists spend so much time exhorting each other to solidarity and unity is because there are so many ways to divide and quarrel, especially in a national organization."[24] Having a group of lower paid workers within the bargaining unit was not likely to lead to solidarity, but to resentment and internal dispute. For this reason also the union pressed for equality among its members, including the part-time workers. "We must not give the employer more ammunition to use to deepen the split between part-timers and full-timers" said a delegate to the 1977 National Convention, arguing for equal pay and benefits for the part-time workers.[25]

By the 1980s the union expressed its philosophy more directly in its written information for members. In a booklet called "Fighting for Equality," equality is broadly defined as equality by sex, race, sexual orientation, freedom from sexual harassment, and equality for part-time workers. Any form of inequality among

---

[24] Joe Davidson and John Deverell, *Joe Davidson*, James Lorimer, Toronto, 1978, p. 67.

[25] Canadian Union of Postal Workers, *Thirteenth Triennial Convention Proceedings*, Halifax, 25–29 July 1977, p. 609.

workers is described as useful to the employer to weaken the bargaining unit and the collective strength of workers:

> This Backgrounder deals with the importance of our fight for equality. Discrimination creates artificial divisions that employers promote and use to undermine workers' collective strength. Equality, on the other hand, helps build unity among workers. Since our ability to fight for individual and collective rights depends upon our unity and solidarity, equality is central to all our struggles.[26]

It was to the advantage of both groups of members to maintain the overall strength of the bargaining unit in order to obtain better conditions for all. Equality for part-time workers was an integral component of the CUPW's perspective.

The Part-Time Workers

Had the union, its full-time members or its leadership demonstrated any reluctance to obtain equal pay and benefits for the part-time workers, the part-timers were present and ready to remind them that the issue was still alive. Part-time workers constituted around 20 percent of the union membership—a very substantial proportion and able to make themselves heard quite clearly. At both the 1974 and 1977 National Conventions part-time workers were vocal in reminding the delegates that part-timers had not yet achieved equality with the full-time workers.

In 1974 there was a discussion on whether part-time workers should pay the same dues as full-time workers or continue to pay less, and a long-time part-time worker stated: "We said we support paying the same as the full-timers, the same dues, on condition that we are treated as pro rata. We are not treated as pro rata as you know. We get less."[27] And in 1977: "We must obtain full rights for part-timers ... Part-timers do not have full rights, especially contractual rights."[28]

In the discussion of seniority at the 1980 Convention there was some heated debate around the issue of pro-rating seniority for part-time workers. From Ontario, one delegate said: "I am a part-time worker who wishes to go full-time at some point. I should not be able to take my full seniority. I should be able to do so on a pro-rated basis."[29] Another part-timer rose to say that the referendum of 1979 had been lost because no pro-rata option had been offered and that this was necessary so that part-time workers could obtain justice. "We are not just a Union concerned with looking out for full-timers. We are supposed to be looking

---

[26] Canadian Union of Postal Workers, "Fighting for Equality," 1984, p. 2.

[27] Canadian Union of Postal Workers, *National Convention 1974, Proceedings*, Quebec, 3–8 June 1974, pp. 1223–4.

[28] Canadian Union of Postal Workers, *Thirteenth Triennial Convention Proceedings*, Halifax, 25–29 July 1977, p. 609.

[29] Canadian Union of Postal Workers, *National Convention 1980, Proceedings*, Ottawa, 28 July–1 August 1980, p. 382.

out for our brothers and sisters, and that includes all of the part-timers."[30] However, some part-time workers disagreed with pro-rated seniority, and one woman delegate pointed out: "I do not want 50 percent of my seniority or 70 percent. I want 100 percent when the time comes."[31]

It is apparent that the part-time workers had no hesitation in voicing their displeasure when they felt that their interests were not being dealt with. However, there was relatively little dissatisfaction expressed with the union's action with regard to negotiating equal pay and benefits for the part-time workers, for obvious reasons. The goal of equality was clearly expressed and progress was made at every round of negotiations.

While organizing the part-time workers into the union in the late 1960s, the CUPW had promised to bargain for equal pay and benefits. During the 1970s the union fulfilled that promise. However, the union had also told the part-time workers that full-time work was the first priority. How the CUPW acted to fulfill that part of its policy is examined in the following chapter.

---

[30] *Ibid.*, p. 384.

[31] *Ibid.*, p. 396.

7

BARGAINING RESTRICTIONS ON PART-TIME WORK

The role of unions in relation to part-time work has provoked considerable criticism, particularly in relation to negotiated restrictions upon the use of part-time employment. It has been argued from a women's perspective that many women wish to work part-time because of their family responsibilities and should be allowed the opportunity to do so. The Royal Commission on the Status of Women stated "Women who need or want to supplement their income should have a chance to do so, a chance many can only get by working part-time."[1] Unions that limit part-time work are regarded, from this point of view, as limiting women's employment opportunities.

In studies of union contracts, controls upon the number of part-timers or their hours of work have been interpreted as a negative approach towards part-time work by unions seeking to protect full-time jobs.[2] Marianne Bossen, for example, suggests that such restrictions are unnecessary and that unions are more concerned with the protection of full-time jobs than the welfare of part-time workers.[3] The federal government established a Commission of Inquiry into Part-Time work that recommended the expansion of part-time employment and criticized unions for reducing or controlling the number of part-time workers in the workplace.[4]

In another study I have suggested that this general criticism of any controls upon the use of part-time work is not appropriate.[5] Restrictions are sometimes negotiated to prevent the misuse of part-time workers by the employer, to the benefit of the part-timers. In some cases protection of full-time positions may be justified if the proportion of part-time work is excessively high or if the part-time

---

[1] Canada, *Report of the Royal Commission on the Status of Women in Canada*, Ottawa, 1970, p. 104.

[2] Joan McFarland, "Women and Unions: Help or Hindrance," *Atlantis*, Vol. 4, No. 2, Spring 1979, p. 57; Marianne Bossen, "Part-Time Work in the Canadian Economy," Labour Canada, Ottawa, October 1975, p. 82.

[3] Marianne Bossen, *Ibid*, pp. 81–82.

[4] Labour Canada, *Part-time Work in Canada, Report of the Commission of Inquiry into Part-time Work*, Ottawa, 1983, p. 93.

[5] Julie White, *Women and Part-Time Work*, Canadian Advisory Council on the Status of Women, Ottawa, 1983, pp. 63–68.

workers themselves would prefer full-time jobs. It is not sufficient simply to consider the contractual arrangements in isolation; it is necessary to understand the context in which such restrictions are negotiated. The purpose of this chapter is to examine this issue within the CUPW, a union that has negotiated extensive controls on the use of part-time work.

Organizing the part-time workers in 1966, the CUPW made it clear that while the union would fight for equal pay and benefits, it also maintained that full-time jobs were the first priority and that part-time work should be reduced in favour of more full-time positions. During the 1970s and on into the 1980s the CUPW proceeded to negotiate restrictions on the use of part-time workers in the Post Office. This chapter examines the methods used by the union to obtain limitations and controls upon part-time work, analyzes the reasons for those actions and explores the reactions of the part-time workers themselves to this process. By controlling the use of part-time work, was the CUPW preventing the employer from abusing part-time workers and enabling women to obtain the full-time employment that they wanted, or was the union protecting full-time work at the expense of the predominantly women part-time workers who needed their part-time jobs?

The use of part-time work in the Post Office was part of the CUPW's larger concern about staffing in general, that also included the use of casual workers, the amount of overtime, and understaffing. The problem of the casuals was the most serious issue for the CUPW since they could not belong to the union under the Public Service Staff Relations Act (PSSRA), so their growth could only weaken the strength of the bargaining unit. The CUPW was opposed to the presence of a large contingent of lower paid workers in the Post Office, both as a matter of justice and because it was likely to act as a downward drag on the standards that the union attempted to negotiate for the regular workers. The union stated its position clearly: "The use of employees with no rights, no prescribed hours and no fringe benefits to perform the work of our members is a complete violation of Union recognition."[6]

The problems of part-time and casual work were interrelated because neither group of workers was guaranteed regular hours of work and the union maintained that both were used by management as available workers, on-call whenever needed. Consequently, the two forms of work were often linked in the union's statements. For example: "Unless casual labour is eliminated and part-time labour brought under much closer regulation, it will be used to destroy the living standards and acquired rights of our members."[7] As the union had expressed to the Montpetit Commission it felt the use of both casual and part-time workers to be excessive, thereby reducing the opportunities for workers to obtain full-time work. At times the union expressed the opinion that casuals and part-

---

[6] Canadian Union of Postal Workers, "CUPW Brief to the Conciliation Board," 18 August 1975, p. 4.

[7] *Ibid.*, p. 3.

TABLE 7: Post Office Wages and Salaries ($ millions)
1970/71 to 1974/75

	1970/71		*1971/72*		*1972/73*		*1973/74*		*1974/75*	
	$	*%*	*$*	*%*	*$*	*%*	*$*	*%*	*$*	*%*
Regular	285	86.2	316	84.9	355	83.8	406	81.6	480	81.3
Casual	16	4.8	22	5.9	31	7.2	36	7.2	45	7.7
Overtime	8	2.4	13	3.4	17	3.9	25	5.1	36	6.1
Other*	22	6.5	21	5.7	22	5.1	31	6.1	32	5.3
Total		99.9	372	99.9	424	100	497	100	593	100

* Other is primarily the cost of wages for revenue, seasonal and sub-postmasters.
SOURCE: Canada, Post Office Department, *Annual Report*, Ottawa, 1970/71 ato 1974/75.

time workers were used interchangeably by management. The struggles the union experienced around the use of casuals affected its policies towards the part-time workers. Consequently, it is useful to examine the union's policies and actions on both casual and part-time work. Restrictions on both types of work were negotiated by 1980, the casual workers being first on the agenda.

Restrictions on Casual Workers

Despite the recommendations of the Montpetit Report to control and limit the number of casual workers, their use continued to increase. In March 1966 the number of casuals employed in the Post Office was 1,177. By March 1969 this figure had increased to 1,997. This was an increase of 70 percent in the number of casuals, while the regularly employed workers in the Post Office had increased by only 36 percent over the same three years.[8] Figures on the number of casual workers in the Post Office are virtually non-existent for the 1970s. However, in its Annual Reports the Post Office Department did publish the amount of money spent annually on casual work, as well as on the regular staff and overtime, so this provides some basis for comparison over time. Table 7 gives this information, with percentages for 1970/71 to 1974/75.

It is clear from Table 7 that over the first five years of the 1970s the Post Office expenditure on casual workers, and also on overtime, was increasing relative to the cost of the regular full and part-time staff, increasing from 4.8 to 7.7 percent over the period. While expenditure on regular staff increased by 68 percent from 1970 to 1975, the cost of casual help rose by 181 percent (and overtime by 350 percent). Moreover these figures are limited in regard to indicat-

[8] Statistics Canada, *Federal Government Employment*, Cat. 72–004, Ottawa, March 1966 and 1969.

ing the quantity of casual work confronted by the CUPW, because the costs for regular workers include all employees in the Post Office, management and letter carriers as well as the inside postal workers, and because the regular staff received higher pay than the casual workers. One year the CUPW estimated the situation from these figures as follows:

> In 1973–74 the overtime represented about 1,900 man-years of work, while the casual pay represented about 4,000 man-years. This is in the order of 20 percent of the labour performed by the full-time employees on regular hours, a ratio the union judges unnecessary and unacceptable.[9]

There is no firm information on the proportion of women casual workers after the 1960s. The latest figure available is for March 1969 and of the 1,997 casuals 996 were women, that is 50 percent.[10] This was a high proportion compared to the number of regularly employed full-time women workers in the Post Office. As mentioned in a previous chapter, union members reported that a higher proportion of casual workers were women. In Montreal casuals had been used as strike-breakers during the 1970 rotating strikes, and at the 1971 National Convention one delegate complained vehemently about the hiring of "400 women to sort the mail, 400 women to dispatch it."[11] Delegates described how casuals were called in as needed and that therefore they were described as "call girls."[12] Whatever the exact proportion of women casual workers during the 1970s, it is clear that women continued to form a major sector of that workforce.

At the 1971 National Convention casual work was a leading concern and the feelings were bitter. There had been local walkouts and wildcat strikes over the use of casuals, and a vote of censure was passed against the national officers for failing to deal adequately with the problem.[13] The outcome was a more determined approach toward "this plague," and in May 1973 the CUPW national officers announced a new round of initiatives on the issue.[14]

The National Executive Board developed the policy that casuals should be used only for a three week period over Christmas because of the high volume of mail, and possibly during the summer to allow regular workers to take summer vacations.[15] Apart from these exceptions the policy was that casual work should

9   Canadian Union of Postal Workers, "CUPW Brief to the Conciliation Board," 18 August 1975, p. 4.

10 Statistics Canada, *Federal Government Employment*, Cat, 72–004, Ottawa, March 1969.

11 Canadian Union of Postal Workers, *National Convention 1971, Proceedings*, Calgary, 31 May–5 June 1971, p. 209.

12 *Ibid.*, p. 215.

13 *Ibid.*, p. 497.

14 Canadian Union of Postal Workers, *CUPW*, Special Edition, May 1973, p. 4.

15 *Ibid.*, p. 2.

be eliminated from the Post Office. Under a newly-developed Hire Permanent Campaign, meetings were held with management to express this policy, and in response the Post Office issued a new directive on the use of casual workers. It stated that "the usage of casual help is to be reduced to a minimum," and that regular staff would be used for predictable increases in mail volume and staff absences.[16]

While the CUPW was not entirely satisfied with this policy, it was accepted as an improvement. But, four months later, in October 1973 the union carried out its own survey of casual and part-time work within the Post Office, only to discover that no progress had been made in reducing the number of casuals. Eighty three percent of CUPW locals responded to a questionnaire about staffing and when these figures were tallied, 15 per cent of the total staff were casual, 11 percent part-time and 74 percent full-time. Moreover, in some locals the proportion of casuals to full-time workers was over 40 percent. Compared to a similar survey conducted in 1972, both the number and the proportion of casual hours had actually increased. As far as the Post Office Department's new policy on casuals was concerned the CUPW concluded that "the entire policy had broken down."[17] This perspective was later confirmed by a Conciliation Board report that stated: "It is generally agreed that this policy yielded no practical results."[18]

In 1974 the union's Hire Permanent Campaign continued at the national level with letters, statements and consultations. Pressure to adhere to the Corporate policy was also applied at the local level, and in 1974 more than 2,000 grievances were submitted on the use of casuals and on infringements due to the use of casuals.[19] However, the grievance procedure proved to be of limited value because of the PSSRA. Under Section 7 of the legislation, staffing is an employer prerogative which need not be submitted to negotiations. Consequently, grievances concerning the proportion of full-time, part-time and casual work in the Post Office could not be submitted to an independent third party for final arbitration, but were decided by the employer. Of the 2,000 grievances related to casual work submitted by CUPW members, every one was denied.[20]

The union declared that the legislation was too restrictive and proceeded in the 1975 negotiations to make demands for articles in the collective agreement

---

[16] Canada Post Office, "Postal Corporation Policy—Casual Help (Postal Operations Group)," Ottawa, June 1973.

[17] Canadian Union of Postal Workers, Research and Information Department, "Statement on the Use of Casual Labour," 22 April 1975, p. 3.

[18] "Report of the Conciliation Board to the Chairman of the PSSRB," Chaired by Jean Moisan, 7 October 1975, p. 90.

[19] Canadian Union of Postal Workers, Research and Information Department, "Statement on the Use of Casual Labour," 22 April 1975, p. 9.

[20] *Ibid.*, p. 8.

that would control the use of casual workers. This round of negotiations ended in a long 42 day strike, during which the employer agreed to contract language that would restrict the use of casuals. The contract signed in December 1975 contained Article 39, which required the employer to use regular full and part-time workers for "predictable workloads and absences," to minimize the use of casuals by maintaining eligibility lists so that vacancies could be filled more quickly, and to have "a sufficient number of regular employees to cover the rate of normal absences due to illness, special leave, vacation leave and leave without pay." Moreover, to deal with unexpected high volumes of mail regular employees were to be offered overtime before casual workers would be hired.[21] Having these provisions in the collective agreement meant that if management failed to fulfil its obligations, grievances could be taken to independent adjudication and would not be subject to automatic denial by the Post Office management.

It seems that this negotiated package on casual work did have an impact on the Post Office. After 1975 the expenditure on casual workers began to decline, a trend that continued over the next five years to 1980. In 1974/75 casual work comprised almost 8 percent of the total costs of wages and salaries in the Post Office. The following year it had already declined to 5 percent and by 1980/81 it had fallen to 3 percent. Over this six year period the cost of regular staff increased by 145 percent, while the expenditure on casual help actually declined by more than 7 percent.[22] Thus, it seems that the agreement negotiated by the CUPW did effect a substantial decrease in the use of casual work. The CUPW continued to protest the use of casual work in the Post Office, its policy remaining that it should be entirely eliminated, outside of specific periods such as Christmas.

Restrictions on Part-Time Workers

The Number of Part-Time Workers

As with the casual workers, throughout the 1970s, and indeed the 1980s, the CUPW continued to express its concern that the use of part-time work was excessive and should be restricted. It is difficult to obtain an accurate picture of the proportion of part-timers in the Post Office and in the CUPW bargaining unit specifically. In fact, even with just the total number of employees in the Post Office there are different and contradictory figures. To give just one example, in 1974 the Post Office in its Annual Report claimed 55,421 workers, the Public Service Commission counted 47,425, while the Pay Research Bureau gave

---

[21] Agreement Between the Treasury Board and the Canadian Union of Postal Workers, Postal Operations (non-supervisory), Code: 608/75, Expiry Date: 30 June 1977, pp. 97–100, Article 39.

[22] Canada Post, *Annual Report*, Ottawa, 1974/75 to 1980/81.

TABLE 8: Dues Paying Employees, CUPW Jurisdiction, 1972, 1973, 1975 to 1977 (Yearly Averages)

Year	Total	Full-time	Part-time	%Part-time
1972	19,449	15,708	3,741	19.2
1973	20,271	16,404	3,867	19.1
1975	22,665	18,401	4,264	18.8
1976	25,919	20,059	5,860	22.6
1977	25,638	20,174	5,464	21.3
1978*	26,056	20,621	5,435	20.8
1979*	24,886	19,631	5,255	21.1

* Figures are averages for only June and July in each year, not for all twelve months.
SOURCE: John Deverell, Director of Education, CUPW, "A Report on Staffing and Work in the CUPW Jurisdiction," April 1976, p. 11; monthly tabulations of the Annual Staffing Record of Dues Paying Employees by region and nationally, 1976 and 1977; Canadian Union of Postal Workers, "Negotiations '80," p. 12, 1978 and 1979.

46,324 as the number of employees.[23] While some part of these disparities can be accounted for by differences in the type of workers included, there is no way to make sense of the different totals. When just counting the number of heads is so inexact, information on particular groups, such as part-time work or the CUPW bargaining unit are few and far between and of questionable reliability. Information on the part-time work force by sex is yet more limited.

For the purposes of this study the most useful information is that provided by the employer to the CUPW on the number of workers paying dues to the union. This material is available monthly for the years 1972 to 1977, excluding 1974, and also for part of 1978 and 1979. (See Table 8.) The material is broken down by full and part-time workers and also by region. It is limited in that the workers who pay their dues under the Rand Formula (i.e. they do not belong to the union, but pay the dues) are not divided into full and part-time workers. These Rand Formula workers have all been added to the full-time figures, and consequently the proportion of part-time workers may be underestimated. With this caveat, this data provides the most reliable information on part-time work within the CUPW bargaining unit. It shows that during the 1970s the proportion of part-time work varied from 19 to 23 percent, a level that seems reasonable given other data sources. For example, the Montpetit Report indicated that 20 percent of the inside postal workers were part-time in 1966.

---

[23] Canada Post, *Annual Report*, Ottawa, 1973/74; Public Service Commission, *Annual Report*, Ottawa, 1973/74; Pay Research Bureau, Public Service Staff Relations Board, "The Composition of the Public Service of Canada," Ottawa, 1974.

There is no doubt that part-time work formed a very substantial proportion of the CUPW bargaining unit, at around 20 percent of the workforce. To compare with the general labour force, part-time work comprised from 11 to 13 percent of the total number of employed workers between 1975 and 1979.[24] Moreover, in some CUPW locals the proportion of part-time workers was considerably higher than the 20 percent national average.

Apart from the generally high rate of part-time work, it is of interest to note the rise in the percentage of part-time work in 1976. A similar trend appears in data from the Post Office Annual Reports, in which the percentage of part-time work rises in 1975.[25] Together, these two sets of data support the opinion that when casual work was brought under stricter control in the 1975 collective agreement, and the proportion of casual work decreased, part-time workers were then hired in greater numbers as an alternative. This trend will be referred to again in the discussion which follows.

While determining the number of part-time workers in the Post Office in the 1970s is hardly an exact science, assessing the proportion of women part-time workers is virtually impossible, the sole available source being unreliable.[26] More accurate data is not available until 1984 when women comprised 71 percent of the part-time workforce.[27] It is likely that during the 1970s the proportion of women part-time workers was higher than in 1984. As wages and benefits for part-time workers were equalized, and as it became increasingly difficult to move into a full-time position without first having worked part-time, a higher proportion of men took part-time positions in the Post Office.[28]

Negotiating Restrictions

Before 1966 the union's policy had supported the abolition of part-time work entirely, but with the unionization of the part-timers, this was changed to the requirement that part-time work be kept to a minimum and be used only for those operations that really required a part-time workforce. Consequently, in the first contract negotiated for the part-time workforce in 1970, part-timers could

---

[24] Statistics Canada, *Labour Force Annual Averages 1975–1983*, Cat.71–529, Ottawa, 1984, table 29.

[25] Canada Post Office, *Annual Report*, Ottawa, 1971/72 to 1976/77.

[26] Information from 1972 from the Pay Research Bureau suggests that women comprised 64.9 percent of the part-time workers in the Post Office. However, data from the CUPW dues check-off indicates that the Pay Research Bureau figures exclude fully 17 percent of the total number of part-time workers.

[27] Information provided by the Canada Post Corporation, Personnel Data Base, 31 March 1984.

[28] This argument is further developed later in this chapter.

not be employed for more than 30 hours per week. Also, the following article appeared in the contracts for both the full and the part-time workers:

> The employer agrees that part-time employees shall be used only for the part-time operational requirements and that, wherever practicable, such positions shall be combined in order to create full-time positions.[29]

Attempting to enforce these provisions was a major concern for the CUPW throughout the 1970s, and a primary source of conflict with the employer.

While further restrictions upon the use of part-time work did not appear in the collective agreement until 1980, the issue of part-time work became more contentious during the 1970s. Attempts to limit the use of part-time work were made in both the 1975 and 1977 rounds of bargaining without success. Before looking at the actual controls that were negotiated, it is important to examine why restrictions upon this type of work became a central issue for the union.

At the 1971 National Convention casual work had created the most concern, but by 1974 part-time had become the more serious staffing issue. A report given by the Western Regional Director suggested that since the union had been pressuring management about the casual situation, more part-time workers had been hired instead. He continued:

> I don't want anybody to think that I am opposed to part-timers, but I am opposed to the use of part-timers when they upset the balance and destroy the power of a local union, when they are being used against the union the way the employer would like to use them, when they are being exploited as workers. Anybody who goes into a department store today knows what staffing can do to any organization. They are run by part-timers and casuals. That's most of the staff in department stores today. They are called in on sale days and whenever the employer wants them, and that's the way the employer would like to run the post office. We've got a major battle over the use of part-timers.[30]

A delegate from Vancouver who had worked for 19 years as a part-timer made the following comment:

> Divide and rule, that is what management has done all the time. Now they are trying to treat us as casuals, because they are trying to please the union by getting rid of a few casuals and increase the ratio of part-timers. We have less full-timers and more part-timers. It is a very serious matter in the major cities.[31]

---

[29] Agreements Between the Treasury Board and the Council of Postal Unions, Postal Operations Group (non-supervisory), Code: 608/10/70, Expires: 26 March 1972, p. 87, Article 42.02, and Postal Operations Group (Part-Time Employees), Code: 678/11/70, Expires: 26 March 1972, p. 47, Article 28.02.

[30] Canadian Union of Postal Workers, *National Convention 1974, Proceedings*, Quebec, 3–8 June 1974, p. 86.

[31] *Ibid.*, p. 1223.

Delegates from the Western region had some cause for concern. Between 1972 and 1975 that region experienced a major growth in part-time work of 62 percent. This was four times the overall growth for the whole union, and was attributed to the automation program that was first affecting the west.[32]

For the first time at the 1974 National Convention the idea was expressed that there should be negotiated restrictions upon the use of part-time work. This was a different concept from the contract clause in place since 1970, which required only that where possible part-time jobs should be combined to create full-time positions. The possibility of a ratio was raised, and it was proposed that part-time workers should only be used for peak periods, when mail volumes were higher and part-time operations could be justified.[33] Although there was no formal resolution on these suggestions, the CUPW's demands in the 1975 negotiations included minimum hours for part-time workers and that they be confined to specific peak periods.[34] However, in this round of negotiations, controls upon casuals were obtained but no changes were made in the use of part-time work.

In the second half of the 1970s part-time work became a more critical issue within the union. As indicated earlier in Table 8, the use of part-time work increased after 1975, following the union's successful bargaining of controls upon casual workers. There had also been a further dramatic decline in the labour relations situation in the Post Office that both affected and involved the part-time and casual situation, and it is necessary to digress briefly to outline the context in which restrictions on part-time work became a central issue for the union.

The major breakthrough obtained in the 1975 negotiations was Article 29 on technological change. The CUPW congratulated itself: "We have won what is probably the best contract language on technological change in North America if not the world, setting a favourable precedent for all working people."[35] Indeed, Article 29 was remarkable in the breadth of protection provided. The definition of technological change was very broad, and any disputes between the union and management over its adverse effects could be submitted to an independent third party for a speedy decision. Meanwhile job, wage and classification security was provided for all workers, as well as paid retraining and no compulsory transfers. Because these provisions were now within the collective agreement, rather than appended in a letter of understanding, grievances on these areas could be submitted to independent arbitration. The CUPW's national newspaper announced:

---

[32] John Deverell, Director of Education, Canadian Union of Postal Workers, "A Report on Staffing and Work in the CUPW Jurisdiction," April 1986, p. 12.

[33] Canadian Union of Postal Workers, *National Convention 1974, Proceedings*, Quebec, 3–8 June 1974, p. 1224.

[34] Canadian Union of Postal Workers, "CUPW Brief to the Conciliation Board," 18 August 1975, Article 40.

[35] Canadian Union of Postal Workers, *CUPW*, Vol. 6, No. 1, p. 2.

"The negotiating committee is very proud of the article negotiated."[36] As a result of obtaining Article 29 the union agreed to drop its Boycott the Postal Code campaign that had been initiated in response to the dispute over the Coders.

The union's elation was short-lived. The new collective agreement was signed in December 1975. By March 1976 the union had submitted a grievance to the Public Service Staff Relations Board (PSSRB) that the employer was ignoring Article 29. Introducing the new machinery into St. John's, Newfoundland and London, Ontario, the Post Office seemed to be claiming that this did not constitute technological change under Article 29, because similar machinery had already been introduced into post offices elsewhere in the country and consequently none of the protective provisions of Article 29 applied.[37] From this perspective the newly negotiated collective agreement was irrelevant to the massive automation program underway, an approach to the definition of technological change described as "specious" and "nonsensical" by the Deputy Chairman of the PSSRB, Mr. Edward Jolliffe.[38]

In July 1976 Jolliffe ruled that the employer was indeed in violation of the law in several respects. The Post Office had failed to give proper notice of technological change, failed to provide information, and failed to engage in meaningful consultation with the union. While this confirmed the union's protests of bad faith on the part of the management, it did nothing to resolve the actual problems occurring, because Jolliffe took no action against the employer, pointing out that there was nothing in Article 29 setting penalties for such violations.[39]

Before Jolliffe's ruling, and perhaps prompted by the union's complaint to the PSSRB, the Post Office management did begin the process of discussion established under Article 29. The disputes between the union and the employer over the introduction of technological change at St. John's, London and Windsor went to mediation and then to a Special Adjudication Committee as laid down by Article 29. However, the purpose of these procedures was entirely negated when on 24th September 1976, Post Office management stated that if the Committee made any rulings contrary to the PSSRA, they would be ignored by the employer. This meant that the Post Office was reasserting its right under Section 7 of the PSSRA to complete control over the introduction of technological change, thereby reneging on Article 29 and the collective agreement it had signed just

---

[36] *Ibid.*, p. 1.

[37] *Ibid.*, Vol. 6, No. 3, April-May 1976, p. 1.

[38] Public Service Staff Relations Board, *Decisions*, File No: 169–2–81/169–2–83, 28 July 1976, p. 69.

[39] *Ibid.*

nine months before. The result was rotating strikes in October 1976, leading to the establishment of a mediator who never presented a report.

Throughout the conflict over Article 29, the CUPW also claimed "a systematic campaign of contract violation," that included the abuse of casual and part-time workers.[40] In the eighteen months prior to the signing of the 1975 collective agreement there had been 1,989 grievances taken to the fourth level of independent adjudication. But, in the eighteen months following the signing of the agreement this figure more than doubled to 4,823 grievances.[41] Over the sixteen months between March 1977 and July 1978 there were fifteen wildcat walk outs and sit-ins lasting from one day to one week, and nine of them involved protests about violations of the contract involving the use of casual or part-time work.[42] Part-time work increased despite the clause that required part-time positions to be combined where possible to form full-time jobs. The CUPW described the employer's failure to honour this article of the collective agreement as "a major factor in the continuous deterioration in labour-management relations."[43]

At the 1977 Convention for the first time a resolution was passed to support negotiating a ratio of part-time to full-time workers in the collective agreement.[44] Consequently, in the 1977 negotiations the union was pressing for a 20 hour minimum work week for part-time workers, and a fixed proportion of part-time to full-time workers in order "to reduce the terrible abuse of part-time labour which has escalated since the introduction of the Employer's program of automation."[45] Despite the strength of feeling among the union's members nothing was achieved in this round of negotiations. A strike commenced on 16th October 1978, but on the following day the government passed back to work legislation. The strike continued until 26th October, when the RCMP raided the union offices and arrested the five executive officers. The CUPW President, Jean-Claude Parrot, received a three month jail sentence for failing to end the strike earlier, and a settlement was imposed from which the union gained little. No changes were made with regard to the use of part-time work and it was not until 1980 that the issue of part-time work was again at the bargaining table.

---

[40] Canadian Union of Postal Workers, *CUPW*, Vol. 6, No. 2, p. 1.

[41] Canadian Union of Postal Workers, "Report of the National Chief Steward to the National Convention," 1977, p. 10.

[42] Canadian Union of Postal Workers, "Negotiations 77," Submission to the Conciliation Board, 10 April 1978, Appendix III.

[43] *Ibid.*, p. 135.

[44] Canadian Union of Postal Workers, *Thirteenth Triennial Convention Proceedings*, Halifax, 25–29 July 1977, p. 1027.

[45] *Ibid.*, p. 60.

The union's determination to resolve the problem of part-time work in the 1980 negotiations was strengthened by several factors. Post Office business plans had established goals for reducing the number of full-time workers while increasing the use of part-time workers and casuals. Plans for the Eastern Ontario District and for London, Ontario specifically suggested that staff reductions be obtained through the increased use of part-time and casual work.[46] The business plan for New Brunswick and Prince Edward Island set goals for adjusting the composition of the work force between April 1979 and March 1980, including increasing casual work from 1.8 to 2.9 percent of the workforce and increasing part-time work from 9.4 to 12.0 percent. This plan expressed one goal as the "general increase in part-time hours," while another was to "examine feasibility of changing F.T. (full-time) to P.T. (part-time) hours."[47] These recommendations were in direct violation of the collective agreement then in force.

Apart from management business plans recommending reductions in the full-time workforce, by 1980 it was already clear that the number of workers in the Post Office was stagnating. From 1962 until 1976 the CUPW had experienced a yearly increase in the number of members, but this came to an end as of 1977 as the impact of technological change asserted itself.[48] In this no-growth situation, the CUPW became yet more concerned to exercise control over the staffing situation to protect the existing jobs and ensure that management did not have the opportunity to misuse part-time work.

Finally, part-time workers had numerous complaints about their hours of work. In some locations they worked split shifts, meaning that in one day they would work part of their hours in the morning and the rest later in the day, making for a long work day even with only a few hours of work. This was particularly common in rural areas, where mail was less likely to arrive predominantly in the evening. Usually part-timers worked 4 hours per day, but sometimes it was dropped back to three hours. In larger centres the work period was often extended to five hours.

> They would come along at night and tap on the shoulder and say "five hour call tonight" so you'd get to work an extra hour, so of course if you had child care responsibilities there would be a fast flurry running for the telephone making child care arrangements.[49]

Weekend work was also irregular. A part-timer might work to 11 at night and find that they were due in to work at 10 the next morning on a weekend. In

---

[46] Canadian Union of Postal Workers, "Negotiations 80," 26 March 1980, p. 9.

[47] Canada Post Office, "Business Plans for 1979–80, New Brunswick and P.E.I.," February 1979, p. 50.

[48] Statistics Canada, *Corporations and Labour Unions Returns Act*, Part II—Labour Unions, Cat.71–202, Ottawa, 1962–1977. See chapter one, table 1.

[49] Interview with Caroline Lee, National Secretary Treasurer, Canadian Union of Postal Workers, Ottawa, 12 October 1988.

Montreal there were particular concerns because the employer was opening new shifts for part-time workers starting at 2 in the morning.

From the union's point of view all the indications were that part-time work was to expand and to be used with yet more flexibility to cover all different periods of the day and night, involving the loss of full-time work and yet more irregular work schedules for the part-time workers.

In the agreement signed in June 1980, the union was successful in obtaining some of its demands on the restriction of part-time work. The Conciliation Board would not support the ratio that the union was demanding, but recognized the problem by recommending that the employment of part-time workers be confined to just one period per day when the mail volumes were higher, called the peak period. This was accepted by the union. Also the hours of part-time workers were limited to a minimum of 20 and a maximum of 25 hours per week. Consequently, part-time workers could not be employed on a full-time basis, but nor could their hours be reduced below 20 hours per week. Under this collective agreement, part-time workers could not be used on a casual basis, and they were assured of regular hours of work. However, these provisions were themselves highly controversial among some groups of part-time workers, and their reactions will be examined in a later section.

The struggles of the union around the use of part-time work continued on into the 1980s. In 1985 the CUPW tried to negotiate a maximum of 10 percent part-time workers, but obtained instead a numerical limit of 4,500 part-time workers. The number of part-time workers then employed in the bargaining unit was less than this figure, but the union perceived it as a way to initiate a limit. In 1986 the union was on strike and was again legislated back to work with an imposed settlement. In the imposed contract decided by Judge Cossette the number of part-time workers was reduced to 4,200. These provisions became effective June 1988 and involved a reduction of approximately 150 part-time positions.

The Cossette award also eliminated the peak period for part-time workers that had been negotiated in 1980. As well the hours of part-timers were changed from a maximum of 25 hours per week to 30 hours per week, these hours to be averaged over 26 weeks instead of over 12 weeks. The impact of these changes has yet to be determined. It will not result in more part-time positions because there is now a numerical limit for part-time workers. It may mean a return to more irregularity in the schedules of part-timers, since the hours can now be averaged over a longer period of time and with the absence of the peak period split shifts may re-emerge. These issues will be considered again in the discussion below of the reactions of part-time workers to the union's policies.

CUPW's Reasons for Restrictions

The CUPW's reasons for wishing to reduce and control the use of part-time work have changed and developed from the 1960s to the present. In the 1960s the union opposed part-time work because it was cheap, deskilled and female labour, and therefore likely to undermine the wages and conditions of the full-time workers. By the early 1970s there were no longer any remarks in articles, briefs or debates suggesting that the number of part-time workers be reduced because they were women. It was no longer acceptable to suggest that women should not be in the labour force, and more women were starting to work in full-time as well as part-time positions.

After 1974 the concern that part-time workers were unskilled also disappeared. Under the settlement of the Coder dispute, the part-time Postal Helpers, who had done different work at a lower classification, were eliminated, and every worker who sorted the mail was classified as a PO 4, with the same requirements for the position and the same job functions.

The CUPW continued to describe the use of part-time workers as "an exploitive cheap labour policy"[50] throughout the 1970s and on into the 1980s. Although the pay and fringe benefits of the part-time workers had been virtually equalized by the 1980s, the employer paid superannuation contributions only for the full-time workers, so that part-time workers remained a cheaper source of labour.[51] However, even if the part-time workers cost exactly the same, there would remain the problem of productivity, namely that part-time workers can work at a higher average speed because they work for fewer hours. As well, if the hours of part-time workers can be easily altered, the employer gains a flexible work force that can be manipulated to meet fluctuations in production, less costly than a regularly employed full-time work force. For these reasons part-time workers may continue to be employed in preference to full-time workers.

Two further arguments for controlling the use of part-time work should be considered: the impact of part-time workers upon the strength of the union and the use of involuntary part-time workers.

Union Strength

In the early 1960s the union had argued that the increase in part-time work threatened the strength of the union, as of course it did before the part-time workers were organized. However, there was also some fear that even once part of the union the part-time workers would be less interested in their jobs than the full-time workers and therefore not contribute to the power of the bargaining unit. Joe Davidson declared this to be untrue, stating that in 1975 the part-time workers were a source of strength within the union, at least as involved and militant as the full-timers. However, the argument that a large part-time work-

---

[50] Canadian Union of Postal Workers, "CUPW Brief to the Conciliation Board," 18 August 1975, Article 40.

[51] Part-time workers were excluded from the Public Employees Superannuation Act. Under the PSSRA pensions were non-negotiable.

force would weaken the union continued to be expressed. In 1976 the Director of Education for the CUPW wrote:

> Full-time employment is the most important staffing consideration for the Union. From a financial point of view, the dues of part-time members are similar to those of full-time members, but from the point of view of control over production and collective bargaining power, there can be little doubt that full-time members are the mainstay of our organization.[52]

The majority of those interviewed for this study suggested that part-time workers are less active within the union that full-time workers. Many reasons were offered to explain this situation, relating to the part-time workers themselves, to the union and to the work place situation. A large number of part-timers are women with family responsibilities, some are students and others have second jobs. With these other commitments, part-time workers may find it difficult to maintain active involvement in the union. The union's policy of reducing part-time work has sometimes created tensions between the full and part-timers and has not encouraged the part-timers to become active in the union. The expectation that part-time workers do not participate may itself lead to inactivity.

Factors related to the workplace may also affect the participation of part-timers in the union. It is now the case that part-time employment is the point of entry into the Post Office since full-time workers are rarely hired from outside (this will be further discussed below). As a consequence new workers, who often understand little about the workplace or the union, are part-time workers and this may contribute to the difficulty in getting them involved. It is also the case that during their five hour shift part-time workers have only one fifteen minute break, which barely gives them the opportunity to discuss any matters of concern to them or have contact with their shop stewards. In some locals it was felt that the part-time workers were subject to closer supervision and more intimidation than the full-time workers. In Edmonton, for example, there is a Part-Time Rights Committee and one issue of their bulletin was entirely devoted to the topic of intimidation.

However, the suggestion that part-time workers are less involved in the union is hotly contested in some locals. In Vancouver, for example, the part-timers have their own shop stewards and elect their own Chief Shop Steward who sits on the executive. The part-time workers from that local have been very active in agitating for the rights of part-time workers. No-one in Vancouver suggests that there is a difference between full and part-time workers in relation to union activity. In Edmonton the Part-Time Rights Committee that deals specifically with the concerns of part-timers, has resulted in part-time workers becoming more active within the union.

---

[52] John Deverell, Director of Education, Canadian Union of Postal Workers, "A Report on Staffing and Work in the CUPW Jurisdiction," April 1976, p. 13.

Involuntary Part-Time Work

Throughout the 1970s and up until the present the union has argued that the part-time workers themselves wanted full-time work and had more opportunity to obtain it if part-time jobs were combined to create more full-time positions. "Many of our part-time members would be interested in getting full-time jobs" said an article in the national newspaper in 1973.[53] While other arguments lost their force through changing circumstances, this one increased in importance. In the 1980 negotiations the union argued that many part-time workers were led to believe when hired that they would obtain full-time jobs, but then were forced to remain in part-time positions.[54] In 1986 a national bulletin stated: "Postal workers have a right to full-time employment and studies show most prefer it to part-time."[55]

In the interviews for this study, part-time workers in locals across the country confirmed that while a proportion of part-timers preferred part-time hours, the majority wanted full-time work. The Edmonton local carried out a survey to examine the preferences of part-time workers, and found that two-thirds would prefer to have full-time employment. Out of a total of 273 part-time workers, 140 completed the questionnaire, 101 women and 39 men. Of these part-time workers, 64 percent had either applied for full-time work, or intended to do so in the near future. The reason why the part-timers wanted full-time work was clear: almost 50 percent were the sole wage earner for their families, and over 60 percent stated that they were experiencing financial difficulties.[56] The preference of the majority of part-time workers for full-time work is a situation that has developed within the Post Office for several reasons.

Once the union had bargained equal pay for the part-time workers in 1975, an increasing number of men took part-time work, prepared to wait for a full-time position. In 1988 with an hourly pay rate of $14 plus shift premium, a part-time job at 30 hours per week in the Post Office meant a weekly income of $450, more than most part-time jobs and even some full-time jobs in other sectors. By 1984 29 percent of the part-time workers in the Post Office were men.[57] While the increased pay made it possible to work part-time while awaiting a full-time job, other circumstances made it obligatory.

By the end of the 1970s full-time opportunities in the Post Office were closing down as the number of employees was no longer expanding. Consequently, it became harder for part-timers to move on into full-time positions just because

---

[53] Canadian Union of Postal Workers, *CUPW*, Vol. 3, No. 9, September 1973, p. 2.

[54] Canadian Union of Postal Workers, "Negotiations 80," 26 March 1980, p. 37.

[55] Bulletin from John Fehr, National Chief Steward, Canadian Union of Postal Workers, "The Fight for Full-Time Jobs Shows Results," 7 January 1986, p. 2.

[56] Canadian Union of Postal Workers, Edmonton Local, "CUPW Part-Timers Survey," October 1985.

[57] Canada Post Corporation, information provided from the Personnel Data Base, 31 March 1984.

Part-time workers protest the use of part-time and casual work, Halifax, 1984. *(Photograph by Michael Creagen.)*

there were fewer full-time positions. After the Post Office became a Crown Corporation in 1981 and the PSSRA no longer applied, the union was able to negotiate that seniority alone would be the criteria for moving from one job to another, including from part-time to full-time. Previously moving into a full-time position was considered a promotion, to be decided by the employer and non-negotiable under the PSSRA. With seniority as the sole criterion, part-time workers automatically had the right to move into any full-time position available. Combined with the stagnation in full-time positions, this meant that it became necessary to first take a part-time position within the Post Office in order to then apply for a full-time job.

When seniority became universal in 1985, one more obstacle to moving from part-time to full-time was removed, again making it less likely that full-time jobs would be available to workers outside of the Post Office. It became an extremely rare occurrence that a full-time worker would be hired "off the street." As a result of these factors the proportion of part-time workers in the Post Office that would prefer full-time work has increased. This development was confirmed in interviews with part-time workers in many different locals. While some part-time workers want their part-time jobs, there was general consensus that the majority are waiting for a full-time position.

Excessive Use of Part-Time

While the CUPW's arguments in favour of reducing the use of part-time work have changed and developed over the period, one argument has been maintained throughout, namely that the use of part-time work has been excessive. The proportion of part-time work in the CUPW bargaining unit has hovered around 20 percent since the 1960s, and the union has always felt that this figure is unreasonably and unnecessarily high. The union has bargained for a 10 percent proportion as reasonable. It is not denied that some part-time work is appropriate and that some workers prefer to work part-time, but the level has always been regarded as excessive.

The Perspective of Part-Time Workers

How did the part-time workers themselves respond to the CUPW's policies over the years? Union officials and activists agree that the union's opposition to part-time work has created tensions between the full and part-time workers, and alienated some part-time workers from the union. One woman recalls part-time workers being hissed at the 1977 National Convention as they rose to speak.[58] Another active part-time woman worker wrote to the national newspaper to complain of the negative attitudes towards part-timers that she had experienced at a union educational.[59] In the interviews carried out for this study, part-time

---

[58] Interview, Vancouver local, 31 October 1988.

[59] Canadian Union of Postal Workers, *CUPW*, Vol. 12, No. 3, May-June 1982, p. 10.

workers sometimes commented that tension existed between the full and part-time workers and while it was often noted that management played a role in creating that tension, it was also asserted that the CUPW was still primarily a union for full-time workers.

Given this environment, it is interesting to note that part-time workers strongly supported the CUPW's policy on reducing the amount of part-time work. In 1974 a delegate to the National Convention who had worked for 19 years as a part-timer said: "I hope that nationally we will see that the ratio of part-time workers is kept lower than it is. You could cut down the ratio immensely and have part-timers doing what they were intended to do and not get rid of full-timers."[60] At the next Convention in 1977 part-time workers had helped to compose the resolution that called for a ratio of part to full-time workers. One part-time delegate said:

> I'm 100 percent behind this resolution and I helped compose it. It's an attempt by the part-timers in this Union to limit their own number for the security of ourselves, the part-time workers, and also that of the full-time workers here. As I said it's an attempt of the part-timers to limit the part-timers. I wholeheartedly concur and hope that it will be passed unanimously.[61]

Other part-time workers rose to support this position, no opposition was expressed and the resolution was carried.

The resolution expressed the concerns of the part-time workers, referring particularly to the lack of work schedules and to changes in hours without notice.[62] Part-time workers saw the need for controls because they suffered from the employer's unfettered use of part-time work, in particular from irregular hours of work. It was also important that the policy of reducing part-time work was never carried out at the expense of any part-time worker's job, so the part-time workers did not fear that such a policy would cost them their positions. Full-time jobs were created only as part-time workers left the Post Office or moved into full-time positions.

However, when controls were negotiated in 1980, the union did not obtain a ratio of part to full-time, but rather the peak period arrangement and a limitation on the maximum number of hours for part-timers. These provisions provoked an outcry from a considerable proportion of part-time workers—in some locals because of the peak period and elsewhere because of the limit on hours of work.

In most post offices the peak load of mail arrives in the evenings, so that became the most common designated peak period after 1980. Part-time workers

---

[60] Canadian Union of Postal Workers, *National Convention 1974, Proceedings*, Quebec, 3–8 June 1974, p. 1224.

[61] Canadian Union of Postal Workers, *Thirteenth Triennial Convention Proceedings*, Halifax, 25–29 July 1977, p. 1028.

[62] *Ibid.*, p. 1027.

already employed on the evening shift were unaffected, and those whose hours had been irregular or who had worked split shifts saw a change for the better. However, in a few locations part-time workers had been employed during the day and were now forced to move onto the less desirable evening shift, starting at 4 or 5 p.m. This was the situation in Toronto, where nine hundred part-time workers were sufficiently incensed to hire a lawyer with a view to taking a case against the union for failure to represent their interests—an initiative that was soon abandoned for lack of a case.[63] A group of 30 part-time workers in Toronto presented a brief to the government appointed Task Force on Part-Time Work that was then touring the country, complaining that the CUPW discriminated against part-time workers.[64] At the 1980 National Convention held just a few weeks after the signing of the contract, delegates from Toronto warned that the part-time workers might refuse to strike with the union again, and in a local with one-third part-time workers that meant no strike. One delegate said: "It will be difficult when we next go on strike to ask these brothers and sisters to support the Union after they feel that they have been betrayed to some extent by the provisions of our last contract."[65]

However, from the point of view of the full-time workers, a full-time worker had to work nights for many years in order to obtain sufficient seniority to move to a day shift. If the employer hired part-time workers directly onto the day shift (and then in some cases gave them eight hours work per day on a regular basis) those part-timers had never had to work nights like the full-time workers. Moreover they filled the day positions, blocking the full-time workers from the opportunity of moving to day work.

Moving from the day to evening shift affected part-time workers in several locals, but a more widespread complaint was the reduction in hours from 30 to 25 per week. In locals where part-time workers had regularly been employed for 30 hours a week, they now saw their hours cut to 25, with a consequent drop in income. The response to this change was "vitriolic" in several large centres.[66] Part-time workers who wanted those extra hours felt it was unfair that full-time workers could be offered overtime, and casual workers hired on a full-time basis, while their hours could not be extended beyond 25 per week.

But, again this negative impact was limited to certain workers and certain locals. While part-time workers who wanted extended hours were dissatisfied, those who only wanted to work 4 or 5 hours a day were unaffected. Part-timers

---

[63] Interview with Geoff Bickerton, Research Director, Canadian Union of Postal Workers, Ottawa, 12 October 1988.

[64] Labour Canada, *Part-time Work in Canada, Report of the Commission of Inquiry into Part-time Work*, Ottawa, 1983, p. 98.

[65] Canadian Union of Postal Workers, *National Convention 1980, Proceedings*, Ottawa, 28 July–1 August 1980, p. 383.

[66] Interview with Caroline Lee, National Secretary-Treasurer, Canadian Union of Postal Workers, Ottawa, 12 October 1988.

who wanted to move to full-time were in a more difficult dilemma, because on the one hand they wanted the extra hours and income, but they also understood that as long as part-time workers continued to work extended hours the possibility of more full-time positions being created was remote. In some rural areas the problem for part-time workers had been that they were offered very few hours of work and often those hours were unpredictable. For these part-time workers it was a great improvement to see their hours increased to the new minimum of 20 per week. They obtained some security of employment and income, as well as regularly scheduled and predictable working hours.

By the time of the 1983 Convention the resentment from the part-time workers had clearly diminished, partly because the experiences were so mixed and by no means uniformly negative, and partly because the 1980 contract provisions had produced some positive results. Reports from different regions indicated that more full-time jobs had been created, jobs which part-time workers had obtained, and that abuse of part-time workers had declined with more regular hours and schedules. The report to the Convention from the Ontario Regional Director stated: "Through the establishment of the peak period over 450 full-time positions were realized in the Ontario region with no part-time members losing their jobs."[67] Also, by this point the referendum on universal seniority had passed and part-time workers could anticipate that this benefit would shortly be negotiated into the contract.

In 1988 the CUPW lost the peak period and the maximum hours for part-timers were returned to 30 per week, and again the response was mixed. In some of the larger locals the part-timers were pleased because they were offered more hours and could take them when they pleased. However, some part-time workers who would have liked to obtain full-time positions were aware that with the extra hours being offered to part-timers, the chances of full-time jobs being created were reduced. Most part-timers were concerned about the loss of the peak period, and some locals had already felt the negative effects of a new midnight shift for part-timers.[68]

Conclusion

The introduction to this chapter referred to several studies that have criticized unions for their attempts to control the number of part-time workers. The material presented here on the CUPW suggests that the reasons for seeking to restrict part-time work are varied and do not arise solely from "the traditional union attitude" of opposition to part-time work.

The CUPW has consistently maintained the position that the number of part-time workers should be reduced, although the reasons for this position have changed and developed over time. In the past some of those reasons have been

---

[67] Canadian Union of Postal Workers, "Report of the National Director, Ontario Region, to the National Convention," Ottawa, 1983, p. 1.

[68] Information from interviews in various CUPW locals, October 1988 to March 1989.

highly questionable, including opposition to part-time work because it was primarily done by women and because part-time workers might reduce the strength of the union. However, the union's concern that part-time work has been used as a source of cheap labour was well-founded, and continues to have some relevance. Whether the numbers of part-time workers are excessive may be open to debate, but it is clear that the proportion of part-time workers within the CUPW bargaining unit has always been high and well above the national average for the general labour force. Most recently it is apparent that a considerable proportion of part-time workers would prefer full-time employment.

In the case of the CUPW, the employer has also played an important role in defining the nature of the union's policies with regard to part-time work. The continuous problems with the use of both casual and part-time work have prompted the union to take determined action. In particular, the employer's use of part-time work as a flexible workforce with changing schedules, shifts and hours has been a concern shared by the union and its part-time members. Given these considerations it is not possible to conclude that because the CUPW has sought to control the use of part-time workers it has therefore worked in opposition to the interests of part-timers.

The reaction of part-time workers has been mixed, including support for reducing the number of part-time workers combined with considerable opposition to negotiated controls upon hours of work and the peak period. There is no question that part-timers within the CUPW have supported, and do support, the union's position in favour of limiting the number of part-time workers. They have participated in drawing up and speaking in favour of resolutions for that policy, and have expressed support for the 4,200 numerical limit on part-time workers. The mixed response of the part-timers to the union's negotiations on the peak period and hours of work is a reflection of the mixed views and situations of part-time workers themselves.

Part-time workers are employed in different ways in different locations and this is reflected in their varied responses to union policy. For example, those who had obtained day shift positions were understandably furious to lose those jobs with the introduction of the peak period, but for part-timers who had been working split shifts it was a major improvement.

Part-time workers themselves are not a homogeneous group, but include men and women, mothers and single women, students and older workers. Some part-time workers want full-time positions and some prefer to remain part-time; some part-timers want additional hours of work while for others it is more important that the hours be steady and predictable. When the maximum hours of work were returned again to 30 per week in 1988, part-timers who wanted the extended hours were delighted; those who preferred to work a maximum of 5 hours per day were unaffected and those who wanted full-time positions saw their chances reduced. The situation also changes over time, both for individuals depending upon their life circumstances and generally in the workplace. For example, a married woman who was satisfied working part-time gets a divorce and needs to work full-time to support her children.

These variations among part-time workers often cut across the issue of gender. Differences in work schedules and preferences, age and other factors are often more important in the response of part-time workers than whether they are male or female. It is the case that a large proportion of part-time workers are women and that often they work part-time as a result of child raising responsibilities, but even among this section of part-time workers very diverse interests emerge. With regard to the peak period, for example, the regularity of hours was a positive factor for women making child care arrangements. But, the minority of women who lost their day positions were understandably just as angry as the men to be forced onto evenings.

One might assume that the evening shift would be disastrous for women with children because they would miss those after-school hours, but this is not always the case. Some women did feel that they only saw their children on weekends, but others said it was a good shift for women with children, because they were at home when the children returned from school, and could prepare and eat supper with the family before going to work, leaving the children with their father, or with a babysitter in the case of single parents. Obviously, this works where the evening shift starts at 6 p.m., and is hardly so convenient where the part-timers begin at 4 p.m. For women with pre-school aged children, they could spend all day with them at home, leaving them in the care of their father or a babysitter for the evening hours. Many couples avoid the cost of child care by thus splitting the time between themselves.

Questions concerning the approach of unions to the needs of part-time workers are complicated by differences among part-time workers and by the diversity of the work situations in which they find themselves. Negotiations to restrict the use of part-time workers must be understood within the context of the specific workplace, in particular the employer's use of part-time work. It is within this diverse and changing framework that the union has to make decisions about how to handle the situation of part-time work, taking into account the needs of both the full-time and part-time workers. One union official said: "As a union I guess you've got to balance off those perceived interests of the individual workers, which are contradictory in many cases, with what you perceive to be a broader collective interest."[69] Making such decisions is not a choice between right and wrong, so much as a delicate balance between many, and often conflicting, variables.

---

[69] Interview with Geoff Bickerton, Research Director, Canadian Union of Postal Workers, 12 October 1988.

SECTION III

WOMEN'S ISSUES IN THE 1980s

"We're Going to Have to Face Up to It"

THE POST OFFICE IN THE 1980s

In 1981 the Post Office became a Crown Corporation with a new management structure operating under the jurisdiction of different labour relations legislation. The CUPW had argued for this change to Crown Corporation status since 1950, and it was meant to alleviate the bitter labour relations atmosphere in the Post Office. Before looking at the emergence of specifically women's issues within the CUPW in the 1980s, it is important to examine the general relationship between the inside workers at the Post Office and their employer. It is not within the scope of this study to assess the failure or success of the Crown Corporation, but it is relevant to consider the relationship between the union and the employer and also to examine relations between management and workers as they occurred on the shop floor.

Labour-Management Relations in the 1980s

In December 1980 the CUPW began its last round of negotiations under the Public Service Staff Relations Act (PSSRA). These negotiations and the strike that resulted in 1981 will be examined in some detail in the following chapter, because one of the central issues was paid maternity leave. On 16th October 1981, the Post Office became a Crown Corporation, a change advocated by the union for many years because from that point the union negotiated under the more liberal jurisdiction of the Canada Labour Code. It also meant direct negotiations with the Post Office management, without the Treasury Board as intermediary. The change to a Crown Corporation had been recommended in many reports on the Post Office since at least 1969. Instead of the cumbersome combination of the Post Office Department, Public Works, the Public Service Commission and Treasury Board, the Post Office would be operated by a single corporate management. The management would be streamlined, and responsible for the general operation of the Post Office, including dealing directly with labour relations and negotiations.

However, the new Corporation did not escape government intervention. Just as the union was preparing to negotiate free of the restrictions of the PSSRA, the government introduced Bill C–124. Responding to a serious economic downturn that sent unemployment and interest rates soaring, the government again introduced wage controls, this time covering just the federal government and Crown Corporations. Under this legislation, the CUPW's 1981 contract was extended for two years and wage increases were determined by the government at six percent the first year and five percent the second. Consequently, it was not until 1984 that the CUPW first negotiated under the Canada Labour Code rather than the PSSRA.

In the meantime the union was able to bargain its own grievance procedure under the Canada Labour Code, which had not been possible under the PSSRA. The new procedure was given a fresh start because the backlog of grievances that had developed after 1975 was handled by special committees established under the 1980 contract provisions. Of the 28,517 grievances referred to these committees, decisions were made on 25,636, and 23,401 were fully or partially sustained, while 2,235 were denied.[1] In 1986 the National Chief Steward, the elected officer responsible for grievances, reported that the legislative change had resulted in "a dramatic impact" upon grievances. For the first time the union could take various forms of discharge to arbitration and argue the cases before an independent third party, and access to the number of arbitration hearings was unrestricted.[2]

Bargaining under the Canada Labour Code also had an important impact upon contract negotiations when they began in 1984. First, there were no legal restrictions upon, nor objections to, the union demands, and no hearings were necessary to determine the legally acceptable issues for a Conciliation Board to consider. Indeed, there was no Conciliation Board procedure, although the Minister could appoint a Conciliation Commissioner to submit a report. The major change was that for the first time the employer submitted management's demands at the same time as the union, at the first negotiation meeting. The CUPW President, Jean-Claude Parrot, described the process as reflecting a real willingness on both sides to reach an agreement and even called it "a rewarding experience."[3] In April 1985 a collective agreement was signed without a strike.

Despite these positive results from the new Corporation other problems were looming. When the Crown Corporation came into existence on 16th October 1981, its first President, Michael Warren, announced three objectives: expanded and improved service, better labour relations and financial self-sufficiency. It was not long before the union expressed concern that the third of these goals was being emphasized to the detriment of the first two. The government's budget of November 1981, announced just one month after the creation of the Crown Corporation, required the elimination of the Post Office deficit by 1986, thereby providing just 4 years for a turnaround in an organization that had last produced a surplus 30 years earlier. This deadline was later extended to 1988, but in neither case was any explanation or justification offered for the time chosen. In the late 1970s and early 1980s the Post Office deficit hovered at around $500

---

[1] Canadian Union of Postal Workers, *CUPW*, Vol. 12, No. 1, January-February 1982, p. 3.

[2] Canadian Union of Postal Workers, "Report of the National Chief Steward," Presented to the Sixteenth Triennial Convention of the CUPW, Ottawa, 7–11 April 1986, p. 1.

[3] Canadian Union of Postal Workers, "Report of the National President," Presented to the 16th Triennial Convention of the CUPW, Ottawa, 7–11 April 1986, p. 5.

million, and in the context of the economic crisis of the early 1980s the government again focused upon reducing the deficit. The pressure, not just to reduce the deficit, but to do so immediately, resulted in further conflict with the CUPW.

The inside postal workers had experienced first a stagnation and then a reduction in their numbers since the impact of the new technology began to take effect after 1976. However, in the early 1980s it became clear that a more determined effort to cut costs and reduce the deficit was to be made at the expense of postal worker positions. In 1980/81 1,100 mail sorting positions were eliminated and in the following three years a further 700 positions were lost,[4] part-time positions sometimes replacing full-time jobs. The CUPW membership of 24,476 in 1978 had fallen to 23,392 by 1982, although by 1987 it had recovered to 23,947.[5] Continued mechanization and work re-organization were only one part of the problem, as the new Corporation took steps to cut back on services and reduce staff by closing postal stations and opening more sub-post offices.

The owner of a sub-post office contracts with the Post Office to provide postal services and receives a commission on sales. In the early 1980s the Post Office management began to increase the number of sub-post offices, thereby drawing business away from postal stations and CUPW members. In October 1982 the employer informed the union of plans to open 19 new sub-post offices and to extend services at another 28.[6] In March 1983 the union noted that there were 2,150 subs in Canada, a figure that had increased to an estimated 2,400 by 1988.[7]

This was a critical issue for the union, because the jobs threatened by this policy were the wicket jobs, involving serving the public in postal stations. Compared to working in a large plant sorting mail, these jobs are clean, interesting and relatively relaxed, and they are also day shift positions. It takes many years of seniority to obtain a wicket position. Reducing their number means fewer day time jobs, longer periods of night work, and a higher proportion of the more monotonous stressful jobs within the sorting plants.

The union's fears were confirmed when the employer announced its Five Year Business Plan in October 1983. The emphasis was on reducing the deficit by reductions in staff and service cutbacks. Suggestions to reduce staff included speeding up the pace of work, restrictions on the use of sick leave, increased use of part-time work, and more contracting out. Service cutbacks to be considered

---

[4] Canada Post Corporation, "Report of the Review Committee on the Mandate and Productivity of Canada Post Corporation," Ottawa, November 1985, p. 7.

[5] Statistics Canada, *Corporations and Labour Unions Returns Act*, Part II—Labour Unions, Cat.71–202, 1978–1985; data for 1987 supplied by the Statistics Canada, Corporations and Labour Unions Returns Act Division.

[6] Canadian Union of Postal Workers, "Final Statement to the Mediator-Arbitrator," 21 June 1988, p. 58.

[7] Canadian Union of Postal Workers, *CUPW*, Vol. 13, No. 2, February-March 1983, p. 7; Canadian Union of Postal Workers, "Final Statement to the Mediator-Arbitrator," 21 June 1988, p. 216.

were closing postal stations, alternate day mail delivery, and offering customers the alternative of free group boxes or payment for home delivery service. Through these methods the Plan's objective was to eliminate 2,535 person years from the Post Office by 1985. The study warned "It must be clearly indicated to the unions, in line with this philosophy, that lay-offs will and must take place if attrition measures do not succeed."[8]

Meanwhile the union was developing an alternative perspective on the Post Office and how to reduce the deficit. In other countries post offices provide a wide range of services to the public, including banking, paying bills and issuing licenses of various kinds. The union proposed a Service Expansion Program for the Canadian Post Office, suggesting that the deficit could be reduced through increased revenues instead of cutting costs. These revenues would be obtained by expanding the range and availability of services at postal stations.[9] The CUPW developed some detailed suggestions on the type of services that could be provided, including: payment of bills; the sale of postal related items such as packaging and wrapping materials, envelopes, stationary and greetings cards; a fee for service arrangement with banks or credit unions to provide banking facilities in the 2,500 communities where there was a postal facility but no bank; selling all types of government licenses and permits; and the sale of transit tickets, lottery tickets and other retail items.[10] The union also proposed expansion into electronic mail and the contracting in of sub-post offices. The union argued that such developments would save and expand the desirable wicket jobs, provide customers with more services, and increase revenues to reduce the deficit.

In the first years of the Crown Corporation these ideas were shared and, on some occasions, adopted by management. The President, Michael Warren, had expressed support for expanded services when he was first appointed. In speeches in different parts of the country he suggested that "the largest retail network in Canada" might be used to provide more services to Canadians, including possibly banking, catalogue sales, travel and insurance.[11]

However, such suggestions were not the focus of the Corporation's Five Year Plan and the CUPW responded by holding demonstrations across the country and initiating a public campaign on the service cuts proposed in the Plan.[12] This was also the year that the union planned to offer cheap stamps at Christmas, stating it

[8] Canadian Union of Postal Workers, "Special Tabloid," November 1983, p. 2.

[9] Canadian Union of Postal Workers, *CUPW*, Vol. 13, No. 2, February-March 1983, pp. 1, 6.

[10] Canadian Union of Postal Workers, "Final Statement to the Mediator-Arbitrator," 21 June 1988, p. 244.

[11] Speeches to the Regina Chamber of Commerce, 12 November 1982, and to the Rotary Club of Ottawa, 21 June 1982, quoted in Canadian Union of Postal Workers, *CUPW*, Vol. 13, No. 2, February-March 1983, p. 6.

[12] *Ibid.*, Vol. 14, No. 1, January-February 1984, pp. 1–2.

would process letters with 10¢ stamps, a protest that was aborted by a decision of the Canada Labour Relations Board. However, union-management meetings reached agreement in February 1984 to conduct the Retail Outlet Experiment. Six sub-post offices were converted to Canada Post outlets staffed by CUPW members, to be evaluated at the end of a year for their success with regard to financial viability, image and service. Post Office management proposed another initiative, called the New Direction outlets, that were post office outlets located in shopping centres, staffed by CUPW members and open longer hours in line with the other stores and services. The employer also agreed not to open any new sub-post offices before January 1985 and the union agreed to postpone its public campaign.[13]

The collective agreement signed without a strike in April 1985 expanded this initiative. The Retail Outlet experiment was extended and provided for nine more conversions of sub-post offices to Post Office outlets if the first six proved successful. The employer agreed to establish 14 more New Direction Outlets and agreed to reduce the number of sub-post offices by 53 during the term of the agreement. The signed agreement went yet further, the employer agreeing to phase in new services at some outlets, provide extended hours of service at some postal stations, implement an Electronic Bulk Mail service and examine the possibility of other services, including transit tickets, bill payment and catalogue sales.[14]

The Corporation did experiment with "Consumers Post" between March and June 1984, whereby customers could order from Consumers' Distributing through their local post office. However, certain business groups were quick to oppose this new initiative, claiming that the Post Office had no place entering into competition with private industry and that it was unfair competition given the network of post offices supported by the government. The experiment was abandoned and in 1985 a government committee established to study the Crown Corporation concluded:

> Although this initiative was widely supported by the postal unions, and may have had the potential to yield significant additional income, it was terminated in response to pressures originating with the business community.[15]

During the early years of the Crown Corporation a contradiction was apparent. Although the Corporation was expected to operate like a private business independent of government support, it was not free to enter into competition with private industry in order to obtain the revenue to achieve that self-sufficiency.

By the end of 1985 the situation within the Canada Post Corporation had altered decisively. In September 1984 the Conservative government was elected;

---

[13] *Ibid.*, Vol. 14, No. 2, March-May 1984, p. 2.

[14] Canada Post Corporation, "Agreement between Canada Post Corporation and the Canadian Union of Postal Workers," Expires: 30 September 1986, Appendices P and Q.

[15] Canada Post Corporation, "Report of the Review Committee on the Mandate and Productivity of Canada Post Corporation," Ottawa, November 1985, p. 8.

in August 1985 Michael Warren resigned as President and in November 1985 a Committee headed by Alan Marchment produced a report on the mandate and productivity of the Crown Corporation. These events marked the end of the tentative agreements around service expansion. The Conservative government was committed to privatization and deregulation, not to the expansion of government services. The Corporation's Annual Reports under the new President, Donald Lander, no longer mentioned improved labour relations within the Post Office, but focused more determinedly upon reducing the deficit through cuts in costs rather than increasing revenues.[16] The Marchment Report criticized the Corporation for failing to control costs, and recommended that the Post Office continue to be required to be financially self-sufficient. Specifically the Report proposed more sub-post offices, increased productivity and greater use of part-time and casual labour, while recommending against competition in any area already well served by private industry and against investment in parcel post processing or electronic bulk mail. The Report further recommended that if the Post Office had not achieved self-sufficiency by 1990, privatization should be considered.[17]

The Five Year Corporate Plan released in November 1986 stated that the Post Office planned to reduce its total staff by 8,700 over the following 5 years, even though the Corporation also predicted that mail volumes would increase by 9 percent. The Plan outlined its methods for staff reductions as follows: privatize through franchising 3,500 of the 5,221 rural post offices and close many others through amalgamation and replacement by mailboxes; privatize an indeterminate number of urban postal stations; provide group mail boxes instead of home delivery; and reduce rural delivery routes. Internally the Post Office Plan called for reduced absenteeism, less job security and more technological change.[18]

During 1986 the Corporation closed 72 rural post offices and several large urban postal stations. Management informed the union that 50 franchises were planned for the first year alone, with hundreds, if not thousands, to follow.[19] The Post Office started to promote and install its "supermailboxes," that is delivery to group boxes instead of home delivery, particularly in new urban subdivisions. Between 1984 and 1987 the CUPW lost a further 1,085 full-time positions.

---

[16] Canada Post Corporation, *Annual Report*, Ottawa, 1985/86, 1987/88.

[17] Canada Post Corporation, "Report of the Review Committee on the Mandate and Productivity of Canada Post Corporation," Ottawa, November 1985, p. 8.

[18] Joan Hannant, "Privatizing Postal Services: The Implications for Women," National Action Committee on the Status of Women, Toronto, November 1988, p. 20.

[19] Canadian Union of Postal Workers, "Final Statement to the Mediator-Arbitrator," 21 June 1988, pp. 74–76.

Meanwhile part-time positions increased by 542, and casual and overtime hours increased.[20] Management also strengthened its determination to reduce the use of sick leave and other types of leave. By 1986 the union was referring grievances to arbitration at an average rate of 460 per month.[21]

Negotiations for a new collective agreement had just commenced when the Five Year Plan was released. The employer's demands included the right to lay-off workers, reducing the restrictions upon the use of part-time and casual labour, and lessening the protection provided against technological change. The union proposed to increase job security by reducing the number of sub-post offices and abolishing the plans to franchise, and wanted an expansion of services, more day jobs and reduced noise levels in the plants. To no-one's surprise a strike resulted in 1987. For the first time Post Office management used replacement workers, thereby creating a new level of hostility among its workers. The CUPW strike was legislated back to work after only 8 days, and a settlement imposed. However, this did nothing to resolve the problems in the Post Office.

In 1988 the CUPW undertook a year long campaign to oppose the privatization of the Post Office. Ten regional coordinators were hired to mobilize union members around the issue, inform the public of the union's position and liaise with community groups. The union was not alone in its concerns. In December 1986 an organization called Rural Dignity was formed to fight the closing of rural post offices and the elimination of rural delivery routes. This group argued that rural post offices were of central importance to many communities, and that service declined when postal facilities were contracted out to private business. In areas where post offices were closed or amalgamated, residents sometimes had to travel remarkable distances for postal services. To give just two examples, since local postal facilities were closed in Ravenscrag, Saskatchewan, residents must travel 68 kilometres round trip to pick up their mail, and in Ruskin, British Columbia, 560 inhabitants must make a 32 kilometre return trip to buy stamps.[22] Apart from the inconvenience, Rural Dignity argued that when residents must regularly travel to other communities for postal services, they carry out other shopping and service requirements at the same time. Consequently, businesses in small communities are threatened, and so are the communities themselves.

An organization called Residents Against Mailboxes was established to represent home owners in their fight to obtain door-to-door delivery in new subdivi-

---

[20] Canada Post Corporation data, quoted in Canadian Union of Postal Workers, "Final Statement to the Mediator-Arbitrator," 21 June 1988, p. 177.

[21] Canadian Union of Postal Workers, "Report of the National Chief Steward," Presented to the Sixteenth Triennial Convention of the CUPW, Ottawa, 7–11 April 1986, p. 19.

[22] Rural Dignity, "Brief to the Standing Committee on Government Operations," Ottawa, 5 March 1987, p. 10.

Demonstration against privatization and closing rural post offices, Toronto, 1989. (*Photograph by David Hartman.*)

sions. While the Post Office suggested that group mail boxes were convenient and attractive,[23] users complained that they were a serious inconvenience to the elderly and disabled, attracted litter and lowered property values. They also argued that it was against the legal mandate of the Corporation to provide them with an unequal and lower standard of service, while nearby neighbours received home delivery.[24]

Women's organizations also condemned the Post Office action to privatize and reduce services. They noted that it was elderly women and women with young children who suffered most when forced to leave their homes or travel to collect their mail in the face of more group mailboxes and reduced rural services. The National Action Committee on the Status of Women pointed out that it was primarily women postal officials who lost their jobs in rural areas. Moreover where services were franchised, workers protected by the pay and conditions of the union contract were replaced by low paid, non-unionised and predominantly women shop clerks.[25]

By 1987/88 the Post Office deficit was reduced to $30 million and the Corporation was planning a profit of over $50 million by 1990.[26] The elimination of the deficit was partly due to large rate increases; the price of mailing a letter doubled from 17¢ to 34¢ between 1981 and 1984, and had risen to 38 cents as of 1989. The reduced deficit was also due to the deep cuts made in staff and services. While Post Office management can claim success in cutting the deficit, not only the union, but also many consumers, are questioning what happened to the other early mandates of the new Crown Corporation, namely improved service and better labour relations.

On the question of labour relations, the Marchment report stated:

> The members of the Committee are unanimous in agreeing that they have never seen labour relations in any jurisdiction that are as acrimonious as those that exist between Canada Post Corporation management and the postal unions. They are poisonous to the point of the potential destruction of the enterprise.[27]

Canadians have wondered for years why labour relations in the Post Office are so unsatisfactory. After all, other workers experience technological change and restructuring, other unions have members who work in large plants under supervision. What creates the level of animosity in the Post Office?

One interesting possibility is to ask the inside postal workers. How do the workers on the job feel about their work, what do they think of the problems in

---

[23] Canada Post Corporation, "Introducing Supermailbox," pamphlet, 1987.

[24] Joan Hannant, "Privatizing Postal Services: The Implications for Women," National Action Committee on the Status of Women, Toronto, November 1988, p. 7.

[25] *Ibid.*

[26] Canada Post Corporation, *Annual Report*, Ottawa, 1987/88.

[27] Canada Post Corporation, "Report of the Review Committee on the Mandate and Productivity of Canada Post Corporation," Ottawa, November 1985, p. 29.

the Post Office, how do they explain the level of hostility? Over the years, many studies have reported on the organization of the Post Office, technological change, management efficiency and even management morale, but not since the Montpetit Report in 1966 has anyone asked the workers on the shop floor for their perspective.

This study was not planned with that goal in mind, being orientated to the union's response to women. Nonetheless information on the nature of the work surfaced constantly during the interviews I carried out with CUPW members working at the Post Office. The material was striking, and ultimately I decided it must be included. Because my interviews were geared to other objectives, the following information only scratches the surface of the issues raised, and omits many questions. It is offered only as the comments of 54 postal workers, employed in post offices in 14 communities across the country. But, perhaps it holds some direction for the future. If we want to know why labour relations are so poor in the Post Office, we might consider asking the people most directly involved.

I spoke almost entirely with women, 51 out of the 54 interviewees, and some of the following material reflects their particular concerns. Whether men working in the Post Office experience their work situation differently from women was not a question explored in my interviews. Certainly some of the experiences described below, such as problems with sick leave, are shared by both men and women.

Working at the Post Office

During the interviews it was impossible not to be struck by the very negative perspective of these postal workers towards their work situation and the remarkable level of tension they experienced. No-one said they enjoyed their work, no-one gave even a qualified positive point of view. In one interview a woman began by telling me that she had no problems at work, but went on to describe numerous difficulties she was experiencing. In this and the following sections, these workers speak for themselves, about what it is like to work at the Post Office, and their explanations for why conditions are so difficult.

> You can see the problems as soon as you get in there. The tension between labour and management—you can feel it as you go up in the escalator the first day that you work there (Edmonton).

> It's an awful job. I find I have to psych myself into going to work each night (Halifax).

> I used to dread for awhile going to work; I hated it (St John).

> I also go to school in the daytime and work in another part-time job, which is kind of what you need because you don't get a lot of job satisfaction working at the Post Office. So you try to get satisfaction in other ways. That's why some people choose to work part-time, so that they can get some sort of satisfaction outside the Post Office (Vancouver).

Personally, I say that now it's humiliating working in the Post Office, humiliating (Montreal).

I think that because of all the other things that happen in the plant the very least of our problems is when we work. It's actually getting to work and putting up with the garbage that we put up with there ... The things that we have to put up with when we're at work is what makes the job hard (Edmonton).

I don't foresee myself ever being happy in the Post Office (Halifax).

Technological Change

Workers employed in the Post Office for some years remembered a different environment prior to mechanization, when more skill was required, when there was more friendship between the workers and better morale. Many of those interviewed were convinced that automation had led to reduced service and slower movement of mail, rather than improvements. Interestingly this perspective was expressed by the Marchment Report that stated:

Indeed, the sharp drop in efficiency of mail processing which coincided with the introduction of the new equipment suggests that, if this were the only variable, continuation of manual sorting operations might have yielded a higher level of productivity.[28]

The report goes on to note that in Australia a large facility was built for automatic mail processing several years before similar plants were established in Canada. Performance deteriorated, remedies failed and it was closed in favour of smaller plants, in which service standards have been restored and labour relations improved.

The majority of CUPW members work in large, mechanized plants and much of the work is described as boring, tedious, and monotonous, especially coding. The noise level in the plants was a constant source of complaint, not only because of potential hearing damage, but also because it meant that talking among the workers was difficult or impossible.

We went into a building with no windows in the processing area. It was really, really a different atmosphere ... People's whole attitude changed. When we were down in the old building on Water Street, it was a friendlier atmosphere and people weren't always really tense ... It's like a dark cloud over your head, it's just a really different atmosphere. The machinery has a lot to do with it. For the first period of time that we were in the building the machines weren't operating and it wasn't so bad. But, once they turned on one machine, even when it was in the testing stages ... then the GDS (Group Desk Suite) and the LSM (Letter Sorting Machine) together and people said "My God, what a racket." And then they got the Toshiba Canceller and they're all there together and once they all started going, people couldn't believe the noise (St John's).

It's a sense of pride that used to be there. I used to go to work and think we're all going to pitch in and it was really like that. And you knew something then. Like, I could sort New Brunswick, and people would come to me and go "You've

---

[28] *Ibid.*, p. 37.

worked here quite a while, where does this little one go?" You had pride. But, now there's nothing to learn anymore (St John).

It (mechanization) made your job more uninteresting because once you are coding, you are coding, that's it. You don't improve, you don't get any satisfaction from your job. While in the past people used to sort and need some knowledge of either their city or the country (Montreal).

From a service point of view, service standards dropped. From a morale point of view, morale just went completely downhill when they started mechanizing. It's partly because of working on the machines, it's partly because supervisors attitudes started to change. They were never really easy to work with or anything, but the priority was always to get the mail out. You went in at the beginning of your shift and you did your work and you got everything done. By the time you left everything that had to be done was done, there was no mail left around for the next shift. When they brought in the machines in St John's they used to stack up the mail all day so that when the Coders came in there'd be enough mail there to run the machine for awhile. Because they always had to get their numbers on the machines (St John's).

When the people were hand sorting and it wasn't being done through the machine, at least the things were sorted into the right place. When it comes to the postal code, sometimes if one letter gets at the top of the pile that has the wrong code on it, maybe fifty or sixty wrong letters will go to Halifax. It happens all the time. When people were sorting it was going into the right case. Our rate for getting mail from one part of the country to the other was within two days and now you should see. My god, sometimes to get it from the south side over to the north side takes a week. I think automation has made things slower (Edmonton).

It's so mechanical now. It could be better done by hand. There are lots of mistakes from the machines. Part of my job is resorting mis-sorts from the machine and there are always lots of mistakes, and it's increased over the years (St John).

The work is boring, the work is repetitious, the work makes you crazy (Vancouver).

I never want to go back in the plant. It's terrible. Coding is the worst job you could get, to sit there for eight hours is terrible. I couldn't handle that. It's terrible (Wicket clerk—Halifax).

Before mechanization it was easy for employees to contact each other. One of the main impacts on us has been the fact of the noise and every employee is alone now. It's very hard to communicate because there's too much noise (Montreal).

I think we're all going deaf … It does damage your ears, especially that LSM (St John).

Mismanagement

Mismanagement, inefficiency and cutbacks in staff and service were cited as further reasons for the poor work atmosphere and the slowness of the mail. The workers interviewed complained that they are moved onto jobs that they are not trained for and strongly discouraged from having any positive input into the organization of the work, or from raising problems concerning the work. The lack of training for managers and supervisors, and the resulting inefficiency and frustration, were mentioned regularly.

Well, I'm sent over to the City section, where they don't train me for the sortation. So, management is accepting that you're producing at a lower rate than you could be. So people are frustrated because you can't do a decent job. Most people have pretty good work ethics; they want to be able to do some kind of work that's meaningful, or at least feel they are contributing in some way. So when they're forced to look up numbers all the time because management is accepting this lower rate of productivity, they get frustrated (Halifax).

We're (part-timers) supposed to be working in forward, short and long ... They just send us wherever they want, they send us all over the plant ... It's turning into a shuffle board lately. They're just very short staffed. It doesn't make sense, because they send us to City sort. We don't have the knowledge. The supervisor told me once that the average trained City person sorts 1,800 letters an hour. The part-timer sorts 300. They don't care, we're just bodies, they send us everywhere ... It's become so ridiculous, everybody thinks "Gee they're sending us here, I'm pretty useless here." Why doesn't management smarten up and train people properly if they want to get the mail out? (Vancouver)

I feel I'm a conscientious person and I'd like to have pride in my job, but the things they do don't allow it. We are always short staffed and management doesn't know what they're doing. There's no consistency ... A lot of places have done away with the relief clerk and everybody suffers for it. The customers get upset because they have to wait (Wicket clerk, Halifax).

What I find the hardest is on the window. Like we have to answer to the public. Now the Post Office cuts out services, but the public never knows this. So, they'll say "Well, how come I could mail a letter to Chatham and it would get there the next day. Now, why is it taking three days?" Well, they cut a service out; it used to go twice a day and now it goes once ... It's the Post Office worker that takes the flak (Wicket clerk, St John).

They don't have a training program for management ... They'll hire someone off the street, they do hire people off the street for APOC positions (front line supervisors), and they have no concept at all. The most they've ever done is put a letter in a mailbox. And they'll put them in a supervisory position over a person with 15–20 years seniority. And tell them what to do. You aren't allowed to say "In the past we've done it this way" or "I do it this way, because of this" or "I find that this works faster" or "I've tried that before but it slowed me down," without risking discipline, and getting yourself in a procedure which leads to dismissal ... You can't go to management and say "This just doesn't work" (Edmonton).

They're so poorly mismanaged. They don't have qualified people doing their jobs—the supervisors and plant managers. They certainly don't make the work area more enjoyable and less stressful (Halifax).

The ones (supervisors) we have now, some of them were never clerks, they have no idea what goes on in that Post Office. They come right in off the street. How can you have respect for someone who doesn't know your job? I mean that's what a supervisor's supposed to do, he's supposed to know what needs to be done, and if he doesn't understand how it's done, how can he really supervise? (St John)

Any kind of change bothers people, simply because they're not asked for their input. Canada Post is really bad. They have industrial engineers and they're paid to make things more efficient, not better, but more efficient. And when they bring in their ideas for efficiency they sometimes overlook the most obvious thing. And if they would have asked the people that worked in the section for any length of time, they could have told them. But, no, they have to implement the change and people have to deal with the implementation (Edmonton).

It got so that I was saying "When I start getting station manager's pay I'll tell you." I was running the office for him. Of course there's all kinds of little things that happen that never happened during his training. He hasn't got a clue what to do with them. He's got that office so messed up… (Wicket clerk, St John).

The Supervision

The workers described an oppressive level of supervision on the job, especially in the plants. Many suggested that front line supervisors are under pressure from higher level management to take the attitude that they do. There were constant references to intimidation and harassment of the workers. There were also complaints that there is no positive reinforcement, no appreciation when work is well done.

You code all day, eight hours, and you stay overtime they make you code some more, which is boring. And they stand behind you all day long … If they think you're having a good time at work they want to stop it right away. You can't enjoy your job … I believe that there has to be a certain amount of supervision, but not the concentration that you're getting now (St John).

If the harassment on the floor is going to be super intense, I'm going to leave after 4 hours (Part-time worker, Vancouver).

There are a lot of problems that don't go to grievance, mainly because in there now there's so much intimidation on the go that everybody's afraid to say "boo." Everybody's totally intimidated (St John's).

I feel bad for her (the supervisor) because she's got to come down and yell at us all the time and she knows we're working. She's got to do it because she's got someone watching her (St John).

Days is the worst shift by far, because there's too much management around and they're (the supervisors) scared to death. When management's around they have to produce the maximum they can put out, specially coding. They just pound on you. If we do 18 (i.e.1800) they want you to do 22, if you do 22 they want you to do 24. We only have to do 18, but the more we do the more they want us to do … They stand behind us (St John).

They don't give us credit at all for what we do. It's always something negative. They're always down on us. Never anything positive … I'd like to have someone congratulate me if I've done way above the required 1800, something to boost the old morale. Instead if you do the required amount they come to tell you that you can do more (Halifax).

In the plants when you're finished there's no reward, there's no thank you, there's no "You've done a great job, go and relax" type of attitude. It's "Come on, we've got more work for you to do" (Toronto).

Anybody who works would like to be appreciated (Halifax).

Specific Issues

The workers interviewed complained about harassment over specific issues, including using the washroom, talking, the use of stools, and the rule introduced in May 1988 that does not allow anyone to take a purse or lunch pail from their locker to where they work. On this last point, Post Office management has explained their reasons as the prevention of theft and use of drugs or alcohol in the work place. However, in 1980 a Commission was established to report on security in the Post Office and management never raised the issue of bags at the work station as a problem.[29] Workers complain that the lockers are often some distance from the work station, and women in particular wish to have their personal belongings with them. Just after the rule was introduced 230 workers in Toronto, mostly women, were suspended for one day for insisting on carrying their purses with them.

It was clear that the workers found the rules unnecessary, petty and sometimes absurd, and that they contributed to an oppressive atmosphere in the workplace and animosity between the workers and management. It was also clear that the rules are not consistently enforced and that what may be permissible one week will be a problem the next. The unpredictability seemed to create as much tension as the rules themselves. Several workers expressed annoyance that such rules imply that everyone is guilty and penalize everyone, instead of warning or disciplining those who actually do abuse the use of the washroom, or talk to the detriment of their work, or steal.

We get timed on our bathroom breaks, we have people come up to you, and like you're a grown adult, and they'll say "You were in the bathroom 8 minutes. What were you doing there?" I'm dead serious. And you have the choice of saying "Well, do you want the details, or do want just a general overview, or would you like to attend with me? What exactly is the problem?" They will tell you "You've gone to the bathroom for this many times, for a total of this many minutes. Do you have a medical problem?" And like I've said to my supervisor that I've gone to my doctor and I've told him how much time I spend in the bathroom and he thinks it's normal (Edmonton).

It's so foolish. The supervisor will follow us into the washroom, will tell us not to spend too long. In November a notice was placed in the book saying that we had to ask to leave our work station. Most just go, the majority refuse to ask. It's another petty little way of trying to get at us ... There is some abuse of the

---

[29] Canada, *The Report of the Commission of Inquiry Relating to the Security and Investigation Services Branch Within the Post Office Department*, Ottawa, 1981.

washroom, but those people should be warned, not just penalize everyone (Halifax).

You can be working and talking. I was in City letters and I could sort 50 letters a minute and if I was talking at the same time it was really a big problem. Socializing is a problem, if you're a social person. It doesn't matter how much productivity there is. They find it really disruptive and it really bothers them (Edmonton).

It's around everything. You're always getting harassed about absenteeism, but its work habits, and how long you spend on your break, you know, if you were seen talking to somebody. It's more if it were the wrong person that you were seen talking to than if it was anybody that they didn't really care about. There are certain people who've been targeted as "We'd like to get these people in trouble" so if you're talking to that person, well you're going to get in trouble (St John's).

They (part-time workers) are really watched, even more so I think than the full-timers. They're criticized, they're watched. And then they start to talk and right away there's a supervisor there, "Move your hands, not your mouth" (Edmonton).

Now they won't let us have purses on the floor, which is ridiculous. If a person is going to steal they're going to find a way. I wrote a letter to the superintendent about it, but he never did answer it ... Yet, you can wear an apron with all kinds of pockets. Isn't that stupid? ... But, I carry my purse because I have to have my medication, and I told them, I said "If I don't, if something happens to me, my family will sue you" (Vancouver).

We have to leave them (purses) in the locker, which means they can't be taken to the washroom. It violates a woman's right. We're women. We all have personal belongings that we need to carry with us. How dare the Corporation tell us that we can't? (Halifax)

I believe in human rights. I believe in a minimum of respect for people at work. In October they said no more handbags. That affected women, because in your purse your carry your sanitary napkins, your pocket book, you don't have pockets like a man. I refused to give up my purse because they said it was because of stealing and it doesn't apply to us because we work with the large letters and packets. So I bought a very small purse that attaches to a belt for my eye glasses and my sanitary napkins. I was suspended for one day (Montreal).

I worked ten years standing up in one place. And then when we got the stools, they only got so many and you were allowed to sit only half an hour. Then you had to pass it to somebody else, you know, which was ridiculous. They're still trying to do away with the stools ... Now I have a heart condition so I have to have a stool, so now they don't say nothing (Vancouver).

Every time you go in you wonder what's going to be new today, because the rules change every day. You never have the same rules ... When the small boss has someone at their back they push you, other times you can do whatever you want and they don't care ... I worked for 14 years. We used to walk in, walk out as we wanted. Then the search started. For 10 years there used to be the possibility of wearing a purse on the job, then no purses anymore. At one time no radios, they fired people for radios, but now they don't ... They don't bother people with that anymore ... Recently they decided no more stools. One day they said "No more stools for anyone." So they took the stools out and everyone has to work standing up for 8 hours ... You have women who are 55 or so and some have problems with the standing up (Montreal).

Absenteeism

Absenteeism includes sick leave, leave for injury on the job, unpaid and special leave. The Marchment Report noted that in 1984 absenteeism among employees of the Post Office was twice the average in industry generally at 16.5 days per worker per year. The average for CUPW members specifically was slightly lower at 16 days per year. This figure was composed of sick leave that accounted for 61.7 percent of the total leave, leave without pay at 19.6 percent, injuries on the job at 14.7 percent and special leave at 4.0 percent of the total figure for absenteeism.[30] In 1983–84 the absenteeism rate had been higher, at 19.1 days per employee. The Corporation initiated a National Attendance Strategy to improve the situation and by 1987–88 the rate was down to 14.7 days.[31]

There are several explanations for a higher rate of absenteeism among postal workers than other employees. The rate of injury on the job is high and in 1986–87 3,983 CUPW members were injured on the job, that is one out of every six postal workers. Two-thirds of these injuries were disabling, requiring at least one day, and an average of 17 days, for recovery.[32] There is little doubt that postal workers are subjected to working conditions that combine to produce high rates of illness. Many studies have linked shift work to increased heart disease and digestive disorders, the result of disturbed body rhythms. Corporation data shows that 43 percent of hours worked by CUPW members in 1986 were evening or night shift.[33] Highly automated work, repetitive tasks and noise have all been associated with higher rates of both physical and psychological illness. At the Post Office, night workers, Coders and workers employed in the large automated plants all have higher rates of sick leave than other workers.[34] A detailed study of the physical and psychological health of postal workers in Edmonton drew the following conclusion:

This study of Edmonton postal workers has added to the mounting evidence that stressors in the workplace take a devastating toll on employee health. Our find-

---

[30] Canada Post Corporation, "Report of the Review Committee on the Mandate and Productivity of Canada Post Corporation," Ottawa, November 1985, pp. 30–32.

[31] Canada Post Corporation, *Annual Report*, Ottawa, 1987/88, p. 17.

[32] Canada Post Corporation data, quoted in Canadian Union of Postal Workers, "Final Statement to the Mediator-Arbitrator," 21 June 1988, p. 79.

[33] *Ibid.*, p. 129.

[34] *Ibid.*, pp. 80, 119, 139.

ings clearly emphasize how jobs that are routine, monotonous, mechanized and oppressively supervised create a variety of stress-related physical and psychological health problems for workers.[35]

The union has claimed that the management's drive to reduce absenteeism has involved the harassment of employees for taking legitimate sick leave provided in the collective agreement, widespread refusal of special leave, and increased pressure upon workers. The workers I interviewed supplied many examples of the problems they or their co-workers experienced with sick leave and special leave.

Sick Leave

According to the CUPW contract postal workers may use their accumulated days of sick leave by taking casual sick leave (without producing a medical certificate) of up to 5 days at any one time and up to 10 days in any one year. After this a doctor's certificate must be supplied. A worker must notify the employer as soon as possible of any illness and indicate the likely date of return to work. Because of the problems experienced with sick leave, another clause was added to the most recent contract that states that a worker using leave "shall not be importuned or disciplined" for taking leave, unless it has been established that it was used dishonestly.[36]

> People are constantly being harassed and counselled and suspended and sent for medical assessments ... Recently I was called in again and told that I had already been talked to once. He told me that I had been away x amount of days, and I said check my files because those x amount of days are all medically certified by my doctor (Ottawa).

> Even when you are sick you hate to stay home because you know what you're going to go through when you go back. I mean you get a letter, then you get an interview, then you get sent to the doctor. You feel like you can't be sick anymore (St John).

> They've really been cracking down on special leave or illness or anything. There are people who abuse sick leave and there are people who don't, but even the people who don't are being harassed ... One woman had diagnosed skin cancer and she had a little lump removed and she came into work that night ... She passed in her note to say why she was off the day before and they came back and said "But, was this leave for illness?" (The note was) signed by an MD, and if that's not harassment ... I mean the poor woman had realized she has skin cancer; she doesn't need anything else on top of that ... If you go to a doctor and the doctor gives you leave, it's none of their business, they shouldn't have to know any details. It's enough they require you to go to a doctor (St. John's).

---

[35] Graham S. Lowe and Herbert C. Northcott, *Under Pressure, A Study of Job Stress*, Garamond Press, Toronto, 1986, p. 109.

[36] Canada Post Corporation, "Agreement between Canada Post Corporation and the Canadian Union of Postal Workers," Expires: 31 July 1987, p. 6, Article 5.02.

We had a woman who filled out a grievance ... in regards to being sent to the hospital when she was working on midnights because she had menstrual cramps, and they forced her to go (Winnipeg).

When you are sick you have to let the employer know, and how long you might be off. They say leave your phone number, in case we need to call you. If you say you will be off sick around 5 days, they telephone you every day at home. If you work nights they call you at night, at 12.30 at night. It's incredible (Montreal).

Special Leave

The contract provides that leave with pay "may be granted" in circumstances beyond the control of the employee, "including but not limited to illness in the immediate family." It further states: "Such leave shall not be unreasonably withheld."[37] The refusal by management to grant special leave was a complaint repeated in locals across the country. The question is of particular significance for women who are most often responsible when their children are sick, and it is complicated by the shift and night work involved. The women are expected to have substitute care available for their children in situations that they consider inappropriate. The examples given here are just a selection of cases that became increasingly familiar as the interviews progressed.

We had the case of J., where she phones in, she works the evening shift, her sitter has crapped out on her, she phones into work, "I can't get into work, my babysitter has crapped out on me." Supervisor says "Well, you'd better get in here." She leaves the child at home, alone, and comes into work, because he's intimidated her so totally. And this child is what 4? 6? This was definite neglect. When other workers found out that this was what J. had done, that she'd been intimidated into coming into work, they were furious with her and said "I'm going to report you, that's not legal what you've done." The supervisor, upon hearing that this has happened, instead of sending her home, moves her to another section, takes her away from those nasty co-workers. And this guy's a father, you'd think he'd think "Oh my god a four year old's at home alone, Jesus, go home, I didn't mean for you to do that." No. That is the kind of mentality that we're dealing with (Victoria).

I'm thinking of one in particular. Her son has cancer, leukaemia, and he's only 3 years old and she's been really hassled a lot for missing work ... Her boy's in hospital and she's been getting called from work, saying "When are you coming back?" (Regina)

People are being interrogated for this, people are being told "Well, you've taken special leave three times this year. Is there something wrong with your child? Get it fixed because we're not going to give it to you any more." We have a list of nursing agencies. You can't get a nurse in Edmonton without at least two weeks notice ... They don't take care of anyone under seven years old. You have to apply months in advance to get night care. So, if you are ready to work and walk out the door at 11 o'clock at night and your child has vomited, unless you

---

[37] *Ibid.*, p. 88, Article 21.03.

know someone that can drop everything, like a friend or family member, that can come over and take care of that child ... you stay home with that child. And if that child happens to get sick two times a year, you're in big trouble (Edmonton).

It's terrible. If your child is deathly ill and is at the hospital they say "Well, we'll give you one day, one day, and you can make arrangements to have somebody else." We've gone into them and said "Well who would you suggest go in and hold your child's hand when it's dying and you have to be at work, tell us who you would send." We had the case of a woman whose child was dying of cancer and the woman had a lot of time off, she had used all her sick time, because she was sick, she was sick at heart about the child, and also she was at the hospital night and day. Finally they were counselling her for absenteeism. They said "Well, we gave her one day and now she should be able to delegate somebody." Well, we said "If it was your child who was dying tell us who you would delegate, your mother? your neighbour? phone up somebody and say would you go and sit with her?" (London)

Union Activity

Apart from the various regulations and the level of supervision on the shop floor, many workers commented that the provisions of the collective agreement are regularly ignored or flouted by the management, and that any problem inevitably has to be put through the grievance procedure. In 1984–85 the CUPW filed 20,797 grievances, and more than 6,700 were referred to arbitration.[38] As a result shop stewards often spend a huge amount of time dealing with the problems raised and handling conflict on the work floor, instead of doing their jobs. While this can be interesting and rewarding, it can also be tense and difficult, and it can lead to more attention from management.

An injustice is done and you can't argue with your supervisor, you've got to go through grievance procedures even though they know they're in the wrong. And then a year and a half later, you may not have all the facts written down, things just get tossed out. Things should be settled within two or three weeks (St John's).

It's a good contract, but since there is no penalty for not respecting it, it doesn't give you anything, because the employer goes against it all the time. He says "Make a grievance." Things will come before an arbitrator three years later, and probably it will be too late for changing things (Montreal).

There are a lot of things in the contract that they (management) just totally ignore ... It's an ongoing Corporate policy I think to ignore the contract completely (Toronto).

I have no control over my work. I can't say "OK, tonight I just have to sit here and code, leave me alone." They'll give an emergency suspension to someone and I have to be at the peak of the knowledge and the training and whatever I have, plus be calm and cool and efficient for that person to keep them from

---

[38] Canada Post Corporation, "Report of the Review Committee on the Mandate and Productivity of Canada Post Corporation," Ottawa, November 1985, p. 29.

going hysterical. And you have no control. And they give out 24 hour notices, like 7, 8 a day ... Tonight I just got out of work, a woman was crying hysterically by the time we were finished, and I'd spent an hour with her. And I felt no better myself (Edmonton).

People see the hassle you get on the floor. Anytime that I want to bring up a problem I get hassled by management. If there's a grievance that I want to prepare and investigate for an individual they put it off. They don't address it that day. They don't address it the next day. You have to persist and persist and persist ... People don't want to have to put up with that because they're already putting up with enough (Halifax).

On midnight shift right now they've isolated L., so she has access to less than half a dozen people.
L: I basically deal with my section and that's it. I cannot see anyone else, except on my way to coffee and on my way to lunch, and I make a point of going all the way to the cafeteria and all the way back, because people do talk to me ... I'm still a presence on the shop floor. And while I'm talking to people on the way there and on the way back I have at least three supervisors from the second floor that watch me all the time to see exactly what I'm doing (Edmonton).

It's hard to find people to be stewards because of the intimidation. It used to be that it was safer if you were a steward, management wouldn't dare harass you, but now it's worse (Halifax).

Conclusion

A woman in New Brunswick perhaps summarized best the feelings expressed by so many of the inside postal workers during these interviews.

We're known as a militant union, and I really believe that Canada Post has made us militant. They're the best union builder in Canada, at Canada Post (St John).

9

PAID MATERNITY LEAVE

During the 1970s the CUPW bargained collective agreements that provided for equality between men and women, and between full and part-time workers, without having regarded those provisions as specifically geared to obtaining equality for women. By the late 1970s and into the 1980s this situation was changing as women became a more significant proportion of the membership, and also a more vocal component on concerns of particular importance to women. Women's issues began to arise both at the negotiating table and in relationship to internal union functioning. Several researchers have pointed out that negotiation items of importance to women have often been dropped early in the bargaining process by some unions, given a low priority in the necessary trade-offs that take place.[1] However, this was not the case in the CUPW with regard to paid maternity leave.

In 1981, negotiations between the CUPW and the Treasury Board broke down and a six week strike resulted. One of the central issues was paid maternity leave, and when the union gained 17 weeks of paid maternity leave in the last days of the strike, it became the first national union to obtain that benefit. At the time of these events the CUPW membership was 43 percent women, a significant minority, but still a minority. There were no women on the National Executive Board, nor on the negotiation committee of the union. Why did maternity leave come to be such an important issue in the 1981 round of negotiations, despite the fact that the CUPW was a predominantly male union?

The first section of this chapter describes what happened during the 1981 round of negotiations, including during the strike. Then follows an examination of why the issue of paid maternity leave emerged as a central concern, considering first events external to the union and then factors within the CUPW itself.

Negotiations 1981

Prior to the 1981 collective agreement, a woman CUPW member taking maternity leave was entitled to up to six months leave without pay. While on

---

[1] Joan McFarland, "Women and Unions: Help or Hindrance," *Atlantis*, Vol. 4, No. 2, Spring 1979; Maureen Baker and Mary-Anne Robeson, "Trade Union Reactions to Women Workers and Their Concerns," Katherine Lundy and Barbara Warme, *Work in the Canadian Context. Continuity Despite Change*, Butterworths, Toronto, 1981; Louise Lafortune, "L'égalité des chances dans l'enseignement ... mais pourquoi pas?" *Canadian Woman Studies*, Vol. 6, No. 4, Winter 1985.

maternity leave a woman did not accumulate sick leave or annual leave credits and the employer ceased to pay superannuation contributions. Under the CUPW collective agreement one day of paid leave was provided to men for the birth of a child and one day for the adoption of a child.

Since no paid leave was provided by the employer, the federal Unemployment Insurance (UI) Act was the only recourse for women on maternity leave. At that time under the legislation a woman was entitled to benefits if she had 20 weeks of insurable employment and if she met what came to be known as the "magic 10 rule." This rule required that a woman have worked for 10 weeks between the 30th and 50th weeks prior to the expected date of birth. The purpose of this rule was to ensure that the woman was employed at the time of conception and did not join the labour force once pregnant in order to obtain the benefits. If she met these requirements and following a two week waiting period, a woman could claim benefits of up to 60 percent of her income up to a maximum of $189 per week (in 1981) for 15 weeks.

Since the 1980 agreement expired in December of that year, preparations were underway by the fall of 1980 for the next collective agreement. In the CUPW, regional wage and contract conferences met in each of the four regions to discuss contract demands and forward resolutions to national office. Resolutions could also be sent direct from locals. Then the demands were collected and reviewed by the President and the four National Directors from the four regions. Decisions were made on what to include based on the strength of membership support and experience with previous negotiations and grievances. This draft program of demands was submitted to the National Executive Board (NEB) for approval and was then sent to every member of the union for a ratification vote. By November 1980 the Program of Demands was submitted to the membership, and its contents were approved. The negotiation committee consisted of a member of the National Executive Board who acted as chief negotiator, and a member from each of the four regions appointed by the NEB.

Health and safety was a top priority in this round of negotiations, and the union was seeking the right to refuse dangerous work situations, reduced weight lifting limits and more regular environmental studies, particularly on noise. Under seven other headings the CUPW's proposals included more day time work and less overtime, increased vacations and holidays, increased job security, more protection from unfair disciplinary action, and limitations on the use of closed circuit television cameras. After health and safety and wages, the third section of the Program of Demands was called "Parental Rights and Social Needs." It stated:

> Female postal workers are financially penalized during pregnancy while male postal workers are not permitted sufficient leave to fulfill the family responsibilities which surround child birth. The provision for adoption leave does not even cover the time that is required to be taken at pre-adoption interviews.[2]

---

[2] Canadian Union of Postal Workers, "National Program of Demands," Ottawa, November 1980, p. 7.

To rectify the situation the union was proposing 20 weeks of fully-paid maternity leave; this meant that the employer would pay full wages for two weeks to cover the two week waiting period under the UI Act, then top up the UI benefits to full pay for fifteen weeks and finally pay another three weeks at full wage. The union was also proposing five days paid paternity leave, and five days paid leave for adoption. Another proposition would give an employee the right to take 5 days of personal leave each year at their own discretion. The article in the contract dealing with these issues was to be changed to read "Parental Rights" rather than "Maternity Leave." Parental issues, and particularly paid maternity leave were given an important position at the start of this round of bargaining.

By January the CUPW had already informed its members that since no real bargaining was taking place, a Conciliation Board had been requested. The chair of the Board commented in June that "no real negotiations had taken place during the months previous,"[3] a not uncommon situation under the PSSRA. On maternity leave, the Treasury Board offered its family package that already covered non-union federal government workers, and had also been negotiated into several contracts. Under this package the employer would pay the equivalent of UI benefits for the two week waiting period for which claimants under the UI Act received no benefits. Unpaid leave was offered of up to 26 weeks, which could be taken by either parent, or by adoptive parents (the collective agreement already provided 6 months unpaid maternity leave). Paid paternity and adoption leave were to remain at 1 day each.

The reaction of the union was that this did not constitute proper negotiations. It was not an offer from the employer in response to the CUPW's proposals and arguments, but a pre-determined policy that Treasury Board had established to cover other federal government workers. The CUPW complained: "it is not acceptable for the employer to impose the collective agreement of other groups onto postal workers."[4] At this time the UI Act and its maternity provisions were under review by a government Task Force and the Treasury Board also insisted that it could not pre-empt possible government legislation on the issue by negotiating independent arrangements with the CUPW. The same argument was presented on the health and safety issue. Because the Canadian Labour Congress had held meetings with the government on the health and safety clauses of the Canada Labour Code, Treasury Board argued that it could not negotiate changes in advance of possible legislation. The union was unimpressed, insisting that its members had expressed their needs, the union was there to bargain for them, and that proper negotiations must take place in response to the union demands, unaffected by external circumstances.

While meetings with the employer and the Conciliation Board continued, the union prepared extensive educational material on the issues under dispute, both to inform the members and to obtain support from outside the union. Five Back-

---

[3] Report of the Conciliation Board, Chair Pierre Jasmin, Ottawa, 11 June 1981, p. 5.

[4] Canadian Union of Postal Workers, *CUPW*, January 1981, Vol. 11, No. 1, p. 1.

grounders were produced between February and May 1981, each providing detailed information on different aspects of the union's demands and the justifications for them. These were Health and Safety (February), Reduced Working Time (March), Parental Rights (March), Night Work (April), Noise (April), Accidents and Injuries (May), and Justice, Equality and Dignity (May). The third Backgrounder on Parental Rights was a substantial document of 12 pages. It stated the union's position that child bearing was a social as well as an individual responsibility, that women workers were penalized financially for their role of child bearing and fathers deprived of the opportunity to fully participate.

This document also pointed out how little cost was involved, given that only one percent of the total number of employees took maternity leave each year. For the employer to top up the UI benefits for 15 weeks and provide another 5 weeks at full pay amounted to just 0.25 percent of the payroll, or 2 cents per employee per hour. It was pointed out that a full-time woman postal worker taking 20 weeks maternity leave lost $4,629 in salary under the current arrangements, while a part-timer lost $2,565. The CUPW proposal would eliminate that loss, while under the employer's offer the full-timer would continue to lose $4,251 and the part-timer $2,285. Apart from lost wages, during the six months unpaid maternity leave provided in the current contract, a woman on maternity leave did not accumulate sick leave credits or annual leave credits and lost the employer's share of her superannuation contributions. The Backgrounder pointed out what it called "government hypocrisy," because the federal government had ratified the United Nations Convention on the Elimination of all Forms of Discrimination Against Women, which includes a commitment to introduce paid maternity leave.[5]

The Backgrounder went on to argue that the absence of adequate paternity leave "serves to reinforce sex stereotyping and inequality by placing the major social and family responsibilities which accompany childbirth on the shoulders of the mother."[6] The employer was rejecting any further paid paternity leave than the one day already provided, but the 26 unpaid weeks could be taken by either the father or the mother (minus the maternity leave of the mother, where both worked for the federal government). The union's position was that unpaid leave would benefit only the few who could afford to take it, and that increased paid leave was the critical issue. On adoption leave the Backgrounder argued that one day was inadequate, whereas 5 paid days would at least help with the requirements made by adoption agencies in regard to interviews. Again the employer was offering only unpaid leave, also of up to 26 weeks.

These Backgrounders were sent to all local officers and shop stewards across the country. In May 2,000 copies of the one on parental rights were sent to unions and another 600 to women's groups, with a covering letter explaining the

---

[5] Canadian Union of Postal Workers, "Parental Rights," Negotiations Backgrounder No. 3, Ottawa, March 1981, p. 6.

[6] *Ibid.*, p. 10.

situation and requesting their support. A one page bulletin was sent to every CUPW member announcing "239 Postal Workers Lose $4,629." The bulletin explained that these were women who took maternity leave in 1980. It also outlined the "employer's non-offer" of just $189 for each of two weeks, and how under such a scheme these 239 women would still have lost $4,251 in income.[7]

The Conciliation Board released its report in June, and supported the concept of paid maternity leave. The report commented that "To justify its position the employer systematically took refuge behind policy established by Treasury Board for all government employees." The Conciliation Board agreed that Treasury Board should have a uniform policy but suggested it was time to change "its entire policy and philosophy regarding maternity leave." And further "The Board considers that maternity leave must no longer be a privilege but a legitimate right, an integral part of the process of achieving full equality for all employees."[8] The report did not support the full union demands for 20 weeks maternity leave and 5 days for paternity and adoption leave, but recommended: 17 weeks of maternity leave at full pay, so that the employer would pay two weeks at full pay and then top up the UI benefits for the remaining 15 weeks; a further 9 weeks of unpaid leave to bring the total to 26 weeks of leave; 2 days of paid leave for paternity and adoption. There is no mention in the report of the paid personal leave that appeared in the union's original Program of Demands, and from this point it is dropped as an issue.

With other recommendations from the Conciliation Board the union accepted the report as the basis for further discussions. In particular the report pointed out that injuries to postal workers "far exceed" acceptable standards, and recommended joint health and safety committees, training in health care, investigations and analyses, and the right for postal workers to refuse dangerous working conditions.

The employer refused to accept the report as a basis for further negotiation. With regard to maternity leave the Treasury Board maintained the same position as before and during the Conciliation Board procedure and no further offer was made. The employer's representative on the Conciliation Board produced a minority report that opposed the union's demands, while at the same time attempting to maintain that the government favoured paid maternity leave. François Grégoire wrote: "It is important to state, at the outset, that the Employer is by no means opposed to maternity leave, or even paid maternity leave. The only difference of opinion is over the extent of this remuneration." However, this difference was the critical one, since the principle of unpaid maternity had long since been

---

[7] CUPW, "Negotiations Bulletin," Number 15, 4 May 1981.

[8] Report of the Conciliation Board Report, Ottawa, 11 June 1981, p. 35.

Woman demonstrates
in support of paid
maternity leave,
Ottawa, 1981.

conceded. Grégoire stated clearly: "I am registering my dissent regarding fully-paid maternity leave."[9]

On the question of paternity and adoption leave, Grégoire opposed Jasmin's recommendation for two days paid leave saying "There does not appear to be any justification for this suggestion in view of the provisions found in the private sector."[10] As with previous rounds of negotiations, one of the government's primary considerations was to avoid establishing any precedent, either for other federal public service workers, or for private industry. Later, during the strike the

---

[9] Report of the Employer Representative, Ottawa, 19 June 1981, p. 11.

[10] *Ibid.*, p. 12.

CUPW President expressed his opinion of that concern. Asked about Treasury Board's fear that paid maternity leave would spread to other government workers and then to the private sector, Jean-Claude Parrot responded "What's wrong with that?"[11]

At this point the major outstanding issues for the union were health and safety arrangements, the use of close circuit television cameras in the workplace, vacations, statutory holidays, and paid maternity leave. Since the Treasury Board did not accept the Conciliation Board report as a basis for further bargaining, the union proceeded to hold a strike vote. Eighty four percent of the membership voted in favour, and the strike began on the 29th June. Three days before that date the Treasury Board President, Don Johnston, stated that he had a further offer to make on maternity leave. When it emerged that the offer was to establish a task force to study the question, the strike went ahead as planned.

As the strike progressed the union continued to maintain its pressure around the issues. At the beginning of July, Parrot sent an open letter to all MPs advising them to apply pressure to the Treasury Board to settle the strike, and pointing out how little cost was involved on the outstanding issues. The press picked up on the question of cost and began to call this work stoppage "the 2 percent strike." The combined cost of the outstanding vacation, holiday and maternity leave demands was just 2 percent of the payroll.

Meanwhile support from both unions and the women's movement began to emerge, particularly around the issue of paid maternity leave. The National Action Committee on the Status of Women (NAC) attended a rally in Toronto at the South Central postal plant, and held press conferences in Halifax and Toronto on the issue. NAC also produced a leaflet calling on women to support the strike and was one of the signatories to a pamphlet that listed as supporters many women's groups across the country as well as other unions. There were letters to the press and to the government in support of the concept of paid maternity leave. In some communities the striking CUPW members were joined on the picket line by supporters, both from other unions and from women's organizations. In Ottawa a group of women formed a committee to support the maternity leave demand of the strike and a demonstration was organized in July with posters that suggested "Treasury Board—It's Time To Deliver." It was at this demonstration that Parrot expressed his determination to win paid maternity leave, insisting that it would have to be part of any agreement and stating simply, "We're going to get it." The next day the press announced "Parrot dead set on maternity leave."[12]

A mediator was appointed to attempt to bring the parties together and resolve the outstanding issues. By the 24th July, the twenty fifth day of the strike, there had been some progress on health and safety issues, and the parties had moved

---

[11] Roswitha Guggi and Bert Hill, "Parrot dead set on maternity leave," The Ottawa Citizen, 24 July 1981.

[12] *Ibid.*

on to deal with closed circuit television within the Post Office. Vacations, holiday pay and maternity leave were still outstanding. The union wanted 5 weeks of vacation after 5 years of service instead of after 10 years and a 12th statutory holiday. On maternity leave the union had reduced its demand to 17 weeks of paid maternity leave (in line with the Conciliation Board report), and wanted 2 days paid leave for paternity and for adoption. On the 3rd August the Globe and Mail called paid maternity leave an "unacceptable demand" and suggested that "Treasury Board should reject absolutely the postal workers' demand for paid maternity leave."[13] The Treasury Board did not seem to require such encouragement since the demand for paid maternity leave was still unresolved on this, the 34th day of the strike.

However, over the following week agreement was finally reached. It seemed clear that the Treasury Board was not improving its public image by its stand on the maternity leave issue. The union had received substantial public support and was not isolated as it had been in 1978, when the government had introduced back to work legislation and arrested the union's executive. Moreover, even those who opposed paid maternity leave questioned whether the issue was worth a continued postal strike given the low cost involved. This was not a strike over money, because the CUPW settled for the same wage agreement as the LCUC had obtained in their last round of negotiations, and very little additional cost was involved. In the final agreement the union gained 5 weeks vacation after 8 years rather than after 10 years, but the 12th statutory holiday was not obtained. On maternity leave the seventeen weeks at full pay were obtained, but paternity and adoption leave remained at just one day each. The maternity leave period was included for the calculation of severance pay, vacation leave, and annual increments, and sick leave credits continued to accumulate.

Members of the CUPW returned to work on the 12th August, after 42 days on strike. This was the longest strike ever for the union, along with the 1975 strike which had also lasted for 42 days. Paid maternity leave was gained only during the last few days of the strike. The following discussion considers why the CUPW made paid maternity leave one of the central issues in 1981, looking first at influences outside of the union and then at factors internal to the CUPW.

The Growing Debate on Maternity Leave and Benefits

For 10 years prior to the CUPW strike in 1981 the question of maternity leave and benefits had been receiving increasing attention from the government, from women's organizations and from the public in general. When the UI Act was passed in 1971, maternity leave was included as an incidental part of the package. However, criticism of the provisions was immediate and became increasingly vocal over the following years, one element of the emerging women's movement and its focus upon discriminatory legislation.

---

[13] "Unacceptable Demand," Globe and Mail, 3 August 1981.

Constrained within the context of provisions for unemployment insurance, the maternity benefit provisions presented various anomalies. It was soon discovered that teachers could not receive maternity benefits during the summer because of Section 158 that prevented teachers on summer vacation from applying for unemployment benefits. After three court rulings that Section 158 was null and void, and with other appeals pending, the UI Commission stopped applying this provision to maternity benefits in 1976.[14] Other women found themselves ineligible for all or part of their maternity benefits because of a technicality around the benefit period, or because maternity benefits could be obtained only 8 weeks before and six weeks after the expected week of confinement. Amendments to the UI Act that resolved these difficulties were introduced in 1975 (Bill C–69 and Bill C–16). The latter bill permitted women to claim their 15 weeks at any time within a 26 week period around the birth.[15]

It was not only the UI Act that came under discussion during these years. Women's organizations also criticized provincial legislation on maternity leave. As late as 1976 four provinces and the two territories had no provision for security of employment during maternity leave.[16] Even where this protection existed in law it was not always provided in fact. In 1976 Pacific Western Airlines dismissed on unpaid leave two flight attendants at the start of their fourth month of pregnancy. Over the following two years the two women fought their dismissal through the courts on the basis that they were covered by the Canada Labour Code that supposedly provided them with job protection in the case of pregnancy.[17] This created considerable public discussion on the question of maternity leave, but even more attention was focused on the case of Stella Bliss and her appeal against Section 46 of the UI Act.

Section 46 prohibited a woman from collecting regular UI benefits even if she was eligible, during the period that she would otherwise be eligible for maternity benefits, the assumption being that she would be unavailable for work. Since the requirements for maternity benefits were more stringent than for regular unemployment insurance (the "magic 10 rule" under Section 30) it was possible, as in the case of Bliss, to be ineligible for maternity benefits, eligible for UI, and yet denied regular UI benefits under Section 46. Stella Bliss was ineligible for maternity benefits under Section 30, the "magic 10 rule," and so she applied for unemployment insurance benefits six days after the birth of her child, stating that

---

[14] Elise Robindaine-Saumure, "Maternity Leave and Benefits," Canadian Advisory Council on the Status of Women, Ottawa, May 1976, pp. 12–13.

[15] *Ibid.*, p. 11.

[16] Canadian Advisory Council on the Status of Women, "The Price of Maternity," The Person Papers, Ottawa, 1976, p. 8.

[17] Elise Robindaine-Saumure, "Maternity Leave and Benefits," Canadian Advisory Council on the Status of Women, Ottawa, May 1986, p. 5.

she was available for work. She was denied again because she was ineligible under Section 46. The case finally appeared before the Supreme Court of Canada in June 1978. Although it was lost, there was considerable publicity around the case and pressure from women's groups to amend the legislation. Meanwhile between March 1978 and February 1979 six complaints were laid against the UI Commission under the newly created Canadian Human Rights Commission.[18] The government announced that there would be a review of the UI Act. In the 1981 Report of the Task Force on Unemployment Insurance, maternity benefits were a central concern, and the report recommended the elimination of the "magic 10" rule and Section 46, and the reduction of the 20 week eligibility requirement to the same 10–14 weeks required for unemployment benefits.

Of specific importance to the CUPW situation, the Canadian Advisory Council on the Status of Women had recommended in 1976 that employers be permitted to top up the difference between the UI benefits and the woman's regular wage.[19] This process had been possible under the Supplementary Unemployment Benefits Plan (SUB) since the legislation had been introduced, but only in conjunction with coverage for illness and temporary lay-off as well. Since few employers were prepared to cover their workers for the more expensive temporary lay-off very few SUBs had been negotiated. In 1978 the regulations were altered, allowing SUBs to cover just maternity leave. By 1981 there were 1,241 of these arrangements in existence, of which the large majority, 1,220, covered only payments for maternity.[20]

Thus, for several years prior to the CUPW strike, maternity leave and benefits had been receiving considerable public attention. At the same time, the question had been taken up by several unions. The SUB arrangement had largely been negotiated by small groups of employees, often at universities, until 1979 when there was a major breakthrough in Quebec. The Common Front, representing government, education and health workers in Quebec negotiated 20 weeks of maternity leave at full pay, plus 10 weeks of paid adoption leave, and five paid days for paternity leave. This collective agreement covered 20 percent of all employed women in the province of Quebec.[21]

This achievement in Quebec prompted action by a group of federal public service workers, thereby bringing the issue much closer to the situation of the CUPW. The Canadian Union of Professional and Technical Employees (CUPTE)

---

[18] Leslie A. Pal, "Maternity Benefit and Unemployment Insurance: A Question of Policy Design," *Canadian Public Policy*, Vol. 11, No. 3, September 1985, p. 557.

[19] Canadian Advisory Council on the Status of Women, "Maternity Leave, Benefits and Related Issues, ACSW Recommendations," Ottawa, 22 September 1976, p. 4.

[20] Leonard Shifrin, "Maternity Benefits: Who Pays?" The Ottawa Citizen, 19 August 1981.

[21] Julie White, *Women and Unions*, Canadian Advisory Council on the Status of Women, Ottawa, 1980, pp. 112–113.

represents government translators, that in 1980 were a group of 1,150 workers, about 55 percent women and over 80 percent Quebecois. Prompted by the benefit obtained in Quebec, and within the context of a socially progressive union, paid maternity leave was one of CUPTE's demands for the translators in their 1980 round of negotiations. The Treasury Board rejected this demand and was also refusing any increase in salary. As a result the translators were on strike for six weeks in the fall of 1980. The government remained determinedly opposed to paid maternity leave and the translators did not win their demand.[22] However, supporters from the CUPW national office in Ottawa had discussed the situation with CUPTE and walked their picket lines in support. Parrot later pointed out: "Postal workers have to thank government translators for putting paid maternity leave on the public agenda as a result of their strike. They did not win it, but they provided the momentum and the focus we needed."[23]

Maternity Leave in the CUPW

The first time that paid maternity leave appeared among the bargaining demands of the CUPW was in 1977. At that time there was a generally stated proposal for "fully-paid maternity leave," which was never made more specific and was not a priority issue.[24] This was the round of negotiations that resulted in a legal strike, back to work legislation, 3 months in prison for the union President, and an imposed contract. Under the arbitral award Judge Tremblay did increase unpaid maternity leave from 17 weeks to 6 months.

In the 1980 Program of Demands unpaid leave was described as inadequate and a general demand was made for paid maternity leave, but again it never was translated into a more detailed demand and was not a priority issue in the negotiations. However, it was the subject of "long discussions" before the Conciliation Board, which nonetheless rejected the demand for paid maternity leave on the basis that it was the responsibility of Parliament to decide the issue through legislation, and that negotiated provisions were still exceptional.[25]

By the 1981 negotiations the situation had changed. Public awareness and discussion of the issue had increased and a government Task Force had been appointed to study the UI provisions. The demand for paid maternity leave from the members was stronger, arriving at head office from several areas of the country, and the CUPTE strike galvanized the leadership to focus more attention

---

[22] Information obtained from Michel Dubois, Canadian Union of Professional and Technical Employees, Ottawa, 14 June 1989.

[23] Address by Jean-Claude Parrot, National President, Canadian Union of Postal Workers, at a conference on Work and the Quality of Family Life, Toronto, 26 April 1982, p. 6.

[24] Canadian Union of Postal Workers, "Negotiations '77," Submission by the CUPW to the Conciliation Board, Ottawa, 10 April 1978, p. 99.

[25] Report of the Conciliation Board, Ottawa, 2 May 1980, p. 35.

on the question. Parrot describes the situation as a gut feeling that the time was right to insist upon that particular demand.[26] Consequently, the demand was formulated more specifically as 20 weeks paid maternity leave, plus 5 days paternity and adoption leave, and it appeared as a high priority in the Program of Demands.

This commitment increased as the negotiations progressed. The negotiating team was involved in preparing the Backgrounder on Parental Rights, reviewing the document and discussing the issues. Their support for the demand increased as their understanding grew, and as a result they were more able to discuss the issue with members and argue its importance at local membership meetings across the country. At the same time it quickly became clear that paid maternity leave was an issue that everyone wanted to discuss. It drew public and media attention, often to the virtual exclusion of the other demands under negotiation. Whatever their opinion everyone wanted to discuss paid maternity leave and the union's position on it.

During negotiations, when the cost of the benefit was analyzed, that also became an important factor. The cost was so minimal that it was simply not an argument that it was too expensive, or that this was something the government could not afford. As well, the union negotiating team was unimpressed with the Treasury Board's argument that it must not pre-empt possible government action on the issue. The argument that no precedent must be set for other government departments had been used in many rounds of negotiation. The CUPW position remained what it had always been; their members had expressed a desire for this benefit, they were in negotiations, and that meant discussing the issue with them, not avoiding the issue because of factors entirely external to the bargaining table.

The union's educational work, documentation and determination on the issue were influential before the Conciliation Board. At this point the provisions obtained by the Common Front in Quebec became important in arguing the case. Paid maternity leave was a central demand for the CUPW and the union was unlikely to have dropped the issue even if the Board's report had opposed the demand. However, the fact that the report supported paid maternity leave, albeit in somewhat reduced form, was clearly a boost to the negotiations. The CUPW had a tradition of insisting upon obtaining at least the proposals of the Conciliation Board.

However, while paid maternity leave was generally supported by the membership as a demand, it was a lot more controversial as a strike issue. In almost all the 14 locals where interviews were conducted for this study, paid maternity leave was described as a difficult, contentious issue. There was a lot of opposition to a strike over paid maternity leave, a lot of argument and debate and difficult discussions. Men complained that there was nothing in this for them and that it was discriminatory, older women felt that they had managed without it and

---

[26] Interview with Jean-Claude Parrot, National President of the Canadian Union of Postal Workers, Ottawa, 1 June 1989.

that young women wanted everything, and even some young women did not support it, feeling as one woman expressed it that it was "a nice benefit" if you could get it, but "ludicrous" to be out on strike over it.

Some of the opposition is understandable given the plain economics of the situation. It was not a major benefit, given that it was a top up to the UI benefits already provided to most women on maternity leave, and it affected fewer than 250 CUPW members for only a short period of time. For this, 23,000 workers were to lose their pay for a period of six weeks. It is one thing to see a demand as a worthwhile benefit to try and bargain for; it is another thing to be prepared to go on strike and lose pay over it. From the interviews it also became clear that although paid maternity leave was a demand, in most locals there had not been any strong demand for the benefit, no groundswell of pressure for this benefit. It had not even received attention from active women within the union, and it had not been raised as an issue of importance to women. Almost everyone I interviewed said that they had been surprised when this demand had become so central.

Nonetheless, once it was on the agenda many women and some men were fully supportive and worked hard to discuss the arguments around it with the members, to explain why it was important. As one woman explained it, the debates and discussions started at local meetings and carried over onto the picket lines once the union was on strike. Many of those interviewed expressed considerable pride in their union that they had managed to obtain the benefit and pave the way for other unions to follow. One woman felt that the national officers and the negotiating team had been "courageous" to press the demand as a strike issue, given the controversy it was likely to unleash.

The negotiating team was aware that it would not be an easy issue, because it affected only a small number of members and minority issues are never easy. However, the CUPW had some experience bargaining for minority groups, including part-time workers, mail handlers, Coders, and night workers. Parrot explained:

> If you want to succeed to make a breakthrough, and if you want to succeed to represent the minorities you have to convince the majority to fight for them. And obviously that means mixing issues. You don't just go with one issue. The role of the leaders is to ensure that if you have to go out on strike then the issues will get the strike mandate out there.[27]

There could not have been a strike over just paid maternity leave because it would not have been crucial enough to sufficient members to obtain the necessary support. However, the strike also involved health and safety demands, the use of closed circuit television, vacations and statutory holidays, issues that affected most or all of the members.

---

[27] Interview with Jean-Claude Parrot, National President of the Canadian Union of Postal Workers, Ottawa, 1 June 1989.

The CUPW was actually hampered in this mixing of issues by the media. Paid maternity leave became the focus of news reports to the extent that CUPW members felt that it was the only issue in dispute. In interviews across the country it was mentioned repeatedly that newspaper reports had angered members because they demanded to know why they were on strike over just that one issue. It was a problem for the leadership, both locally and nationally, throughout the strike, to communicate effectively with the members that paid maternity leave was not the only issue. At the same time it was seen as an educational process, an opportunity to discuss the question of maternity leave and women at work. The dynamic of the situation is captured in the following comments from the CUPW's National Director for the Western Region:

> There was a lot of shouting and yelling from inside the union, "What the hell am I on strike for—maternity leave?" We overcame that ... We just had drag it out, beat it out discussions and we were more determined than they were. And I think it bears the fruit today. It wasn't an easy task, but I wasn't going to back down from anybody on the issue. And as we went along we convinced those that weren't convinced, and the momentum swayed ... That was just another segment of the educational process on the rights of women and the problems of women. It woke a lot of people up ... It was a big hurdle we had to jump. Because at one point it got to the stage where they were even saying, "We're not staying out for maternity leave." They were focusing the whole issue, whether it be rightly or wrongly, on maternity leave and we would say "Well, maternity leave is one issue, here are the other issues, and in the process you're wrong in your stance on maternity leave."[28]

Conclusion

While paid maternity leave was a demand that emerged from the CUPW membership, it did not become a central issue in the 1981 negotiations because of a strong groundswell of membership support, either from the members in general or from women in particular. The importance of the issue in the initial negotiations was related more to the commitment of the union's leadership and their recognition that paid maternity leave was a demand likely to muster public support and therefore create pressure on the government to provide the benefit. Thus, the attention focused on the issue by women's organizations over the previous ten years was important in creating a climate in which such a struggle would be successful.

The union leadership saw the opportunity that had been created and was prepared to take advantage of it, despite the fact that it might be controversial among their own members. It was important that the CUPW had a tradition of being a generally progressive union, concerned with broad social issues rather than just the more narrow concern of wages and strictly work-related benefits. Also the union, both leadership and members, had experience with minority

---

[28] Interview with Pat Miller, CUPW National Director for the Western Region, Ottawa, 20 October 1988.

issues, that is issues that affect only a small proportion of the total membership. The leadership knew that this demand must be linked to others that were of a more general concern, and they knew it would be necessary to explain the importance of the issue to their members. Consequently, the contention among the members was met with bulletins, meetings and discussions on the issue. The controversy was regarded as a useful opportunity for debate and education, rather than a reason to drop the demand.

At this point it was critical that local activists, including many women, supported the issue and were prepared to meet the members' criticisms and concerns once the demand had become more central. In the final analysis paid maternity leave was obtained because the members of the CUPW were prepared to stay on strike despite the disagreement and questioning. There is no doubt that without a strike paid maternity leave would not have been obtained.

Since 1981 the CUPW has bargained other provisions of particular importance to women. In the most recent contract that expired July 1989, paid adoption leave was equivalent to the paid maternity leave, which remained at 17 weeks at full pay. Unpaid leave had been expanded to 24 weeks following the paid leave and was available to either the mother or the father, adoptive or natural. This contract also contained provision for a joint management-union study of child care as a basis for future negotiations on the subject, a complicated issue within the CUPW because of the shift work.

The insistence upon equality that marked the CUPW negotiations in the 1970s carried over into successful bargaining around specifically women's concerns in the 1980s. The reasons include the impact of the broader debate on women's issues raised by the women's movement, the increased proportion of women within the bargaining unit translated into negotiation demands of concern to women, the generally forward-thinking nature of the union on social questions and in regard to minority issues, and the dynamic relationship between progressive leaders and a militant membership. The following chapter turns from negotiations with the employer to examine how the CUPW has responded to women's concerns on issues internal to the union.

WOMEN'S ISSUES INSIDE THE UNION

A s with other unions, women's issues in the CUPW have arisen not only in relation to the collective agreement and negotiations with the employer, as in the case of paid maternity leave, but also on questions related to the internal structure and functioning of the union. Extended debates have occurred within the CUPW on women's committees, sexual harassment, child care for union meetings, and education. Before analyzing the union's reactions to these concerns, it is important first to look at the participation of women in the union, comparing their proportion within the general membership to their participation at union conventions, and looking at how many women have become union officers at the local, regional and national levels.

Women's Participation in the Union—Facts and Figures

The most recent data available on membership in the union is for 1987. For that year the total number of union members was 23,947 while the number of women members was 10,209, that is almost 43 percent.[1] Table 9 shows the number of women participating in the union, as members, as local presidents, as delegates and speakers at National Convention, and as full-time union officers at the local, regional and national levels.

With women membership in the union at 43 percent, it is clear that the participation of women in the union is not equivalent to their proportion of the membership, whether assessed by participation at Conventions or election to official positions within the union. It is interesting to note that although women comprised 28 percent of the delegates to the 1986 National Convention, they constituted less than 15 percent of the speakers, indicating that the presence of women at such events does not necessarily ensure that their voice is heard.

The table indicates that the participation of women declines the higher the position within the union. While women were over 33 percent of local presidents, they comprised only 29 percent of the full-time paid presidents of locals, and less than 17 percent of the full-time elected officials of the union at the regional and national levels. Of the 5 women in positions above the local level, one sat on the five-member National Executive Board, one was a National Union

---

[1] Data obtained from Statistics Canada, Corporations and Labour Unions Returns Division, Ottawa, for 1987.

TABLE 9: Women's Participation in the Union			
	Total	*No. Women*	*% Women*
Members, 1987	23,947	10,209	42.6
Delegates to National Convention, 1986	279	79	28.3
Speakers at National Convention, 1986	1,109	164	14.8
Local Presidents, as of October, 1988*	188	63	33.5
Full-time Local Officers, as of 1986	24	7	29.2
National/Regional Officers, 1986	30	5	16.6

* *Note:* Excludes 4 locals where the presidents were not identified.
SOURCE: Statistics Canada, data for 1987 supplied by Corporations and Labour Unions Returns Act Division, Ottawa: Canadian Union of Postal Workers, *National Convention 1986, Proceedings*, Ottawa, 7–11 April 1986; Canadian Union of Postal Workers, "Report of the National Secretary-Treasurer," Presented to the 16th Triennial Convention, Ottawa, 7–11 April 1986, pp. 1, 12; Canadian Union of Postal Workers, computer printout of local presidents, 11 October 1988.

Representative, and the remaining three worked at the regional level, one in the West, one in the Atlantic and one in Ontario.

The participation of women as presidents of locals deserves a little more attention, since there was a striking variation between the four regions of the union. Table 10 shows the proportion of women as local presidents, as well as the percentage of women members of the union for each of the four regions.

Comparing the percentage of women CUPW members in each region to the percentage of women presidents of locals, there is a clear difference between the West and the Atlantic on the one hand and Quebec and Ontario on the other. In both the Western and Atlantic regions there is actually a higher proportion of women presidents than there are members of the union. In the West this is very slight, with 54 percent of the membership women and 55 percent of the presidents women. In the Atlantic it is more pronounced with women at 27 percent of the total membership, while 31 percent of the local presidents are women.

The situation in Ontario and Quebec is quite different, for in both of those provinces the proportion of women local presidents is less than half the proportion of women members of the union. In Ontario women are almost 46 percent of the membership, but less than 22 percent of the local presidents. In Quebec while women comprise 28 percent of the union membership, they constitute only 13 percent of the local presidents in that region. Differences between the regions will be referred to again in the discussion that follows.

TABLE 10: Local Presidents by Sex and Region for 1989, and the Percentage of Women in the CUPW by Region for 1987

	Total No. Presidents	No. Women Presidents	% Women Presidents	% Women in CUPW
West	66	36	54.5	53.5
Ontario	60	13	21.7	45.7
Quebec	30	4	13.3	28.1
Atlantic	32	10	31.3	27.2
Total*	188	63	33.5	42.6

* *Note:* Four locals, one from each region, are excluded because the presidents were not identified.
SOURCE: Canadian Union of Postal Workers, computer printout of local presidents, 11 October 1988; Statistics Canada, data on membership by region supplied by Corporations and Labour Unions Returns Act Division, 1987.

Some of the information on the participation of women in the union is comparable, or partially comparable, over time. The proportion of women members within the union has remained stable since 1980, hovering between 41 and 43 percent over those years.[2] Meanwhile there has been an increase in the participation of women in union activities. As Table 11 shows, the proportion of women delegates, of women speakers and of women elected as regional or national officers all increased from the 1980 to the 1986 Conventions. There is no information on the change in the number of local presidents over time.

Women's Issues Within the Union

Beginnings

The first National Convention of the CUPW, with the new name and the right to negotiate took place in 1968. At that time women were 12 percent of the membership and over the three day Convention two women spoke. Miss Jones, a part-time worker from Vancouver, was introduced as a "fraternal delegate" and spoke on the support of the part-timers for the union. An unidentified woman from Montreal rose to express her support of this position.[3]

By the time of the 1971 National Convention the proportion of women members had leaped to over 21 percent. In the Convention proceedings women were

---

[2] Statistics Canada, *Corporations and Labour Union Returns Act*, Part II—Labour Unions, Cat.71–202, Ottawa, 1980–1986.

[3] Canadian Union of Postal Workers, *Tenth Triennial Convention Proceedings*, Montreal, 27–29 May 1968, p. 352.

TABLE 11: Percentage of Women Delegates, Speakers and Elected Officers at CUPW National Conventions, 1980, 1983 and 1986

	1980	1983	1986
% Women Delegates	22.6	-	28.3
% Women Speakers	10.3	12.1	14.8
% Elected Officers	0.0	10.0	16.6

SOURCE: Canadian Union of Postal Workers, *National Convention Proceedings*, Ottawa, 1980, 1983, 1986.

identified as "female delegates" and during the six day event they spoke on seven occasions. Their interventions were largely confined to two issues. The first was a resolution to support the *Report of the Royal Commission on the Status of Women* that had been published the previous year. The Resolutions Committee recommended rejection of the resolution, but a woman delegate rose to explain that the Report was "just a recognition of the basic rights of all women."[4] After a brief discussion, the Committee's recommendation was defeated and the resolution was passed. Perhaps motivated by this success, a woman delegate rose to propose an emergency resolution on pensions that would equalize contributions for men and women and provide improved protection for widows. It was passed without opposition.[5]

The Proceedings of the 1974 National Convention do not indicate whether the delegates speaking were male or female and no issues arose of particular importance to women. However, for the first time a woman appeared as an invited speaker, Maria Elena Serna, representing the United Farmworkers of America. Also a woman delegate rose to complain to Joe Davidson, the President and chair, that he kept referring to "brother this and brother that" but she was a delegate as well and a "sister delegate."[6] Indeed, the language of this Convention

---

[4] Canadian Union of Postal Workers, *National Convention 1971, Proceedings*, Calgary, 31 May–5 June 1971, p. 1108.

[5] *Ibid.*

[6] Canadian Union of Postal Workers, *National Convention 1974, Proceedings*, Quebec, 3–8 June 1974, p. 799.

was decidedly male-orientated, with references to hiring "men," the "men" needed for the job and "I'll take the men out" in the case of a strike.[7]

Outside of Conventions other developments were taking place. The national journal was re-established in 1971 and there began to appear indications that more women were becoming involved in the union. Jacquie Horkey was the full-time Secretary-Treasurer of the Vancouver local, the third largest in the country, and congratulations appeared in 1971 when she also became a member of the Executive of the British Columbia Federation of Labour.[8] Announcements of elections to local executives began to indicate that women were becoming increasingly involved at the local level.[9] Sexist cartoons were printed sporadically in the journal, but the last one appeared in September 1973.[10]

By the 1977 Convention women were 39 percent of the union membership and this was the first National Convention at which women's issues were raised in earnest. It was the first Convention at which resolutions were debated that related directly to the status of women within the union. A resolution from the Atlantic region proposed a new clause in the Constitution to state that wherever masculine terms were used the feminine was also included. This passed with no opposition after one delegate pointed out that during the strike "women 'womanned' the picket line, they didn't man it, they 'womanned' it with their kids."[11] Although no further resolutions appeared on the topic, following the 1980 National Convention the revised Constitution was drawn up using male and female alternatives (his/her, etc.) throughout. However, the collective agreement continues to use he/his throughout with a disclaimer that this applies also to women.

From the Western region came a far more controversial resolution to the 1977 Convention, suggesting that a room be set aside at all conferences and conventions for a women's caucus. Also an emergency resolution was presented on the floor of the Convention proposing that the National Executive "include in their education program policies pertaining to the further involvement of women at all levels of the Union" and "recognize the right of women to organize women's committees at all levels of the union." The resolutions committee recommended rejection of both resolutions and the majority of delegates agreed. A woman delegate complained "you're begging for favours for crying out loud" because if women wanted to get involved in the union they just had to get out and do it. Another woman delegate stated: "we work with our brothers, we stand with them

---

[7] *Ibid.*, pp. 379, 745–750.

[8] Canadian Union of Postal Workers, *CUPW*, Vol. 1, No. 2, November 1971.

[9] *Ibid.*, Vol. 2, No. 1, April 1972.

[10] *Ibid.*, Vol. 7, No. 9, September 1973, p. 3.

[11] Canadian Union of Postal Workers, *Thirteenth Triennial Convention, Proceedings*, Halifax, 25–29 June 1977, p. 232.

on the picket line, we work under the same contract for the same boss and why do we need separate education." The issue was not regarded as significant by some delegates because someone had to protest: "Rather than laughing and sneering as if it's some big joke, Union members should take it very seriously."[12]

From Vancouver, where the resolutions had originated, the delegates argued that there were proportionately fewer women at the Convention, at the national office and in the larger locals, that this needed to be dealt with, and that the purpose of the resolutions was to encourage the participation of women in the union. Despite the defeat of the resolutions, in one sense the delegates who had argued in favour had the last word:

> We're putting our heads in the sand if we think we can just glibly say women are equal and that's all there is to it. It's ignoring the reality of the world around us and at some point in time we're going to have to face up to it.[13]

At the 1980 National Convention and from that point on the delegates had to face up to a flood of resolutions on topics of concern to women and far more vigorous and extensive debates on the issues. These issues included women's committees and caucuses, sexual harassment, child care at union meetings, and union education. The reactions within the union to each of these issues will be examined in the following sections.

Women's Committees and Caucuses

The first women's committee to be formed within the CUPW started in the Vancouver local in 1976.[14] There had been a series of incidents involving women who finished work at 1 a.m., including a purse snatching and an attempted rape. The committee organized a meeting with a speaker on rape, and later planned a course on self-defense which did not materialize. The Committee lasted only a few months at this point, but was resuscitated two years later.

From 1978 on the Vancouver women's committee organized within their own local to encourage women's participation, developed and taught a course on sexual harassment for shop stewards, held a course on self-defense, worked on the issue of abortion and were involved in the local events for International Women's Day. They also discussed their concerns with other women within the Western region, proposed resolutions at the local and then regional levels, and worked to educate the members in preparation for the debates. Many of the resolutions on women's questions that have appeared on the floor of National Conventions have originated from the Vancouver local.

---

[12] *Ibid.*, pp. 1015–1020.

[13] *Ibid.*, p. 1017.

[14] All information on specific locals provided in this chapter was obtained from interviews with members of those locals, conducted October 1988 to May 1989.

Between the 1977 and the 1980 National Conventions the climate had changed. The growing impact of the women's movement and further development on women's issues within the general trade union movement had wrought some changes in attitude. Within the CUPW, women now comprised almost 44 percent of the membership, the Vancouver local women's committee was reconstituted and stronger than before, and in other regions of the country, particularly in the Atlantic provinces, developments had taken place with regard to women's issues. For the first time the Report of the National President to the Convention commented on the status of women. It noted that nearly one-half of the members of the union were women, and concluded: "Over the years the Union has done a good job of representing them, but there is still much to be achieved."[15]

In response to a resolution calling for a caucus at National Conventions, the National Executive Board organized an evening session on women's issues. It was separate from the regular Convention, but chaired by the President of the CUPW like the rest of the Convention, and it was open to both men and women. It did not involve resolutions, but was an open discussion of problems of importance to women. The discussion included the lack of child care for union meetings, the lower participation of women in positions of power, sexual harassment, the absence of education on women's questions, the union's insufficiently serious approach to these concerns, and the need for women's committees as a forum to discuss all these issues. Both men and women took part in the debate, and although there was some opposition, the majority of participants were agreed that action was needed to deal with the points raised.[16]

On the floor of the general Convention there was less agreement. The resolution proposing that a women's caucus be held at all National Conventions was debated. The Resolutions Committee recommended rejection, commenting: "We felt that this would discriminate against men and also other groups such as the handicapped, or the deaf, or any other group. We recommended rejection so that the Convention would not consist of a multitude of caucuses without any unity." Delegates opposed to the resolution argued that women did not need separate meetings because they were equal within the union, that such arrangements would only isolate or ghettoize women, and that equality is created by participation in the union, not by caucuses. One delegate said: "I do not want to be isolated because I am a woman. This Union never said that women should not be involved in its work. If the women in the locals of any region want to be involved in this Union, there is nothing to hold them back." And another: "This is equality: right here, right now ... We do not need separate meetings. If there are any problems get them out here and now."[17]

---

[15] Canadian Union of Postal Workers, "Report of the National President," Presented to the 1980 National Convention, Ottawa, 28 July–1 August 1980, p. 46.

[16] Canadian Union of Postal Workers, *National Convention 1980, Proceedings*, Ottawa, 28 July–1 August 1980, Women's Caucus, Evening Session, 29 July 1980.

[17] *Ibid.*, pp. 198–200.

Those in favour of the resolution pointed out that in some unions there had been women's committees for many years, that the British Columbia Federation of Labour had withstood a women's committee for a full ten years without signs of collapse, and that when women became more involved in the union it was strengthened, not weakened. One woman complained about all the noise during the debate of this resolution and asked, if women were really considered equal within the union, would it be possible for the delegates to regard this issue no less seriously than others. One male delegate pointed out that this was a trade union convention, that some delegates were expressing a problem and that it should be dealt with and resolved just as if a union member came to a shop steward with a complaint:

> I think anybody here that is a trade unionist should take all these complaints seriously and help these women as much as they can to try and solve their problems in their own way. It is only following trade union philosophy to do so … As trade unionists, when your brothers and sisters come to you with a problem, you deal with it. You do not tell them that you do not understand.[18]

The majority of delegates did not agree and the resolution was rejected.

Women's meetings were the cause of further heated debate three years later at the 1983 National Convention. One resolution from the Atlantic region called for support and encouragement for women's committees at all levels within the union, plus a women's caucus at National Conventions. The Constitution Committee dealing with the resolutions recommended the adoption of a meeting at National Conventions. However, the suggestion for women's committees in locals was excluded because there had been such strong opposition within the Committee, again on the grounds that there were many groups that might wish to have separate meetings. The resolution as it appeared therefore constituted a compromise, enabling the Committee to recommend adoption rather than rejection. A second resolution, this time from the Vancouver local, proposed to add women's issues committees to the list of committees in the Constitution that were to be established in the locals. On this the Committee recommended rejection.

Much of the debate echoed that of three years earlier. Those against argued that women were already equal, that meetings behind closed doors were divisive, and that it was not a question of women's rights but of workers' rights, since the issues affected everyone. "There are no men, or no women in this Union, we are workers, one solid entity."[19] Those in favour argued that women's meetings would open up the discussion instead of keeping it behind closed doors, that these problems would remain women's issues unless they could be raised and thereby become everyone's concern, and that talk of equality was fine, but what

---

[18] *Ibid.*, p. 205.

[19] Canadian Union of Postal Workers, *National Convention 1983, Verbatim Report*, Ottawa, 2–6 May 1983, p. 257.

about reality, since women had yet to obtain full equality in society and in the workplace. One delegate stressed: "There has to be some movement in our union towards addressing the issues of women workers ... We, as a union, are far behind many other unions and organizations on this matter."[20] Despite these arguments, the resolutions both for the caucus and for the women's committees were defeated.

These resolutions were raised within the context of changes to the union's Constitution, always dealt with first at CUPW Conventions. Another method of raising issues was through the union's general policies—statements of the union's position on various matters. However, since 1977 the National Conventions had failed to deal with the policies of the union because of lack of time, and there were no union policies on any women's issues. In 1980 many policy resolutions, including those on sexual harassment, child care, and equal rights for women had failed to reach the Convention floor. In 1983 the Western region presented a group of resolutions containing a thorough coverage of union policies, reorganizing those previously adopted up to 1977 under general headings and adding many new ones, including a comprehensive package on women's issues. There were also several resolutions from the Atlantic region covering some of the same issues of concern to women. Again the majority of policy resolutions were not dealt with, even though a second Convention was called to try to complete the work. At the close of the second Convention a motion was passed referring all the outstanding resolutions to the National Executive Board.

The Board proceeded to draw up an extensive list of policies, based upon the outline from the Western region. Under the heading "Social Issues" are policies on many questions of concern to women, including support for 9 months paid parental leave, 24-hour universal non-profit child care, equal pay, access to non-traditional jobs, and lesbian and gay rights, as well as opposition to violence against women, sexual harassment and limitations upon abortion. Also included is a statement that the union encourages the formation of committees at a local level to develop more awareness of women's issues.[21] Thus, although there is no requirement to establish women's committees within the Constitution, there is a statement of support for those who might wish to form one. The policies are attached to the union Constitution and are therefore distributed to every member of the union.

In 1986 no resolutions appeared on the floor of the Convention on the topic of women's meetings and consequently there has been no further debate of this issue at this level in the union. An ad hoc women's caucus was held during the Convention. A group of women decided that they wished to discuss issues with other women and asked the union President to announce the time and place, which was done. Marion Pollack, then Vice-President of the Vancouver local,

---

[20] *Ibid.*, p. 530.

[21] Canadian Union of Postal Workers, "National Constitution Adopted 1986," National Policies Adopted at the National Convention, pp. 17–20.

chaired the meeting and the 44 women and men present discussed various issues, including the resolutions specific to women's concerns that were to appear before the Convention. There were plans to continue to keep in touch through a newsletter, but nothing further was done.

In summary, the CUPW has a statement of support for the development of local committees to deal with issues of concern to women. Such committees are not identified as "women's" committees and are, like other committees, open to all members, men as well as women, an arrangement that has caused difficulty in some locals. There is no other committee, caucus or convention for women in the union.

At the time of writing there are some women's committees within the union, although this no longer includes Vancouver. The Vancouver women's committee declined in 1983 for various reasons. Some of the women were tired and burnt out, while others had taken on active positions within the union and did not have time for additional meetings. As well, the situation within the union changed and other issues became more pressing as the Crown Corporation pushed towards privatization and the question of job security became of paramount importance. Despite the lack of a formal women's committee there has continued to be a group of active women within the Vancouver local who have raised issues and made their presence felt, not only locally, but also at the regional and national levels.

There has been a women's committee in Winnipeg since 1985, first inspired by the successful push to obtain improved washrooms and lockers for women working in the transfer section. Transfer is the section where the mail trucks arrive to be unloaded, the work is heavy and relatively dirty, and it has traditionally been a job done by men, Mail Handlers and Dispatchers. The women's committee has existed since 1985, though meeting only as the need arises. The committee has presented a course on sexual harassment to shop stewards, has looked into the question of child care for local meetings, and has worked to inform other women's committees and groups of the detrimental impact of privatization upon women postal workers. This committee is established under the formal constitutional provisions of the union and includes both men and women, which according to the women involved, has not proved to be a problem. The local president (male) has supported the women's committee.

In Toronto an initial attempt to establish a women's committee was derailed because of the involvement of men, who did not take the issues seriously and undermined the meetings. Another committee had just recently been established at the time of my interviews at the end of 1988, and this time only women were involved. This committee was just beginning to discuss its agenda.

In Montreal an effort was made to organize a women's committee in 1982, and a group of women met over a period of three months to discuss issues and gain support. However, the resolution to formally establish a committee met with concerted opposition from the local president (male) and executive, and was consequently defeated at the union's local meeting. The women involved were scandalized by the tactics used and some of them no longer participate in the union.[22] There has been no further effort to establish a women's committee in Montreal.

In the Atlantic region a women's committee has been formed on an ad hoc basis at the regional level, and has received support and encouragement from the male officers at the union's regional office. The committee draws women from across the maritime provinces, who meet at regional educationals and do so separately from men, despite some negative comments. The committee has discussed a wide range of concerns for women, has provided education on sexual harassment at the regional meetings, has encouraged increased participation from women at the educationals, and was in the process of organizing a trip by CUPW women members to Nicaragua. The committee was planning to press for formal recognition from the National Executive of the union and to request a budget to facilitate activities.

Sexual Harassment

Sexual harassment at the workplace is a difficult issue for unions to handle because it is not only supervisors who harass workers, but also other workers. The difficulty is partly a practical one concerning how a union prevents harassment when it is required to represent both the victim and the harasser as union members. It is also a contentious issue because union members are expected to be united in obtaining improved working conditions, not themselves contributing to an uncomfortable workplace atmosphere. Since men are most commonly the harassers and women the victims, sexual harassment is a problem that not only affects women differently, but also recognizes a source of conflict between men and women workers.

There were three resolutions on sexual harassment sent to the 1980 National Convention. The Western, Ontario and Atlantic regions suggested that the CUPW adopt a policy opposed to sexual harassment. Like other policy resolutions, these did not reach the floor of the Convention because of time limitations. However, the topic was raised and discussed by members from different parts of the country at the evening session on women's issues organized at that Convention. Following this identification of the problem, the National Executive Board arranged for a course to be available on the topic.

Meanwhile the Vancouver local women's committee had developed and taught a course on sexual harassment, starting in 1981. It is a three hour section of a course for shop stewards and, as of 1988, continued to be taught by women within the local. A similar course has been taught by the women's committee in Winnipeg, and the Atlantic regional women's committee has done educational work on sexual harassment.

---

[22] Despite numerous telephone conversations with the Montreal local President and a letter requesting interviews, attempts to make contact with members of the Montreal local who might have held a different position on this subject were not successful.

From the Vancouver local originated a group of seven resolutions on sexual harassment that were steered through the Western Regional Conference to appear at the 1983 National Convention. These resolutions dealt not with union policy, but with changes to the Constitution that would provide a definition of sexual harassment and a mechanism for dealing with the problem when it arose between members of the union, first informally with the help of the shop steward and then through a formal complaint procedure. The Vancouver women were well-organized. They had prepared information kits on sexual harassment, which were available at the Convention and had also been mailed to many locals in advance. The women planned to make an initial presentation and then speak on various aspects of the issue.

The Constitution Committee dealing with the resolutions grouped those on sexual harassment into one resolution for the Convention. The Committee also changed the resolution so that instead of referring to any member harassed by another member it qualified this by the phrase "in the course of union activities." The Committee had wanted to clarify that including the problem in the Constitution was appropriate because it was an issue within the union and not just at the workplace.[23] While the intention was worthwhile, the phrase in fact limited the scope of the resolution rather strangely, because it covered member to member harassment only during union activities and not at other times.

The debate on the resolution lasted for more than 2 hours. From Vancouver and the Atlantic region women outlined the need for recognition of the problem, describing how courses had been developed in their regions to help deal with the issue. Other delegates in favour of the resolution argued that something in the Constitution was necessary to show that the union was clearly opposed to sexual harassment and thereby enable women to raise the problem knowing that they would have some support. The topic was not a comfortable one to deal with. Initially some opponents insisted that really there was no problem, at least not within the CUPW, and one delegate from Quebec suggested that perhaps sexual harassment was only a problem in the Western and Atlantic regions.

Some delegates called for specific examples to prove that such a problem existed. Several were provided. "I will give you a specific fact that happened at this Convention on Monday night ... A sister from our region who happens to be down the hall from me had someone at her door for about half-an-hour, banging on the door. I call that harassment ... That happened at this Convention."[24] But, the most telling example occurred on the Convention floor during the debate. Suddenly a woman jumped to the mike, interrupting a speaker, and demanded an apology. She had overheard a male delegate commenting in no uncertain terms on the body of the woman then speaking at one of the mikes. The apology was

---

[23] Canadian Union of Postal Workers, *National Convention 1983, Verbatim Report*, Ottawa, 2–6 May 1983, p. 497.

[24] *Ibid.*, p. 490.

given and the speaker continued, pointing out: "Obviously, I will not have to address the question of whether or not such harassment happens at union activities."[25]

Some delegates did not take the issue seriously and there was considerable noise on the Convention floor, particularly at the beginning of the debate. One woman complained that the definition was too rigid and men and women would have to keep their hands over their eyes, ears and mouths "like the three little monkeys" in order not to be harassing someone. Another woman opponent joked before she left the mike "I wish to apologize to the 50 men or so that I must have harassed this week."[26] It was a male delegate who pointed out: "That is usually the way people deal with sexual harassment; they laugh it off and pass it off as a joke. But, obviously, it is no joke to those that are being harassed."[27]

Delegates who admitted there was indeed a problem raised other objections. It was argued that sexual harassment had already been dealt with by the union because the negotiated contract prohibited discrimination based on sex or sexual orientation. In contradiction to this approach, other delegates suggested that it was premature to deal with the issue, to take any action, because there should be more discussion and education first, and then perhaps an improved resolution could be brought to the next Convention. It was further suggested that action by the union was unnecessary because there was human rights legislation that dealt with the issue. There was also concern that if the union dealt with sexual harassment it would pit one worker against another and the employer might find a way to use it against the workers. Finally it was argued that there were technical problems with the resolution and that it should deal with workplace harassment and not just harassment during union activities.

A delegate complained that "people have a funny way of supporting this resolution," recognizing the problem but then not wanting to do anything about it.[28] It was pointed out that if a problem existed it needed to be dealt with, so why wait another three years before passing a resolution. There was no mechanism for handling complaints and action was necessary now, and the union did not have a history of relying upon legislation to solve its problems. Other unions and labour organizations had supported similar arrangements and it was time the CUPW did the same. Delegates argued that it would not pit worker against worker anymore than the rest of section 8 of the Constitution, that treated how the union disciplined its members for a variety of offenses. The employer was already involved because the union did not handle it and a case was cited where the employer had disciplined two workers for sexual harassment. Finally, this resolution was to deal with sexual harassment within the union, leaving the

---

[25] *Ibid.*, p. 494.

[26] *Ibid.*, p. 491.

[27] *Ibid.*, p. 497.

[28] *Ibid.*, p. 497.

contract to deal with the problem on the work floor; it was a step forward and should be supported, any technical difficulties notwithstanding.

A standing vote was required because the support and opposition were so equally divided. Finally, the resolution was defeated by 118 votes against to 109 votes in favour. The same resolution was put forward by the Atlantic region in 1986, but did not come before the floor of the Convention due to lack of time. Consequently, there remains no formal mechanism within the CUPW for dealing with worker to worker sexual harassment.

However, there is a policy that states the opposition of the union to sexual harassment and commits the union to educating its members through shop steward courses and information to new members.[29] This became a policy of the CUPW in 1983 when the National Executive Board dealt with a wide range of policy issues that had not reached the Convention floor.

With regard to sexual harassment from management, there is no specific clause within the union contract that deals with the issue. However, the contract contains a general "no discrimination" article including that there shall be no "harassment" because of "age, race, creed, colour, national origin, political or religious affiliation, sex, sexual orientation, or membership or activity in the Union."[30] The union has taken arbitration cases under this article, including several cases of sexual harassment by supervisors.

Child Care

Participation in union activities is often difficult for parents who have children to look after. This affects women particularly because mothers usually take primary responsibility for the children, whether within couples or in the case of separation or divorce. Consequently, the issue of child care for union meetings has been one of special concern to women.

Within the CUPW the question of child care in relation to union activity was raised briefly at the evening session on women's issues during the 1980 National Convention. However, it was not until 1983 that resolutions on the question were proposed to the National Convention. Although child care was provided at the 1983 National Convention, the first resolution proposed adding the provision of child care for National Conventions to the Constitution to formalize and ensure its existence.

Even on this resolution there was considerable debate and although the Constitution Committee recommended adoption, there had been disagreement among its members. One member of the Committee said:

---

[29] Canadian Union of Postal Workers, "National Constitution Adopted 1986," National Policies Adopted at the National Convention, p. 18.

[30] Canada Post Corporation, "Agreement between Canada Post Corporation and the Canadian Union of Postal Workers," Expires: 31 July 1989, p. 6, Article 5.01.

Really I was shocked to find out that the Committee was split on this particular issue. It is about time that we recognize, not only the problems of women workers but, also, the other single parents and allow them to fully participate within this union.[31]

Some delegates argued that it was not necessary to make the provision of child care obligatory, and others countered that it should be a right rather than a privilege and written into the Constitution so that women could see that the union supported their participation. It was also argued that since there was another resolution on child care, the issues should be brought to the Convention floor together. Supporters of the resolution contended that many of the resolutions debated on the floor were interrelated and that issues needed to be dealt with separately. When the vote was taken the resolution was passed.

The second resolution was more controversial and raised more debate. Originally the resolution from the Western region had proposed that on-site child care or reimbursement for off-site child care be provided to participants for all Conventions, regional conferences and other meetings under the Constitution (with the exception of local meetings). However, in order to recommend adoption the Constitution Committee excluded the provision for off-site child care in the resolution it presented to the Convention. Delegates complained about this limitation, for example: "I am from Vancouver. If I was to follow through on using your recommendation and bring my children here, it would cost me $1,500 and be a huge inconvenience. I have two four-year-old children ... With off-site child care, I could arrange personally for it near my place of residence."[32]

The chair of the Committee sympathized, but explained that there had been "a very heavy debate" in the committee, not just around on-site versus off-site child care, but whether to have any child care at all. Excluding the off-site child care provision had enabled the Committee to compromise and recommend adoption of the revised resolution. Following the rules of order for the Convention, had the Committee recommended rejection, delegates could only attempt to refer the resolution back to the Committee with instructions for an altered resolution or a different recommendation. In theory the Committee would then return to the Convention at a later date with the required revision, but in practice the opportunity rarely arose for a resolution to reappear because of time constraints. The Committee chair advised delegates to vote for the resolution because at least it provided on-site child care at more than just the National Convention and it could be improved upon at a later point.

Even without the off-site provision, some delegates expressed a major concern for the cost of the child care arrangements. It emerged that the union had paid $1,000 for the May 1983 Convention and two children had used the facility.

---

[31] Canadian Union of Postal Workers, *National Convention 1983, Verbatim Report*, Ottawa, 2–6 May 1983, p. 211.

[32] *Ibid.*, Ottawa, 18–20 November 1983, p. 37.

It was suggested that in rural regions it would be far more expensive to organize child care and that a study should be made in advance to determine the costs. "I cannot but wonder what our union dues would be like if this resolution is adopted, not to speak of the additional obligations it would impose upon the concerned officers."[33] Delegates argued against this perspective, saying that good quality day care was expensive, but it was worthwhile to get the full participation of women in the union, stating that $1,000 was measly and calling the fears around costs "hysteria." One delegate pointed out:

> It costs us $400,000 to be here this weekend. We could have totally avoided that cost if we had stuck to the time limits of the Convention we had in May ... It is not a question of the money. If we can encourage and increase the participation of women and single parents in this union, then whatever money we spend it is worth it.[34]

Another argument against the resolution was that the government had a responsibility to provide child care, not the union. "Some people in our union have such a yearning to try to solve so many problems that we have reached the point where they want our union to take up the responsibilities of the government in all fields ... some would like to see our union do the job in spite of our financial situation." One delegate responded that the union should be trying to solve society's problems as well as its own, but that was not the point with this resolution. She continued: "But the issue here is not fighting for society's deficiencies; it is having the maximum participation of your members. That is the issue."[35] When the resolution was put to the floor it was adopted, thus providing on-site child care for union conventions and meetings (excluding locals).

At the 1986 National Convention the issue was again debated at length when another resolution was proposed to fill the gap by also providing reimbursement for off-site child care expenses of up to $60 per day. Several delegates described the problems they experienced in participating in the union because they had children. A part-time worker from Vancouver explained that before she could run as a delegate to the National Convention she had to arrange, as a pre-condition, for friends to take care of her child for most of the week, but it was still costing her $60. She had also been a delegate to the Western Region Wage and Contract Conference and that had cost her $40 for child care. "I am not asking for sympathy, I am not asking you to pass the hat and I am not asking for a husband to help take care of my child because I am a single parent. I am asking for change."[36]

---

[33] *Ibid.*, p. 40.

[34] *Ibid.*, p. 45.

[35] *Ibid.*, pp. 40, 41.

[36] Canadian Union of Postal Workers, *National Convention 1986, Proceedings*, Ottawa, 7–11 April 1986, p. 372.

Not all the delegates were impressed by these examples and one claimed "The child care issue is raised to play with feelings and squander Union funds." Again the finances were cited as a critical problem. "The union's finances are important; without financial means, we risk getting smashed up in the review of bargaining units, in organization. This is what is at stake here. Wake up."[37] It was pointed out that child care had cost $1,368 at the 1983 May Convention and $1,079 in November, but there was still concern that many more requests would be made for off-site child care and that receipts would be easy to obtain. Again it was argued that parents should be able to participate equally and one delegate mentioned that in his local there were not many dishonest union activists who would be likely to claim for expenses they had not genuinely incurred. At the vote the resolution was adopted.

Thus, the union provides child care upon request at all meetings above the local level, and will reimburse child care expenses up to $60 per day for participants who choose to make their own arrangements. While locals are not required to provide these arrangements, a few do make provisions for local meetings.

However, another problem quickly emerged with the child care allowance. The constitution states that it is for use by delegates to meetings. Consequently, a woman elected as a regional officer discovered that when she attended regional educationals to give seminars her child care was not covered, although it had been provided when she attended as a delegate. On appealing this to the National Executive, it was interpreted that regional officers would receive child care allowance for attending regional and national conventions, to which they are considered delegates, but not for attending regional seminars where they may be organizing educationals as part of their work. It is anticipated that this problem will be rectified by a resolution to the next National Convention, since the purpose of providing child care is to encourage the participation of women within the union at all levels, not just as delegates.

Union Education

Education on women's concerns was one of the earliest issues raised in the CUPW. At the 1977 National Convention a combined resolution that dealt with both women's committees and education was defeated. In 1980 there was a resolution calling for the inclusion of women's concerns in the list of courses to be developed at the national office. In its presentation to the Convention the Committee excluded the course on women's issues from its recommended changes to that section of the Constitution. However, with some manoeuvring it was adopted, partly due to the intervention of the CUPW President, Jean-Claude Parrot.

At the 1980 Convention the defeat of the resolution concerning women's committees and the evening session on women's issues had both occurred the day before the resolution on education came to the Convention floor. Activists

---

[37] *Ibid.*, p. 373.

within the union were expressing their concern on women's issues, and yet the resolution on women's committees had been defeated and it seemed likely that the resolution on education for women would also be defeated. Parrot declared that while he also was not in favour of separate committees to deal with the issue, there was no reason not to have education on the topic. He said:

> I think that we are generally agreeing that this is a problem we have to deal with. We don't want to create a ghetto and we don't want to discriminate but we cannot deny that certain problems exist which have to be examined. The only way we can do this within our Union is in the context of a Union education program.[38]

The resolution had to be referred back to the Committee so that the additional point concerning women's issues could be included. This was done and when the Committee later returned to the Convention floor with the revised version, it passed without further debate. Since that time the Constitution has a list of 20 different types of courses that are the responsibility of the 2nd National Vice-President, including the "problems of women workers in Canada Post and women workers in general."[39]

By the beginning of 1983 the national journal reported that various courses had been developed at the national office for distribution to local and regional offices, including one on sexual harassment.[40] However, it remains the only course concerned with women's issues.

The CUPW'S Reaction to Women's Issues

Acceptance of women's issues inside the union has been cautious and often reluctant in the CUPW, although changes have been made. Union policy formally supports the formation of women's committees and in some locals and regions they have been promoted, but they have not received any active encouragement from the national level. Compared to some other unions and union organizations the CUPW is hardly well-endowed with women's committees, has never held a women's conference or even regular women's caucuses, and has never considered other methods of affirmative action, such as a national women's committee or creating a position to animate issues of concern to women. The CUPW has developed a course on sexual harassment and handled arbitration cases on the issue, but there is no explicit clause on sexual harassment within the collective agreement and no established mechanism to deal with worker to worker harassment. Child care provisions are generous for national and regional educationals and conventions, but they were obtained only after

---

[38] Canadian Union of Postal Workers, *National Convention 1980, Proceedings*, Ottawa, 28 July–1 August 1980, p. 231.

[39] Canadian Union of Postal Workers, "National Constitution Adopted 1986," p. 36.

[40] Canadian Union of Postal Workers, *CUPW*, Vol. 13, No. 2, February–March 1983, p. 4.

some struggle and delay, and there remains the loophole that denies child care to women union officers if they are attending in their official capacity.

The CUPW is a progressive union that has achieved enviable gains for women in its collective agreement, and yet it has been relatively circumspect in its handling of women's issues that affect the internal functioning of the union. This section considers the factors that have contributed to the manner in which this union has handled internal issues of concern to women.

The Role of Women

One obvious factor contributing to the emergence of specifically women's issues related to the internal structure of the union, has been the increasing number of women in the union. As the proportion of women members has risen from less than 6 percent in 1965 to more than 42 percent twenty years later, there have been more women involved in the union, more women delegates to conventions and more discussion of women's concerns.

This numerical influence has been reinforced by the development of the women's movement and its impact on society in general and within the union movement in particular. In the CUPW the Vancouver local has played a particularly important role in raising and developing women's issues and it is no accident that in British Columbia the women's movement was generally more advanced and active than elsewhere in the country. The British Columbia Federation of Labour was the first to establish a women's committee, in 1970, and it was in Vancouver that two independent women's unions developed, the Association of University and College Employees and the Service Office and Retail Workers Union of Canada. Active women in the Vancouver local obtained support for their perspective from the women's movement in that region years before their ideas were acceptable within the CUPW.

However, while the role of women is certainly one factor in explaining the emergence of women's issues, it is not the only factor and cannot sufficiently explain how those issues have been handled within the union.

The Union Leadership

If the leadership of a union is opposed to the emergence of women's issues it may be very difficult for those issues to be heard and dealt with, regardless of the number of women within the union and their degree of activity.

The national leadership of the CUPW is perceived by women within the union as generally supportive of women's issues, although the perspective varies considerably. Among the women interviewed for this study, some saw the national leadership as very supportive, while others described them as fairly supportive in general but also neutral on some issues. The National Executive did arrange an evening on women's issues at the 1980 National Convention and did incorporate a range of social issues of relevance to women in the union's policies after the 1983 Convention failed to deal with them. The President did speak in favour of education on women's issues in 1980 and announced the informal women's caucus in 1986. There has been no attempt to prevent issues from being raised and openly discussed on the floor of the Convention.

On the other hand there has also been no enthusiastic encouragement on behalf of women's issues, no initiatives from the national office to promote women's questions, no rush to provide education on the topic. Some women pointed out that men cannot be expected to champion women's issues within the union and the national office is still predominantly male. Others mentioned that the national office is often not aware of issues, but has taken up concerns once they are brought to their attention. Some sympathized with how many issues the national officers have to deal with and suggested that they do not always have time to deal with everything.

In 1983 the President of CUPW, Jean-Claude Parrot, expressed the ambivalent position of the union towards women's issues in an interview. He said:

> We don't have a women's committee at the national level like other unions. We never pushed for that and we were almost against it. We felt sometimes that there are other ways to take up women's issues without creating a separate body. On the other hand I think that the union has also become conscious that if you want to be able to deal with women's issues you have to know what they are. And in order to know what they are you have to allow women to sit together and discuss them, because they won't do it in front of men ... We don't discourage locals in the union from having women's committees, but at the same time we're saying we had better be careful not to create divisions, because there are differences among women.[41]

At the local and regional levels the situation varies from some very supportive men who have actively promoted issues of concern to women and even initiated women's committees, to clear opposition. Most women's committees had experienced some opposition from men when they were first established. In Vancouver in the mid–1970s the President at the time was not supportive and there had to be a lot of discussion to convince the men that it was not a threat. The committee established in 1985 in Winnipeg was encouraged and supported by the local male President and has always been open to men. Still there was some opposition, including questions as to why there was not a men's committee, and at first men joined the committee to check its activities rather than out of interest. However, there continues to be a man involved in the committee who is genuinely concerned and supportive. In Edmonton some women had attempted to form a committee, and their suggestion that men not join the committee met with "extreme and malicious opposition." However, several women in other locals expressed the opinion that it would be unfair to exclude men because some are genuinely interested in and knowledgeable about those issues.

To some extent it may be that the union leadership was placed in the position where it had to concur with some demands on women's issues for political reasons. By the early 1980s it was becoming clear that women were an increas-

---

[41] "Jean-Claude Parrot: An Interview," *Studies in Political Economy*, No. 11, Summer 1983, p. 58.

ingly active force within the union, that there were a growing number of women activists demanding some changes and that any overt opposition would have created considerable discontent. On the other hand the majority of members within the union, represented by their delegates at Conventions, were not demanding dramatic changes. The democratic process within the union was critical in deciding the union's direction on these issues, and the national leadership's position of providing some support without fully embracing every issue reflected the mood of the membership. The question is not just how union leadership has responded to issues, but also why the membership, including the women members, has not been prepared to support some issues of concern to women.

Democratic Process

Democratic processes within unions allow the expression of the views of the membership and permit changes to occur as they are seen to be necessary. This is important to women because the entry of women into unions has brought concern for different issues and the need to make changes to accommodate those issues. The CUPW is widely recognized as having a highly democratic constitution and structure.

However, while democracy permits issues to be openly raised and discussed, it does not guarantee the outcome. In locals, regional conferences and national conventions members and delegates have the opportunity to decide what issues to support and what changes to make. In the CUPW these processes have resulted in fairly cautious movement on women's issues. It might be argued that since women do not form the majority of members of the union, and since they are not proportionately represented as delegates at conferences and conventions, this is hardly surprising. However, while this is doubtless a factor it is clearly not the only one.

It has not been the case that men have opposed women's issues while women have supported them. There is no way of knowing how men and women have voted, but the speakers at national conventions are some indication. In most of the debates discussed above women as well as men have opposed the resolutions, while they have been supported by men as well as by women. For example, during the 1980 debate on having a women's caucus at the national convention, three women and three men spoke in favour, three women and four men spoke against. In 1983 on the resolution on sexual harassment seven women and seven men spoke in favour, while six women and five men spoke against. On having women's committees in locals one man and one woman spoke in favour, while two women spoke against. On the question of providing child care at National Conventions five women and three men spoke in favour, while two women and two men spoke against. The same pattern of mixed responses from men and women can be traced in most of the debates.

There is no question that other factors than gender have been important to the outcome of these debates, the most obvious being regional differences. During the debates delegates from the Western and Atlantic regions, both men and women, generally spoke in favour of resolutions that raised issues of concern to women. Delegates from Ontario have not held a uniform or consistent position and have spoken on different sides of the debates and varied with the issues. Delegates from Quebec have opposed the resolutions on issues of concern to women in almost all instances, and were in particular responsible for the failure to obtain the off-site child care allowance in 1983. When it was later passed in 1986, 48 delegates exercised their right to record their dissidence from the vote. Of these, 47 were from Quebec, 1 was from Ontario, and 6 were women.[42] One union official commented: "Our union from the point of view of women's issues is behind the rest of the union movement and my view is that the main reason we're behind is because of Quebec."[43]

A democratic process allows for the expression of opinion and often different opinions. There have been very diverse points of view expressed within the CUPW, not only among men and women and not only among different regions, but also among women themselves. It is not the case that women comprise a unanimous voice on the direction the union should take with regard to women's issues. The following section explores the perspectives of women, based upon interviews with 55 women CUPW members, of whom four were also officers of the union. Of these two worked at the national office, one at the regional level, and one was the full-time President of the Vancouver local. Three other women were hired by the union for just 1988 to work full time on the campaign against privatization, and were then returning to their jobs in the Post Office. The remaining 48 women were working as inside postal workers at the time of the interviews in 14 locations across Canada, and of these, twelve were members of their local executives, holding various positions.

Women's Perspectives

There was no question among the women members of the CUPW that they were the equals of men, and that they should be treated as such both in the workplace and within the union. The women interviewed all supported the need for equality for women and felt that the union should continue to move in that direction. No-one suggested that men were perhaps more knowledgeable or more capable, or that they should for any reason be in positions of power within the union more than the women.

This is not always the case, particularly in work situations where women work in different and lower paid jobs than do the men. Other research has found that where sex-based inequalities exist in the workplace, women as well as men

---

[42] Canadian Union of Postal Workers, *National Convention 1986, Proceedings*, Ottawa, 7–11 April 1986, pp. 366–367.

[43] Interview with Ted Penny, Regional Grievance Officer, Atlantic Region, Canadian Union of Postal Workers, Halifax, 11 January 1989.

tend to accept that there are reasons for that inequality based upon differences in capability or need between the sexes, and many women will even express opposition to equal pay for women.[44] It has also been discovered that in workplaces where women do different jobs for lower pay, this inequality shapes women's union participation and is reflected in inequality between men and women within the union. Members for union executives are drawn from the better paid, supposedly more skillful jobs within the bargaining unit, jobs usually dominated by men. The women in such a situation sometimes express the opinion that the men are better placed to be union representatives.[45]

Men and women in the CUPW are equal on the shop floor, they get equal pay, they do the same jobs. There are no inequalities to be explained or to be carried over into the functioning of the union. It might be difficult for a man in the CUPW to argue that men should have a superior role in the union, when no such superiority exists in the job or in the pay packet. Likewise the women, equals on the shop floor, do not expect to be regarded as anything less than equal in the union. As one woman said: "We feel on an equal footing with the men. I don't feel any better or any less than them. We work right along side them, we do the same job they do" (St John). Another woman directly linked the situation within the union to the workplace: "CUPW for me is equal. I work alongside men and I do exactly what they do, they do exactly what I do, and there is absolutely no discrimination" (Frazer Valley).

While there was agreement between women over the general direction of the union in supporting the participation and equality of women, there were different opinions over how that should be accomplished. The main difference was whether women's issues should be handled as worker's issues through the mainstream union with no special committees or arrangements for women, or whether they should be dealt with as women's issues with the support of women's committees and other special mechanisms that would allow women to work together.

Women's Issues are Worker's Issues

One point of view held by women CUPW members is that women's committees or other special arrangements to deal with women's issues are not necessary. This is not to say that women's concerns do not need to be dealt with, but that they have been handled and should continue to be handled by the general union, so specific arrangements are not required. It is argued that the CUPW contract is excellent for women, that the leadership is progressive and that there is no discrimination within the union.

Among all the 55 women interviewed there was general agreement that the contract is very advanced for women. It was described as "great" and "the best in

---

[44] Nicola Charles, "Women and Trade Unions," in Feminist Review, *Waged Work, A Reader*, Virago Press, London, pp. 170–172.

[45] Charlene Gannagé, *Double Day Double Bind, Women Garment Workers*, Women's Press, Toronto, 1986, pp. 170–184.

the country" and there is little doubt in the minds of women in the CUPW that the union has done a good job of protecting women's interests. The women have equal pay, equal job opportunity, equality between full and part-time workers in pay and almost all benefits, paid maternity leave and parental leave with all benefits and seniority protected, and there is no lower paid ghetto of women's work. They are aware that they are not fighting the battles that remain to be fought in many other unions.

One critical element in obtaining these contract provisions has been the degree of solidarity among CUPW members. Many issues, such as equal pay and equality for part-time workers, have been argued as necessary not only from a perspective of justice, but also because they create solidarity between the workers, preventing the employer from finding means to weaken the union through internal divisions. It is considered essential to have a united front to face the employer in order to make gains for everyone, including women. Since this strategy has obviously met with considerable success, for some women there is no reason to alter it. The union has accomplished a great deal for women without the benefit of special arrangements and consequently some women felt that they could continue to work directly with men to obtain improvements. They opposed women's committees as being either unnecessary or divisive. One woman said: "Keep it as its always been. The union fights for everybody whether you're male or female" (St John).

For the same reasons it was argued that women's issues do not need to be identified as such. Some women said that they liked the approach that dealt with all concerns as "worker's issues" rather than women's issues because they perceived that to be real equality. They felt that women's issues were also men's issues, for example concerning child care or parental leave. Feeling equal to men in their jobs, some women felt it was a retrograde step to identify women or women's issues separately in any way. For example, one woman commented:

> I like to ignore women-male stereotyping at work ... I try to make it, I'm neuter, like I'm not female, I'm not male on the floor, that's got nothing to do with my job. And I try to encourage that attitude, not segregating people into male and female. Like it has no place there to me ... And I don't complain "I can't do that because I'm a woman." I hate that kind of attitude. It's just dividing women from men (Regina).

Women who opposed the idea of specifically women's issues also stated that there was no discrimination within the CUPW. This is not to say they denied that there were ever any sexist comments or sexual harassment, but these women felt that the large majority of men regarded them as equals, did not attempt to prevent them from participating in the union and listened to their concerns with respect. One woman described the situation within the union as "wide open" and another said:

> For a long time, even including myself, we felt there wasn't a need for a women's committee because our union was very forward and progressive. And for a long time a lot of us felt there was no need to have a women's committee

because we certainly didn't feel discriminated against. Women's issues have always been in the forefront and have always been given a lot of dignity by the union as a whole (London).

These women had not experienced negative reactions from male union officials, and felt confident that they would receive a sympathetic and helpful response to any problem they might raise. They credited the union leadership for obtaining a good contract, for being prepared to recognize the importance of women's concerns, and for insisting upon equality between all members of the CUPW, regardless of sex or any other factor.

Women with this perspective came from locals where male union officials had been sympathetic to women's concerns and where women had participated fully in the union and its executive, if not actually dominating it. There are some locals where the executive is entirely, or predominantly, women. For example, women from the Victoria local said: "We haven't had a women's committee or anything like that and yet we've had the majority of the executive have been women for years now ... It seemed to be a natural development" (Victoria). Holding a women's committee meeting was likely to draw just the same group of activist women, so there was little reason to do so.

A good number of the women interviewed did not feel that they were battling against inequality in the workplace or discrimination within the union. Consequently, many women did not see the need for women's committees. They sometimes indicated that they saw the need for women's committees in unions where women were fighting for equal pay or equal opportunity, but this was not the case within the CUPW. Some were genuinely puzzled as to what such a committee would discuss, what it would be seeking to obtain. Added to their reservations was the comment that women active within the union were not prepared to go to any more meetings without a very specific purpose and concrete goals.

Women's Issues are Women's Issues

There are also women in CUPW who feel that women's issues need to be dealt with as just that, and that locals should have women's committees in order to ensure that it happens. A variety of arguments for this perspective were expressed.

While these women agreed that the leadership had not generally opposed the emergence of women's issues, still they were aware that the leadership is predominantly male and not likely to recognize issues until they are made aware of them, and they questioned how that is to happen unless women raise the issues. Some would agree that women are not discriminated against in the union, but argue that women may still lack the confidence to raise issues or run for official positions, and that women's committees have an important role in supporting women and enabling them to feel comfortable. While they would agree that the collective agreement is very good, still they feel that there are issues to be dealt with and improvements to be made. As one woman explained:

I just know what it's like when you're in a meeting of women and they're discussing a problem and it's to do with working with brothers on the workfloor and there's a lot of things they don't feel comfortable saying in a group of men ... There are times when it's more appropriate to meet alone ... We really want to encourage women to become active in this union. I think we're going to have to identify the problems and throw out some solutions and the best people to do that are women (St John's).

One woman expressed the tension between wanting and yet not wanting to identify women's issues: "I hate things being women's issues, but we do wind up having quite unique problems" (Winnipeg). Some women argued that avoiding women's committees and dealing with "workers' issues" rather than women's issues simply makes the problem invisible, but it's still there. While the union has a strong political and ideological philosophy that everyone should be equal, it takes another leap of consciousness to realize that it does not exist, as much as they would like it to. There are problems for particular groups and differences between people that may need to be addressed. "Pushing everything as workers' issues has been partially based on an inability and a refusal to understand that women are socialized and affected differently" (Vancouver). One woman described the resistance to the sexual harassment issue as based on the union's difficulty in accepting that one member would mistreat another member, when everyone was supposed to be equal and united.

Supporters of women's committees find the argument that they might be divisive, laughable. It is very clear to them that they encourage women to become more active within the union, giving them a place to raise their concerns and support to become more involved. In Vancouver the President noted that the women's committee had worked only too well, in that those women had become so active on various issues within the union that they no longer have the time or energy for a women's committee. However, one woman noted, perhaps with some perception, that women's committees were divisive only to the extent that the men opposed them. It was the case that every woman's committee established had initially met with some resistance and critical comment, even where it later became accepted.

There are also women with the union who support the need for women's issues receiving special attention because they have experienced, or they are aware of, overt sexism and discrimination by male members and officials. It is worth outlining a few examples to make the point. A woman in Winnipeg started working in the transfer section and was the only woman employed there for the first six months. She described a situation in which the younger men particularly had a lot of trouble accepting her presence, "and once they get going, there's nothing you can do to control it, you just remove yourself from the situation." She said "It's been a very difficult year. There's many nights when I leave in tears."

A woman who had worked in Edmonton described the situation when she moved to the transfer section in that post office:

The place was just walls of sunshine girls and calenders. It was just plastered. I'd never been down there ... but we had to go down and work there. And there were a whole bunch of women and we went down there day after day and complained half-heartedly. Finally ... three of us went down there and we tore down everything ... we tore down walls and walls of this stuff.

Two women at opposite ends of the country, in Vancouver and Halifax, described the negative and abusive reactions they received from male members because they had each written an article on sexual harassment for union publications. A woman in St. John's was blunt about the need for a women's committee: "It's a lot easier talking to women than a bunch of chauvinists."

While this kind of experience from male members is difficult to handle, sexist attitudes and/or discrimination on the part of union leaders is more destructive and can have a broad impact on women within a local or region. In Montreal I spoke to women who felt that their participation in the union was discouraged because the President's longtime control over the local had resulted in opposition to any independent activity by the members, including by women. They felt that their attempts to establish a women's committee had been sabotaged by undemocratic and sexist methods.

In Toronto the newly established women's committee was attempting to deal with a case of harassment of a woman union officer. Her office had been ransacked and disturbing sexist and racist comments had been written over some personal photographs. A committee of union activists and shop stewards had access to her office, but the local executive was reluctant to investigate and refused to publish an article written on the incident. Another woman who had once sat on the Toronto local executive made the following comment: "I thought I knew them. I thought I knew the guys I was working with on a personal basis as well as what they were about within the union. When I sat on the Executive I found such a double standard that it was mind boggling." In Ottawa a woman was harassed by two shop stewards because she was seeing a supervisor in her private life. She finally complained to the Human Rights Commission and both men received fines. It is hardly surprising that women who have experienced such situations are more likely to perceive a need for women's committees within the union.

One further argument was presented in favour of women's committees, and it was simply that if women felt the need for them, then they should have them. The following comments were made by a member of the Atlantic region's women's committee, a woman who had previously opposed women's committees in the union:

The argument that's been used all along is why separate us from each other because in this union you don't need that. But if the women feel they should have a committee of their own, then certainly by all means we should have it. And I don't think it's going to in any way isolate us from the mainstream ... I don't feel our brothers in the union have anything to fear. If the women feel they have to have a committee, then we'll have it whether they like it or not. Of course we'd like them to understand that it's not because we're anti-men or anti

WOMEN'S INCREASING PARTICIPATION IN THE UNION

Deborah Bourke was elected National Union Representative in 1983, the first woman elected as a national officer.

Caroline Lee was elected National Secretary-Treasurer in 1985, the first woman to sit on the National Executive Board.

anything in the union. But if there's women that feel the need for that committee then we're going to have it and that's all there is to it.

Women's Participation in the Union

This issue raised so much discussion and such strong arguments from so many women, that it is dealt with separately here. During the interviews I asked why there were fewer women than men in leadership positions within the union. A few women felt that it was simply a natural progression, that given time women would move into those positions. They pointed to the fact that this was happening, that there were more women as local presidents, a few women at the regional level, and the first woman on the National Executive. Women were moving up into positions of increased responsibility and this would continue to develop until complete equality was obtained.

However, this was not the perspective of the majority of women interviewed, who felt that there were undeniable barriers to women's equal participation in the union. Again and again women raised the same concern, namely responsibility for family and children. Women members of the CUPW may be equal with men in the workplace, but the union does not represent them in regard to domestic labour, where they continue to find themselves responsible for an unequal share of the work. One woman explained: "The woman of the family the majority of the time has to provide the child care and is left with that responsibility" (Winnipeg). Another said, more bluntly: "I saw a T-shirt that said 'Every mother is a working mother.' I think every mother is a single mother" (Edmonton). Even those few women whose spouses fully share the domestic labour remain at a disadvantage, because many men have wives who relieve them of that work entirely, freeing them for union activity to an extent that few women can match.

Sharing the work at home is not the only problem. Women expressed their concern at working all week and then disappearing on the weekend to a conference or an educational. One women who worked part-time on evening shift felt that she only really saw her school-aged children on the weekends. For workers on other shifts it was difficult to attend a lot of evening meetings, even if day care was provided by the local, because they wanted to spend time with their children.

The impact of these responsibilities upon women's involvement in the union is critical. One woman had been active in the union since the early 1970s and described how she had once been approached to run for office at the national level. She had little doubt that she would have won, but declined because she would have had to uproot four young children and move them to Ottawa. She partly regretted her decision, and noted that although the men who took those positions also had to move their families, they seemed to feel far less compunction about it.

In one local the full-time President resigned when she took maternity leave. By the time she became pregnant for the second time she was chief shop steward and this time decided to remain in the position during her maternity leave, attending as many meetings as possible. She had some support and some opposition to this decision within the local. In another local a woman explained how she and other mothers can manage the position of shop steward, because the work is largely carried out during working hours. But she had resigned herself to the fact that for the next ten years she can have no further participation in the union because she has a young child.

Many women expressed the opinion that women could only become active in the union in the more demanding positions if they were childless, or if their children were older and therefore required less time. One woman described her experience attending a weekend educational: "I was the only one there from our local that has children that aren't capable of staying home on their own ... the only woman. There were lots of men there that have children that can't stay home alone" (Winnipeg). When she was elected as the first woman member of the National Executive, Caroline Lee pointed out "I'm not really a role model because I don't have children or a spouse to consider when I decided to run. If I did, I probably would not have been able to run."[46] Likewise, Marion Pollack, President of the Vancouver local, was quick to point out that she is single and childless. There are a few exceptions, but clearly the majority of women feel that children and union activity are difficult or impossible to combine.

Asked if the union could do anything to deal with this problem, some women felt that it was not amenable to solutions from the union, since this is not just a question of providing child care, but a much more difficult issue. Some women felt that there had to be something that the union could do about the situation, but were not sure what it was. However, a good number of women had begun the process of thinking about what should be done and had developed some ideas, at least about the general direction. These women identified the problem as the degree of involvement required by the union in order to participate.

There is certainly agreement that the union demands everything of its officials. They have to work long hours, give up their weekends, and sometimes travel a good deal. "The union has worked to get decent working conditions, decent working hours for the members. But if you're a union activist you're expected to put in a 14 hour day" (Edmonton). Women are disadvantaged in attempting to meet these requirements: "It's really hard to do that kind of job unless you have a wife to do your laundry for you" (Vancouver). To obtain a full-time union position it is also necessary to "pay your dues," meaning that union commitment must be demonstrated by extensive activity over a long period of time. This is more difficult for women who carry the major responsibility for child rearing.

Some women were not happy at their sense of exclusion and a few contemplated changes in the union, a reorganization that would allow a less frenzied existence for activists, a flexibility that would enable people to participate at various levels of intensity, a recognition that unionists might also have other

---

[46] Canadian Union of Postal Workers, *CUPW*, Vol. 15, No. 3, July-September 1985, p. 3.

things in their lives besides the union. One mother with a young child said: "I want to participate in this union and I feel I have a right to participate in this union, and the only way that is going to happen is if the system changes and we have a loosening up" (Edmonton). But it was not only mothers who wanted to reduce the stress associated with union participation. Childless, single women lamented the absence of any social life because of their union involvement, and some simply dropped out from fatigue. It was a single woman who said:

> The whole labour movement has got to restructure itself and how it gets its work done. We can't participate under these rules. We really can't. You can't cope with the level of stress. You can't have a real family life. You can't do the things that you want to do as a woman and still be a leader in the union (Vancouver).

Like this woman, many recognized that it was not just a problem within CUPW but in other unions and throughout the labour movement.

Still To Be Dealt With

In the Contract

While the women members of the CUPW are generally very satisfied with their collective agreement, they could point to further improvements that would have special importance for women. The following list was compiled from the suggestions of the women interviewed, almost all of whom had some proposal to make, though none supplied the whole list.

1. *Special Leave.* Women want special leave for the care of sick children, or in the case of other family emergencies, that would be specified within the contract, rather than at the discretion of management as at present.

2. *Personal Leave.* A few women mentioned the need for a new kind of leave, a certain number of days per year that could be used, not for illness or emergencies, but for personal reasons, which might be medical and dental appointments, or the chance to attend a child's school concert for a parent working evening shift.

3. *Modified Duties During Pregnancy.* Another common complaint was that pregnant women were not always permitted to work at those jobs requiring less heavy work, a situation described as "criminal" by one woman (Frazer Valley). In one local an arrangement for modified duties had been introduced and women had then been told that pregnancy did not qualify for eligibility. Women would like to see a clause negotiated that would ensure lighter work during pregnancy.

4. *Child Care.* This is a critical issue for many women within the union, particularly given the difficulties engendered by shift work. "I used to work a shift 6 at night until 2 in the morning. You try and find a babysitter who's going to work 6 at night until 2 in the morning. There isn't one. It's a major, major issue" (Victoria). The last contract provided for a union-management study of the issue, because it is not clear what the

best form of provision would be, child care centres or some form of allowance.

5. *Extended Maternity/Parental Leave.* Women felt that these provisions need to be extended in a number of ways, including a longer period of paid leave. Women in Quebec particularly felt that 17 weeks with pay is not particularly progressive, since public service workers in that province receive 20 weeks at full pay.

   Women would also like an extension of unpaid leave beyond one year, especially since it has become harder to move between full and part-time work due to the general stagnation of the workforce. Some women suggested that unpaid leave up to school age would be desireable, and that it exists in some contracts.

6. *Pensions For Part-Time Workers.* I spoke to several women who had more than twenty-five years seniority with the Post Office as part-time workers, but would receive no pension upon retirement. The union was not able to negotiate this issue until 1984 because of legislative restrictions, and did not achieve it in the last round of negotiations. It is regarded as a very high priority by many part-time workers.

7. *Hours of Part-Time Work.* Most part-time workers would prefer to see the peak period re-instated because they either have been moved or fear being moved to undesirable shifts such as the midnight shift. Part-time workers support a numerical limit or a ratio upon the number of part-time workers, but many want to have the opportunity to work longer hours before overtime is offered to the full-time workers or casuals are hired.

8. *Shorter Work Week.* Negotiating a generally shorter work week was considered as important for all women, since it would enable them to spend more time with their families.

9. *Lower Weights.* For women working in the transfer section, or as Mail Handlers in postal stations, it was important to them to reduce the weights that they are required to lift. The present requirement is a maximum of 55lbs.

10. *Sexual Harassment.* There needs to be a specific clause within the collective agreement to deal with sexual harassment by management, so that the problem would be clearly identified, women would be aware that protection was available and therefore encouraged to report any problems.

In the Union

As with the previous section on improvements in the contract, the following list is a collection of suggestions made by different women interviewed. I have already discussed the differences of opinion over how women's issues should be handled by the union.

1. *Women's Committees.* More support is needed for women's committees in locals and at the regional level, including a stronger national policy of

support for such committees. Women's committees should have a budget available with which to pursue their activities, including reimbursing committee participants for lost pay for attending meetings.

There should be a national women's committee as well as a network of regional committees to follow up on issues as necessary at those levels within the union.

2. *Women's Conferences.* To enable women to meet and discuss issues of concern and to facilitate contact between women in different parts of the country there need to be women's conferences at least at the national level, and preferably also regionally. It was commented that women in just one local or region cannot come up with solutions to problems on their own, that there needs to be input from women across the country.

3. *Child Care Facilities.* Several women commented that the provision of child care at conferences is not well organized. Parents are not happy to leave their children in a hotel room for a week, and want improved facilities, with more organized and interesting programs and activities, preferably located away from the hotel at least during the daytime.

It was also noted that the child care facilities or allowance are not provided outside of Convention hours, nor for the period prior to the Convention when the committees considering resolutions meet to prepare for the Convention. This considerably limits the possibility for women to become committee members for the Convention.

The child care provision should be extended to include women employed at the regional or national level when they attend regional or national educationals or conventions.

4. *Sexual Harassment.* Many women felt that there should be a clear mechanism within the Constitution to deal with cases of worker-to-worker sexual harassment. Now it is dealt with in some locals and regions, but not in others. There needs to be a more consistent message to women members that they will be protected from harassment and a clear message to men that such behaviour will not be tolerated by the union.

In many locals there has never been any education on the topic of sexual harassment, and women felt that there should be more encouragement to hold such educationals at the local and regional levels.

5. *Integration of Women's Issues.* Some women commented that they would like to see women's concerns better integrated into union courses and publications. There should be more courses that consider the impact of issues upon women. There should be more articles in union publications that document and provide information on issues of concern to women. The struggle around privatization was offered as an example where this was successfully accomplished.

6. *Family Responsibilities and the Union.* Many women felt that there had to be a more serious consideration of how to involve women within the union and enable them to participate despite their family responsibilities.

Some women suggested that a national women's conference and committee would be able to discuss such a problem, as well as others, in more detail, obtain the input of women across the country, and begin to consider solutions.

Conclusion

It is clear that changes have taken place within the CUPW in response to the massive entry of women into the Post Office and into the membership. Increasingly women have become active at the local level, moved into official positions within the union and attended union conventions. However, it may be that this trend is limited by women's responsibilities outside of the workplace and therefore will not produce equal representation unaided. Also the women involved in the union may be predominantly women who are relatively free of family responsibilities, while men in all family situations and of all ages will continue to participate.

From my interviews I noted the extent to which women move in and out of union positions, depending upon family considerations, but also because of fatigue and the desire for a life outside of the union. For example, during the course of this study the woman president of the Vancouver local resigned from that position, as did the woman regional union official in the Atlantic region. It may be that this is the same for men, or it may be that men move more steadily through the ranks and up into senior union positions. A comparative study would be necessary to explore this question further.

Perhaps ironically, the CUPW's record of achievements on bargaining issues of concern to women has created an environment of equality and solidarity in which women's committees or other special attention for women's issues are considered as unnecessary, or even a step backward, by a considerable number of women within the CUPW. This view is not held because women are unsympathetic with the goals of the women's movement, but because of the culture of solidarity and equality within the CUPW and the real benefits that have been obtained for women in the bargaining process. There was general agreement among almost all the women interviewed that at the national level of the union there was considerable support for women's concerns and that this had been translated into action, especially with regard to contract negotiations.

However, it was also apparent that sexism and discrimination continue to present problems for women, in some locals more than others and in some regions more than others. Consequently, while some women were certain that discrimination did not exist within the union, others were just as certain that it did. In particular the attitudes of local and regional union officials were quite critical in encouraging or repressing the involvement of women in the union and the development of women's committees. In some situations, and Vancouver is the primary example, women were able to obtain support for their union activities from the general women's movement outside the CUPW, but elsewhere women needed internal union support for their activities, and it was difficult, if not impossible to function without it.

The CUPW has obviously found some issues easier to deal with than others. Paid maternity leave was supported in the union, partly because it fell within the traditional field of conflict for the union, that is to say conflict with the employer. While it was an issue that was potentially divisive of the membership, nonetheless it involved obtaining improved benefits for members within the context of the collective agreement. The union has a long tradition of obtaining equal treatment for members through the negotiation procedure. Child care for union meetings also presented less difficulty than other issues. It did not raise the notion of division between men and women within the union, but rather like maternity leave, simply recognized the fact of women's additional family responsibilities and the need to account for them.

Women's committees and sexual harassment have been far more contentious. Both of these issues directly suggest not only differences between men and women, but that those differences might be conflictual. Women's committees suggest that there might be problems that men and women do not share, while sexual harassment suggests that women have problems that men cause. Consequently, these have been the questions that the union, committed as it is to solidarity and equality, has had most difficulty dealing with.

The national office of the CUPW has trod a carefully democratic path, relying upon convention delegates to decide the extent of the union's commitment to women's issues without providing much guidance or education on the questions concerned. If the CUPW is to increase the participation of women and move to resolve some of the issues outlined above, it is likely that more direct encouragement and leadership will be necessary. For example, if the National Executive were to indicate its clear support for women's committees, recommend the establishment of a national women's committee, and undertake some education to reach that goal it would send a clear signal to all its locals that the issue was considered to be an important one.

This is not to suggest that the national level of the union should, or could, impose its perspective upon the union generally. Delegates to National Convention must still decide the issue and it is anyway of little use to have a national office policy without local understanding and support. However, there is also a dynamic interaction between leadership from those responsible for the overall direction of the union and democratic input from the membership. On women's issues inside the union there has, thus far, been little education or leadership.

Women within the CUPW are increasingly organizing women's committees and pressing the need for consideration of women's concerns. This trend seems likely to continue because despite the equality provided on the shop floor by the union contract, women continue to experience inequalities in the broader society. Sometimes those inequalities are reflected within the union in the form of sexism and discrimination; more often they establish limits to the equal participation of women in the union. It remains to be seen to what extent societal limitations imposed outside the union might be compensated for, and thereby overcome, within the union itself.

11

CONCLUSION

This final chapter attempts to place the foregoing research on the CUPW within the context of the developing research on women and trade unions. It considers the evidence to date on the role of unions with regard to the status of women, first in the workplace and then within unions themselves. The various arguments offered as explanations for union policies and actions are examined in relation to their relevance to the history and current practice of the CUPW.

The literature on the role of unions in women's lives abounds with criticism of unions for their lack of recognition and support for women in paid work. Historical research in Canada and elsewhere has revealed a substantial history of discrimination on the part of the labour movement.[1] The evidence indicates that, in the past, unions adopted policies to exclude women—either from the labour force, or from certain positions within it—in order to protect the pay and positions of male workers. Such exclusionary policies have included the promotion of protective legislation for women, defending a higher wage for men on the basis that they support dependent wives and children, and outright proposals to ban women from the labour force in general or from specific occupations in particular. There are examples of unions that have refused to accept women as union members, ignored the struggles of women for improved working conditions and failed to support demands for equal pay. As a result, it has been argued that unions participated in the segregation of women into low-skilled, low-paid occupations.[2]

---

[1] For example, see Joan Sangster, "The 1907 Bell Telephone Strike: Organizing Women Workers, *Labour/Le Travailleur*, Vol. 3, 1978; Sarah Boston, *Women Workers and the Trade Unions*, Davis-Poynter, London, 1980; Philip S. Foner, *Women and the American Labour Movement*, The Free Press, New York, 1980; Ruth Frager, "No Proper Deal: Women Workers and the Canadian Labour Movement, 1870–1940," Linda Briskin and Lynda Yanz, *Union Sisters, Women in the Labour Movement*, The Women's Press, Toronto, 1983.

[2] Michèle Barrett, *Women's Oppression Today, The Marxist/Feminist Encounter*, Revised Edition, Verso, London, 1988, pp. 170–171; Dorothy Smith, "Women and Trade Unions: The U.S. and British Experience," *Resources for Feminist Research*, Vol. X, No. 2, July 1981.

Previous research suggests that unions are most likely to respond with such exclusionary policies during periods of technological change, when employers introduce unskilled and lower paid women workers to carry out the newly created monotonous tasks that require little or no training. In protecting the positions, pay and status of their male members against the inroads of cheap labour, unions have attempted to exclude women workers.[3]

Research on the current status of women in unions has presented a similar, though perhaps less severe, picture of the role of unions. It is argued that unions have failed to organize women, resulting in a lower rate of unionization for women than men, have not given priority to women's specific concerns and have therefore neglected to negotiate clauses in collective agreements on these issues, and have continued to bargain lower rates of pay for women and percentage pay increases that widen the pay gap.[4] Some researchers have concluded that since existing unions do not benefit women, separate independent feminist organizations are necessary.[5]

Explanations for the policies adopted by unions towards women workers stem from two different approaches. One stresses the strength of the general and long-standing belief in women's inferiority, arising primarily from the expected role of women within the family.[6] From this point of view, trade unions share the general ideology that women's primary role is in the home while men's proper sphere is the labour force. Consequently women should be protected from the work force, do not have the same attachment to the labour force as men and,

[3] Cynthia Cockburn, *Brothers: Male Dominance and Technological Change*, Pluto Press, London, 1983; Johanna Brenner and Maria Ramas, "Rethinking Women's Oppression," *New Left Review*, No. 144, March-April 1984.

[4] Patricia Marchak, "Women Workers and White Collar Unions," *Canadian Review of Sociology and Anthropology*, Vol. 10, No. 2, 1973; Joan McFarland, "Women and Unions: Help or Hindrance," *Atlantis*, Vol. 4, No. 2, Spring 1979; Carla Lipsig-Mummé, "Organizing Women in the Clothing Trades: Homework and the 1983 Garment Strike in Canada." *Studies in Political Economy*, 22, Spring 1987.

[5] Bank Book Collective, *An Account to Settle: The Story of the United Bank Workers (SORWUC)*, Press Gang Publishers, Vancouver, 1979; Jackie Ainsworth, *et al.*, "Getting Organized in the Feminist Unions," Maureen Fitzgerald, *et al.*, *Still Ain't Satisfied: Canadian Feminism Today*, The Women's Press, Toronto, 1982.

[6] Heidi Hartmann, "Capitalism, Patriarchy and Job Segregation by Sex," Martha Blaxhall and Barbara Reagan, *Women and the Workplace*, University of Chicago Press, Chicago, 1976; Michèle Barrett, *Women's Oppression Today, The Marxist/Feminist Encounter*, Revised Edition, Verso, London, 1988.

since they do not support a family, do not need the same wages as a man.[7] Thus, protecting men's jobs and wages is a first priority for unions. Further, it has been proposed that working class men in unions ally themselves with male employers where it is in their common interest to ensure the subordination of women.[8]

The second approach prefers to locate the major part of trade union reaction to women in the social and economic conditions produced by the economic competition of capitalism. From this point of view women enter the labour force disadvantaged, as a source of cheap labour by employers, and union policy is a response to that situation rather than a cause of it. For example, Brenner and Ramas state:

> It is entirely unnecessary to resort to ideology to explain why trade unions were particularly adamant in their opposition to female entry into their trades. It is quite clear that when unions were unable to exclude women, a rapid depression of wages and general degradation of work resulted.[9]

It is argued that union responses must be understood within the limitations placed upon them by the organization of the workplace and the labour market. For example, I have argued elsewhere that in certain industries the fragmentation of the labour force and the virulence of employer opposition have played a major role in inhibiting the unionization of women;[10] and that the employer's use of part-time work as a form of cheap labour has been influential in determining union response to that issue.[11]

The unresolved debate over the relative strength of ideology versus material conditions forms the backdrop for the developing research on women and unions. The purpose of this analysis of the CUPW is not to attempt to resolve this debate, but to consider a different aspect of the problem. In terms of examining the CUPW the difficulty with both perspectives is that they have each sought to explain the negative responses of unions towards women. The initial response of the CUPW to the entry of women into the labour force was predictable within the context of the research outlined above. When women part-time workers were employed as a source of cheap labour by the Post Office in the 1950s, the union moved to protect the predominantly male full-time jobs by calling for the aboli-

---

[7] Charlene Gannagé, *Double Day, Double Bind, Women Garment Workers*, The Women's Press, Toronto, 1986; Gillian Creese, "The Politics of Dependence: Women, Work and Unemployment in the Vancouver Labour Movement Before World War II," Gregory S. Kealey, *Class, Gender and Region: Essays in Canadian Historical Sociology*, Committee on Canadian Labour History, St John's, 1988.

[8] Cynthia Cockburn, *Brothers: Male Dominance and Technological Change*, Pluto Press, London, 1983.

[9] Johanna Brenner and Maria Ramas, "Rethinking Women's Oppression," *New Left Review*, No. 144, March-April 1984, p. 45.

[10] Julie White, *Women and Unions*, Canadian Advisory Council on the Status of Women, Ottawa, 1980.

[11] Julie White, *Women and Part-Time Work*, Canadian Advisory Council on the Status of Women, Ottawa, 1983.

tion of part-time work and excluding the part-time workers from the union. The source of this response might be traced both to social and economic conditions and to more ideological considerations. From the materialist point of view the threat of cheap labour was unquestionably real and increasing for the union. Nonetheless, the fact that it was women who were working part-time is itself directly related to the responsibilities of women within the family, and certainly sexist arguments were used by the union to bolster those strictly related to the labour market issue.

Whatever the exact weight of the factors, of more striking interest is that this initial, predictable response was not the enduring one. The union did organize the women part-time workers and proceeded not only to bargain, but also to strike for equal pay and conditions. Similarly, the introduction of the Coder position was a further example of the use of women as a source of cheap labour in the context of technological change and deskilling. Again the union did not resort to exclusionary policies but fought with great determination for equal pay. Why did the CUPW produce these responses to the threat of cheap labour in the form of women workers?

In the CUPW the explanation does not lie with the increasing number of women in the union. The expression of women's interests has been felt on issues of particular concern to women since the late 1970s. Women played a part in supporting the negotiations for paid maternity leave in 1981, and have been particularly active on questions internal to the union. However, in the struggles during the late 1960s and early 1970s to obtain equality for part-time workers, parity for the Coders and equality of pay in general, women within the union did not play any special role. It was not pressure from women that particularly created these policy responses, although all union members, male and female, played their part in obtaining the final results.

Previous research has indicated that in some situations unions have pressed for equal pay for women as a veiled attempt to follow the same exclusionary policies and keep women out of the labour force.[12] Where this strategy was successful, employers proved uninterested in hiring women if there was no advantage in lower wages. However, this was not the case in the CUPW with regard to the Coder dispute. When the Coders were introduced to operate the new machinery no question was raised concerning whether they were male or female. Only the level of pay was in question and no attempt was made to preserve those jobs for men. The situation with the part-time workers was slightly more complex since the union was undoubtedly interested in containing their numbers, and in the mid–1960s pay equality was proposed as one method of accomplishing this goal. However, the union was attempting to maintain a proportion of full-time positions in the bargaining unit, whether for men or women, and this approach was and is supported by the part-time workers them-

---

[12] Ruth Frager, "No Proper Deal: Women Workers and the Canadian Labour Movement, 1870–1940," Linda Briskin and Lynda Yanz, *Union Sisters: Women in the Labour Movement*, The Women's Press, Toronto, 1983.

selves. Once part-time workers were members of the union, part of the rationale was to enable part-time workers to move into full-time positions, not eject them from the workforce. The CUPW's successful push for equality of pay was not an attempt to preserve jobs for men compared to women.

Another possible argument has been raised. Following on from the position that unions reflect the dominant social ideology, it has been suggested that unions change their attitudes as they change in society generally.[13] This argument has some relevance for the late 1970s and 1980s, as the force of the women's movement became increasingly influential. The obvious example with regard to the CUPW is paid maternity leave, and the considerable public attention that had been focussed on the issue by women's organizations, creating a climate of support for the union's demand. However, this factor was not influential in the late 1960s and early 1970s when the union was grappling with the problem of women as a source of cheap labour. The union's perspective was to view all workers, including men and women, as equals, which was not the dominant social ideology at the time, but quite exceptional.

In the context of the CUPW it is only possible to understand the response of the union to women workers by considering not only when the interests of men and women diverge, but also when common interests provoke a united reaction. In this regard the particular circumstances of technological change, the nature of the employer, restrictive legislation and general economic pressure all combined to produce responses from the union, including those that affected women particularly. These factors need to be examined in more detail.

As Harry Braverman describes it in his research, the drive to accumulate capital in an economy based upon the demands of competition has resulted in a relentless push to control and reduce labour costs. This has been accomplished through the division of labour into fragmented parts, each part entailing one small element of the overall labour process. Whether through the reorganization of work or automation, the achievement of this goal has systematically reduced the skill involved in work processes, thereby both reducing the cost of unskilled labour and reducing the control exerted by workers over their work. He recognizes the role played by women as a source of cheap labour in this process.[14]

---

[13] M. Baker and M.A. Robeson, "Trade Union Reactions to Women Workers and their Concerns," Katharine Lundy and Barbara Warme, *Work in the Canadian Context, Continuity Despite Change*, Butterworths, Toronto, 1981.

[14] Harry Braverman, *Labor and Monopoly Capital, The Degradation of Work in the Twentieth Century*, Monthly Review Press, 1974.

Other researchers, critical of Braverman, have argued that this deskilling process may not be accomplished without resistance from the workers who experience a loss of control, of status and of financial reward. An interaction occurs in which the workers may influence the outcome of the deskilling process and the extent to which the employer benefits from it.[15] On this point Veronica Beechey has suggested that women have entered particular industries and occupations not only because of the demand for labour and the recruiting practices of employers, but also as a result of "the attempts of male-dominated trade unions to define certain kinds of jobs as "men's jobs" or "women's jobs," thereby leaving a restricted range of occupations open for women."[16]

In the case of the Post Office, the processes described by Braverman can be seen as one fundamental explanation for the trends that have developed. Handling mail was in the past a labour intensive process that relied, until the 1950s, upon the knowledge of the expert sorter. As mail volumes expanded with the business prosperity of the 1950s and 1960s, and prodded by rising annual deficits, the Post Office moved to cut labour costs, first by reorganizing and simplifying the work, and then through a massive program of automation. However, Braverman's analysis related to the private monopoly corporations, not the situation of the Post Office which has always been a public sector operation, a department of the federal government and since 1981 a Crown Corporation. However, the analysis is applicable although the processes are somewhat different.

The government is not driven by the requirement to accumulate capital in order to compete, as is the case with private corporations. Its options are not limited to increasing prices or cutting costs to produce increased capital. Taxes can be raised to produce revenue, to cover expenditures, and deficits can be withstood over long periods. However, these options are severely limited in themselves by the demands of the economy. Taxes on corporations reduce their capital, while taxes on individuals are unpopular and may have unwelcome political consequences. Rising government deficits create in themselves a squeeze on capital, because government borrowing reduces the amount available to companies for investment.[17]

---

[15] B. Schwarz, "On the Monopoly Capitalist Degradation of Work," *Dialectical Anthropology*, Vol. 2, No.2, 1977; R. Coombes, "Labour and Monopoly Capital," *New Left Review*, No. 107, 1978.

[16] Veronica Beechey, "The Sexual Division of Labour and the Labour Process: A Critical Assessment of Braverman," Stephen Wood, *The Degradation of Work? Skill, Deskilling and the Labour Process*, Hutchinson, London, 1982, p. 56.

[17] Rick Deaton, "The Fiscal Crisis of the State and the Revolt of the Public Employee," *Our Generation*, Vol. 8, No. 4, October 1972; David Wolfe, "The State and Economic Policy," Leo Panitch, *The Canadian State*, University of Toronto Press, 1977.

These pressures on the government have been clearly in evidence over the last 20 years—with periods of inflation, high interest rates, and increasing government deficits. One response to the situation has been for the government to cut costs within its own ranks, cutting programs, laying-off public sector workers and holding down pay increases.[18] Within this general context the Post Office has experienced its own related problems. The Post Office deficits created continuous criticism and pressure to reduce costs. Moves to obtain cheap labour, the introduction of automation, the shift to a Crown Corporation and, most recently, the trend to privatization have all been attempts to limit costs and achieve self-sufficient management. The old notion of the Post Office as a service to the population and therefore worthy of subsidy has paled in the push to eliminate the deficit.

While this perspective certainly throws some light on the situation within the Post Office over the last 20 years, how does it relate to the particular policies of the CUPW with regard to women? Indeed it has been suggested by other researchers that it is precisely within this context of technological change, cost cutting and job loss that unions might be most inclined to protect existing male members against the inroads of female labour. However, in the Post Office technological change was introduced in particular circumstances, with remarkable speed, in a climate already heavy with animosity and distrust between the workers and their employer, and in a context of legislative restriction. It is the combination of these factors and their cumulative impact upon the union that requires consideration. It is worth reviewing briefly the specific circumstances within the Post Office.

Prior to 1967 the union did not have the legal right to negotiate or strike to improve pay and conditions. As conditions in the Post Office deteriorated during the late 1950s and early 1960s, postal workers found themselves powerless to influence events. Over the eight years between 1957 and 1965 inside postal workers received only two pay increases instead of the customary annual raise, and they had seen their wages steadily fall behind those of other workers employed in public services. When the government announced a pay rise in 1965 of just half what the union had been demanding, postal workers walked off the job. It was the first strike since 1924.

While pay was the major catalyst behind the dissatisfaction in the Post Office and the 1965 strike, many other grievances irritated the postal workers on a daily basis. These grievances were aired through the Montpetit Commission established by the government in September 1965 as a result of the strike. The grievances covered every aspect of the work, including health and safety, the hours of work, night and weekend work, timing of pay cheques and late payment of overtime, boot and clothing arrangements, vacations and other kinds of leave, and examinations and promotions.

---

[18] John Calvert, *Government Limited, The Corporate Takeover of the Public Sector in Canada*, The Canadian Centre for Policy Alternatives, Ottawa, 1984.

The complaints were embittered by the perception of the workers that the Department management did not treat the complaints seriously and made little effort to deal reasonably with the problems raised. To the Montpetit Commission the union stated that grievances were often ignored, or were channelled up the bureaucracy to become subject to endless delays, and that too often management made decisions without reference to the union or its concerns. The atmosphere in most post offices was described as disciplinarian and intolerant. The military style management, complete with a Code of Discipline and pay reductions for infractions, derived in part from the large number of veterans given preferential hiring in the Post Office after the war.

In response to union pressure and growing dissatisfaction the Public Service Staff Relations Act (PSSRA) was passed in 1967, giving federal public servants the right to negotiate collective agreements and the right to strike under certain conditions. Clearly the legislation did nothing to relieve worsening labour relations, since strikes recurred in the Post Office in 1968, 1970, 1971, 1974, 1975, 1978 and 1981. The PSSRA is a restrictive piece of legislation, and the union was legally prohibited from negotiating hiring, appraisal, promotion, demotion, transfers, lay-offs, duties or classifications. This meant that during the period of rapid technological change in the 1970s the union was legally prevented from bargaining many of the issues that were most critical for its members. Throughout the Coder dispute, for example, the employer steadfastly maintained that the union had no legal right to involve itself in classification, which was a management prerogative under the Act.

The CUPW was subjected not only to the restrictions of the PSSRA but other forms of government intervention in the negotiating procedure. In 1975 general wage controls were introduced, and in 1982 legislation that specifically affected federal government workers limited wage increases and suspended collective bargaining for two years. In 1978 and again in 1986 the union was legislated back to work after legal strikes and on the first occasion the CUPW President received a 3 month jail sentence.

These legislative restrictions, combined with an autocratic and incompetent management style, inhibited the resolution of the many problems created by the reorganization of work in the process of technological change. Thus, the CUPW was responding to several factors: a management style creating discontent on the shop floor, the introduction of massive technological change by an employer reluctant to negotiate many of the implications with the union, legislation that restricted the union's capacity to protect its members, and the increasing pressure to cut labour costs in response to general economic recession and rising deficits. One part of understanding the Post Office in recent years is to grasp the intense conflict of interest between the workers, suffering deskilling, loss of control, the threat of cheap labour and loss of jobs, and the employer, intent upon reducing labour costs through technological change, cutting the work force and, most recently, reducing services.

The result was to produce continuing frustration and dissatisfaction among inside postal workers, which lead in turn to the election of local and national leaders increasingly capable of channelling that discontent for effective bargaining. The dynamic relationship between the membership and its elected officers was supported by changes in the structure of the union. The change in name from the Canadian Postal Employees Association to the Canadian Union of Postal Workers symbolized a fundamental shift in the union. A new and democratic constitution was adopted, an extensive programme of education developed and a comprehensive network of communication established.

The union has developed what might be called a culture of struggle that includes the belief that management has no interest in the welfare of its workers, the attitude that only when forced will the employer concede any improvements, and the development of the institutions necessary to work in such an environment. This approach has been fuelled by management actions on the shop floor that continue to produce a remarkable degree of hostility from rank and file members. It has also been supported by the relative success of a militant approach. Negotiation, mediation and conciliation have repeatedly failed to produce results in the Post Office—the Coder dispute being an outstanding example. Critical in this regard has been the fact that this union represents postal workers, employed by a high-profile, nationwide, monopoly operation. A strike by postal workers cannot be ignored; it affects every person and every business in the country and is immediately the source of public debate and concern. The inside postal workers hold more bargaining strength than most workers.

In this context, with a battle line drawn between the workers and the employer, the consciousness of solidarity among the workers dominated potential differences by sex, and the union stressed the importance of solidarity over the many possible internal disputes in order to face the employer from a position of strength. The union developed an internal perspective that valued solidarity and equality, that was opposed to, or at least disregarded, the general ideology based on sex differences. The CUPW could be described as sex-blind during the late 1960s and 1970s, concerned with the protection of its members without consideration for their sex, or indeed any other characteristic. Consequently, confronted by the threat of cheap female labour the union's response was based upon the interests of all its members rather than just the immediate concerns of the men, upon class rather than gender interests.

Within this context the union developed a progressive perspective on social issues, concerned initially with equality between its own members but also in society more generally, thus creating the context in which the CUPW would bargain for paid maternity leave. Moreover, once equality for women in the workplace was established, this reality itself influenced the union's approach by reinforcing the ideology of equality—there being no material division of the labour force to foster attitudes of female inferiority. In circumstances where women do different work for less pay, the sexual division of labour feeds the perception of women as less capable, less skilled, less strong, or less responsible.

Equality on the shop floor meant that neither men nor women members of the CUPW had any basis to question the role of women. It also meant, as the interviews indicated, that the consciousness of many women in the CUPW was geared towards a united response from all the workers, rather than to specifically women's issues. To understand the CUPW it is necessary to deal with the extent to which actions by the employer produced a united response from both men and women postal workers.

One feminist researcher has outlined the relationship between class and gender interests in explaining the negative responses of unions to women:

> The failure of the labour movement in the past to take up the interests of women workers has not merely resulted in the oppression and exploitation of women. It has militated against a unified working-class consciousness and unified militant action. In short, it has constituted a failure to resist the political division in the working class that capital's division of labour creates and profits from.[19]

Apparently the opposite result is also possible, namely that a unified working class consciousness can overcome the divisions among men and women, creating a situation in which a union acts in the interests of all its members, both male and female.

Unions respond to women not only as workers but also as union members. Previous research has shown that women are under-represented as union officials and on union executives in proportion to their numbers as union members.[20] Several explanations for this situation have been proposed: sexist ideology exists among male unionists who discriminate against women obtaining union positions; it is a reflection of the workplace, where the higher paid workers, usually men, are considered more capable of taking on those positions; women's family responsibilities make the additional union work unmanageable; and the organization, structure and processes of the unions are geared to male needs and interests, often making it difficult if not impossible for women to participate.[21]

To deal with these problems women's committees, caucuses, and educationals have been developed to educate women about unions, and provide them with support and encouragement to participate. In some unions women's coordinators

---

[19] Michèle Barrett, *Women's Oppression Today, The Marxist/Feminist Encounter*, Revised Edition, Verso, London, 1988, p. 171.

[20] Charlene Gannagé, *Double Day, Double Bind, Women Garment Workers*, The Women's Press, Toronto, 1986; Grace Hartman, "Women and the Unions," Gwen Matheson, *Women in the Canadian Mosaic*, Peter Martin Associates, Toronto, 1976

[21] Grace Hartman, "Women and the Unions," Gwen Matheson, *Women in the Canadian Mosaic*, Peter Martin Associates, Toronto, 1976; Lesley Lee, "A Woman's Unionism," National Action Committee on the Status of Women, *Status of Women*, November 1984; Charlene Gannagé, *Double Day, Double Bind, Women Garment Workers*, Women's Press, Toronto, 1986; Miriam Edelson, "Making it Work Takes a Little Longer, Feminist Process and Union Democracy," *Our Times*, Vol. 6, No. 2, March 1987.

have been hired to deal with these concerns, and in some cases special positions have been created on union executives to ensure the representation of women.[22]

Within the CUPW, although there have been some changes since the late 1970s, the same problems occur as in other unions with regard to the lower participation of women and their under-representation, especially at the higher levels of the organization. Despite the conditions of equality within the workplace and the culture of equality within the CUPW, sexist attitudes have not been eradicated and women's family responsibilities continue to place real limitations upon their union involvement. This raises the question of how far a union, or for that matter any other organization, is constrained by the conditions of the general society.

It is also the case that the various structures to deal with the under-representation of women have not been popular within the CUPW, despite its generally progressive stance, and perhaps indeed because of it. This relates in part to two different definitions of equality, and whether it means treating men and women the same, or whether it means special arrangements for women. The CUPW has tended towards treating women the same as men, a positive position in the 1970s when women were accorded the same place as men within labour force, and not viewed as a special group in terms of skills or strength or need for income. But there has been a shift towards recognising that women may require special treatment in order to achieve equality: special encouragement to participate, protection from sexual harassment, women's committees to discuss women's concerns more comfortably, and perhaps changes in union structures to accommodate a women's perspective.[23] The CUPW has been less willing to provide special treatment than the same treatment.

The union's strong emphasis on solidarity has militated against special arrangements that would recognize a conflict between men and women, that would cut across the class solidarity regarded as essential for the welfare of all. Consequently women's committees and sexual harassment between members have been particularly contentious issues, regarded as potentially divisive of the membership. The union's emphasis upon equality and solidarity has produced positive results, so that it is not only men who are sceptical of special arrangements for women. The women interviewed for this study were not always convinced of the need for women's committees, and very few supported hiring a women's coordinator or creating special positions for women on local or national executives.

However, it is also necessary to add that there is great variation within the union on these issues, particularly according to region, and it is apparent that the role of local and regional leadership has been one critical factor. The CUPW offers a salutary warning of the danger of simplistic assumptions with regard to

---

[22] Linda Briskin and Lynda Yanz, *Union Sisters, Women in the Labour Movement*, Women's Press, Toronto, 1983.

[23] Nadine Jammal, "Les Femmes Dans le Discours Syndical," *Canadian Woman Studies*, Vol. 6, No. 3, Summer/Fall 1985.

union reactions. There is not necessarily a clear-cut union position on women's issues, but a more complex interaction that varies according to the issue, the location, the perspective of women as well as men members, and even the definition of equality. Moreover there may be no immediately obvious relationship between the union's position on specifically women's issues within the union and negotiation of fundamentals such as equal pay and job access with the employer. The CUPW's progressive collective agreement has not meant an easy acceptance of women's issues within the union. Likewise, women's committees, conferences and coordinators within unions may not translate into equality in the workplace.

Final Words

In the development of research on women and unions, it has been necessary, as in other areas, to re-write history from a women's perspective, given that earlier studies simply ignored women in their analyses.[24] Consequently, there has been an emphasis upon the differences between men and women, why women were and are less unionized, the different responses of unions to women than to men, and women's particular experiences of unions. The debate between the two approaches emphasizing either the role of ideology or the impact of capitalist competition has centred around the question: why have unions responded negatively to women? There has been a concentration upon the conflicting interests between male and female workers, based either upon the sexism of male unionists or the competition wrought by capitalism.

However, another aspect of reality has been considered here, namely a union that has acted to protect both its male and its female members. In this case pressure from the employer, combined with other factors, created a solidarity of interest between men and women workers, who struggled together for interests of concern to both. In this instance a level of unity was achieved that overcame (perhaps sporadically, perhaps only temporarily) the divisions brought about both by sexist ideology and capitalist competition.

An analysis that takes this possibility into account must not simply assume workers' solidarity in resisting the employer. In the past this assumption has usually meant the exclusion of gender from the analysis. The intention must be to understand the dynamic relationship between gender differences and tensions on the one hand and the common interests of male and female workers on the

---

[24] Harold A. Logan, *Trade Unions in Canada*, MacMillan, Toronto, 1948; Charles Lipton, *The Trade Union Movement of Canada 1827–1959*, Canadian Social Publications, Montreal, 1967; Martin Robin, *Radical Politics and Canadian Labour*, Industrial Relations Centre, Queen's University, Kingston, 1968; Stuart Jamieson, *Industrial Relations in Canada*, MacMillan, Toronto, 1973.

other.[25] This relationship is shaped by factors affecting the specific workplace, the internal organization and membership of the union, and the impact of both ideological and social conditions.

From this study it is apparent that the convergence of these factors, even within the same workplace and the same union, may produce different results over time, between regions and according to the issue. There is no automatic consistency between policies concerning internal union affairs and strategies at the bargaining table. Nor is the result pre-determined as to the reactions of men and women, who vary not only between themselves, but also among themselves. The important point is that unions have been neither homogeneous nor consistent in their response to women, and we need more detailed analyses of what creates the different responses.

There is general agreement that the labour movement has been changing in its response to women workers. If we are to understand this process, without relying on the sole and insufficient explanation of the activity of women themselves, we must begin to explore not only why unions have acted to the detriment of women's interests, but also why they have supported women and their concerns.

---

[25] This is, I believe, a somewhat different formulation than that offered by the excellent work of Ruth Milkman, who refers only to the competing interests of gender and class among men, without reference to the interests of women. See Ruth Milkman, *Gender at Work, The Dynamics of Job Segregation by Sex During World War II*, University of Illinois Press, Chicago, 1987, pp. 7, 158.

POSTSCRIPT

During the course of this research unforeseen events occurred that radically altered the nature of the CUPW. In May 1985 the Canada Post Corporation applied to the Canada Labour Relations Board (CLRB) for a review of the bargaining units in the Post Office. However, it was not until February 1987 that the CLRB ruled that the operational category of Post Office workers should bargain as one unit. This decision meant that inside postal workers, letter carriers and a small number of clerical and maintenance staff would belong to the same union. This decision was supported by the CUPW, since the union had always adhered to the position that one large union would be a stronger bargaining agent in negotiations with the employer.

Since the two major unions involved, the CUPW and the Letter Carriers Union of Canada (LCUC), were unable to reach a merger agreement, the CLRB ordered a vote of the members. From November 1988 to January 1989 the unions were campaigning to convince the members to vote for them. When the result was announced on 17th January 1989 the CUPW had received 51 percent of the ballots and therefore became the union to represent both inside postal workers and letter carriers.

This is the beginning of a new phase in the history of the postal workers. The membership has instantly expanded from 24,000 to 46,000 and there continue to be some very contentious issues that remain to be resolved between the two sets of members and officials. It means the end of the CUPW as the union representing just the inside postal workers.

It also means new circumstances for the women of the CUPW. In 1987 the LCUC had a membership of 20,005, of which just 2,351 were women, that is almost 12 percent. The proportion of women in the new union of postal workers is now around 29 percent, compared to over 42 percent within the old CUPW. The women I interviewed commented upon this new balance in the membership and were contemplating what it might mean for women's issues in the union. Most felt that it would mean a step back in time, a starting over again with education and some of the same battles to be struggled through a second time. However, some were looking forward to working in the same union with the women letter carriers. Others commented that the LCUC did have a national women's committee, which the CUPW did not.

Another study will have to analyze the outcome of these changes.